Nordic Neoshamanisms

Palgrave Studies in New Religions and Alternative Spiritualities

Series editors: James R. Lewis and Henrik Bogdan

Palgrave Studies in New Religions and Alternative Spiritualities is an interdisciplinary monograph and edited collection series sponsored by the International Society for the Study of New Religions. The series is devoted to research on New Religious Movements. In addition to the usual groups studied under the New Religions label, the series publishes books on such phenomena as the New Age, communal and utopian groups, Spiritualism, New Thought, Holistic Medicine, Western esotericism, Contemporary Paganism, astrology, UFO groups, and new movements within traditional religions. The Society considers submissions from researchers in any discipline.

A Study of the Movement of Spiritual Inner Awareness:
  Religious Innovation and Cultural Change
Diana G. Tumminia and James R. Lewis

India and the Occult: The Influence of South Asian Spirituality
  on Modern Western Occultism
Gordan Djurdjevic

Reading and Writing Scripture in New Religious Movements:
  New Bibles and New Revelations
Eugene V. Gallagher

Sexuality and New Religious Movements
Edited by Henrik Bogdan and James R. Lewis

Nordic Neoshamanisms
Edited by Siv Ellen Kraft, Trude Fonneland, and James R. Lewis

Nordic Neoshamanisms

Edited by
Siv Ellen Kraft, Trude Fonneland, and James R. Lewis

NORDIC NEOSHAMANISMS

Copyright © Siv Ellen Kraft, Trude Fonneland, and James R. Lewis, 2015.

All rights reserved.

First published in 2015 by
PALGRAVE MACMILLAN®
in the United States—a division of St. Martin's Press LLC,
175 Fifth Avenue, New York, NY 10010.

Where this book is distributed in the UK, Europe and the rest of the world,
this is by Palgrave Macmillan, a division of Macmillan Publishers Limited,
registered in England, company number 785998, of Houndmills,
Basingstoke, Hampshire RG21 6XS.

Palgrave Macmillan is the global academic imprint of the above companies
and has companies and representatives throughout the world.

Palgrave® and Macmillan® are registered trademarks in the United States,
the United Kingdom, Europe and other countries.

ISBN: 978–1–137–46139–1

Library of Congress Cataloging-in-Publication Data

Nordic Neoshamanisms / edited by Siv Ellen Kraft, Trude Fonneland,
and James R. Lewis.
    pages cm. — (Palgrave studies in new religions and alternative
spiritualities)
    Includes bibliographical references and index.
    ISBN 978–1–137–46139–1 (alk. paper)
    1. Shamanism—Scandinavia. I. Kraft, Siv-Ellen, editor. II. Fonneland,
Trude, 1977– editor. III. Lewis, James R., editor.

BF1622.S34N46 2015
201'.440948—dc23   2014035189

A catalogue record of the book is available from the British Library.

Design by Newgen Knowledge Works (P) Ltd., Chennai, India.

First edition: February 2015

10 9 8 7 6 5 4 3 2 1

Contents

Part III   Neoshamanism in Secular Contexts

Figures

Introduction: Nordic Neoshamanisms

During the mid-1970s, Ailo Gaup, then a young Sami journalist from
Oslo, traveled to Finnmark, the homeland of his ancestors, in search
of a Sami shaman. Gaup had studied scholarly accounts of the pre-
Christian Sami religion, commonly understood as a form of shamanism, but had not found descriptions of how – in practical terms – to
initiate a trance and embark upon journeys. At the Tourist Hotel in
Kautokeino, he met Ernesto, a Chilean refugee with the necessary
qualifications from South American contexts. Gaup's first visit to
the spirit world of his ancestors took place with the help of Ernesto,
Chilean traditions, and an African djembe-drum (Gaup 2005:86–98).
Over the next decade, he further developed his skills, through training at Michael Harner's Foundation for Shamanic Studies in Esalen,
California. By the late 1980s, he was back in Oslo, established as a
professional shaman and ready to take up the task of reviving the
spiritual practices of his ancestors. There is, according to Harner's
perspective, a core content in the multitude of traditions that together
constitute "world shamanism." Each of these should be recovered
and reconstructed, in order for their richness and complexity to come
forth, and each of them offers unique contributions to the common
source.

Indicative of the complex interactions behind Nordic neoshamanisms, Gaup's story speaks of global influences as well as local traditions,
including – in the case of the Sami – intersections between cultural and
religious revival. One aim of this book is to take seriously such interactions, through case studies from Nordic settings. Another aim is to
explore the relationship between neoshamanism and New Age spiritualities on the one hand and secular contexts on the other. A third is to
take seriously the ethnic dimension of these currents and intersections,
through a specific focus on Sami and Norse versions of neoshamanism.
Nordic shamanisms have become part of the international scene, but
are also "home grown" – on local lands and through the use of local

traditions, including the Sami and Norse religions of the ancient past. Both have been central to the shape and inventory of neoshamanism in the Nordic countries, and by 2014 constituted their most active and profiled parts. Together, they offer rich opportunities for watching second- and third-generation neoshamanism evolve, and challenge some of the central assumptions of neoshaman and pagan research—for instance, that these religions cater primarily to urban romantics for whom connections to nature have in practice been lost, that the noble savage depends upon distance in time and space, that pagans tend to be either reconstructionists (oriented toward the reconstruction of "their own" pasts and traditions) or eclectics (mixing elements from various traditions, see Srtmiska 2005), and that they differ substantially from New Age spiritualities. Through the chapters in the present book, contributors question these presuppositions. Nordic shamanisms, we argue, attract people in cities as well as in rural areas; the "noble savage" is no longer limited to distant landscapes; the distinction between reconstructionism and eclecticism is difficult to maintain among entrepreneurs like Gaup and his followers, and boundaries between neoshamanism and New Age have become increasingly blurred.

In substantial ways, scholarly research has contributed to the globalization of neoshamanism. Nordic neoshamans, like their colleagues elsewhere, turn to studies by anthropologists and historians of religion in order to revive and reconstruct the religions of their ancient past, both with respect to descriptions of particular religions, and to what – more generally – shamanism *is*, as an *ism*. The contemporary study of religion is, as Friedrich H. Tenbruck phrased it, "confronted with the effects of its own systematizations" (cited in von Stuckrad 2003). Neoshamanism is an unusually clear example, as a movement in which

> Academic specialists (mostly anthropologists holding a PhD) act as religious specialists on a "shamanic field of discourse," which cannot be understood without taking into account the formation of euro-American concepts in early modern times. (Stuckrad 2003: 264)

In academic circles, "shamanism" has been highly contested during the past several decades, due partly to these historical trajectories and to their results, including widespread notions of shamanism as an *ism* (Rydving 2011, Znamenski 2007, Svanberg 2003, Stuckrad 2002). In this book we take as our starting point emic vocabularies, that is, the ways in which notions of "shaman" and "shamanism" are today used by practitioners and others who relate to them, as designations of religious choices, preferences, and lifestyles. Our concern, then, is not with shamanism as an analytical concept or with the issue of whether this concept makes sense historically—outside of the areas of its origin—in Siberia. We are concerned with sensemaking on emic grounds, including ways in which contemporary shamans anchor their practices in ancient pasts, or what they see and experience as ancient pasts. Notions of traditions and authenticity, similarly, are approached from the perspective of ongoing religion making. "Traditions," as we view them in these pages, are authentic to the degree they are articulated as such. We leave it, that is, for the shamans to discuss and to decide upon what is or is not "authentic," and relate this issue to their ongoing concerns rather than to matters of historical continuity.

We will return (in chapter 1) to the contribution of Carlos Castaneda and Harner, both of whom began their careers as anthropologists, then gradually went native, shaman style. Harner's ideas are today contested among practitioners, but many of the pioneers behind Nordic-style neoshamanism, including some who are today critical of his ideas, themselves received their first training at Harner's center in the United States. Ongoing debates and controversies also indicate their continuing relevance.

The US influence was particularly pronounced during the first stages of neoshamanism in Nordic countries. Indian-style shamanism reached this region during the 1980s, along with New Age and occult impulses. The turn to local traditions occurred at different times, notably through the energy and enthusiasm of individual entrepreneurs (Lindquist 1997: 189). A leading figure of Swedish paganism, Jørgen I. Eriksson, was already criticizing Harner during the 1980s, and encouraged people to search for local traditions. In Denmark, Annette Høst, who had received her initial training from Harner, began including *seidr* by the early 1990s, a ritual practice known from Norse religion, as a part of her courses. In Norway, as mentioned above, Ailo Gaup established himself as a Sami shaman in the late 1980s.

Our concept of "Nordic shamanism" refers both to the geographical frame (Denmark, Finland, Iceland, Norway, and Sweden), and to historical resources. Estonia, which is represented in one chapter, is widely thought of as a Baltic state, but belongs geographically to Northern Europe, and has historically been connected to what is today considered the Nordic countries, and is regarded by many Estonians as culturally Nordic (see Parks, in this volume).[1] Ties among the Scandinavian countries (Norway, Sweden, and Denmark) have been particularly close, historically and today. People in these countries speak mutually comprehensible languages (the Sami excepted), have adopted similar welfare systems, cooperate through Nordic political organizations, and their populations are among the wealthiest and best educated in the world. Religious similarities are also substantial. Norway, Sweden, and

Denmark share a history of predominantly Christian populations and strong national churches.

All three countries have during the last decades become religiously more diverse, due to immigration, secularization, and the influx of new religions and New Age spiritualities (Christensen 2010). The latter started out as fairly marginal countercultural movements during the 1960s, gradually became established as economic markets, and increasingly catered to mainstream audiences, for secular as well as spiritual orientations, and crisscrossed established religious and secular boundaries. The sheer size and turnover of Nordic New Age markets indicate that mainstream populations are involved. Products like alternative medicine attract clients with various religious and secular mindsets (Kraft 2011, Frisk 2013, Sorgenfrei 2013). New Age-style coaching and mindfulness have been described as contemporary religious revivals (Hornborg 2012), and increasing interests in so-called "paranormal" experiences among Christians are expressed in terms of New Age vocabularies (Henriksen and Pabst 2013). The increasing presence of New Age spiritualities in films, music, and television similarly indicates mainstream appeal – if "only" as entertainment (Kalvig 2013, Endsjø and Lied 2011). In the following, we try to paint Nordic neoshamansim in its cultural context, relating it both to the local mainstream cultures in which they are situated and to contemporary neoshamansim globally.

The development of economic markets may to some extent explain the blurring of boundaries between the sacred and the secular, on the one hand, and New Age spiritualities and neoshamanism on the other. Both the specialization (niche developments) and the hybridization of products (products catering to both religious and "secular" needs) make sense from the perspective of the market mechanism – of entrepreneurs trying to make a living from their religious interests and talents (Kraft 2011). Many neoshamans specialize in one particular tradition, but allow for combinations, cater to clients with different needs and interests, and offer their products in typical New Age arenas like festivals and fairs. At times, little but the title (shaman) signals an orientation toward "shamanism." The most publicly-profiled book on "shamanism" to come out of Norway in 2012, *Shaman on High Heels*, was written by a woman who appears to have no interest whatsoever in "shamanism," but nevertheless chooses to designate herself as a shaman, and is known in Norwegian popular media as such.

Adding to this wide range of products and specializations, both Norse and particularly Sami shamanism are used in various tourism settings, and in festivals and place-marketing strategies, as part of the cultural heritage of particular places. These forms of shamanism are offered by professional Sami shamans and secular agents, and they draw on trends in the spiritual milieu as well as in the experience economy. Secular and spiritual actors and institutions share an interest in landscapes of wilderness and opportunities to experience the past, and they draw – to some extent – upon the same spiritual vocabularies.

Recent developments in the form of organizations reflect the diversity and hybridity referred to so far. The most important among new comers is *Sjamanistisk forbund* (the Shamanistic Association), which in 2012 was established as a Norwegian religion in the legal sense of the term (Fonneland 2014). The Shamanistic Association (SA) has from the start included both Sami and Norse-oriented shamans and shamanistic practices, and combines a view of shamanism as a universal path with an emphasis on local roots and connections. Its goal, according to official statements, is to serve as a tradition keeper for northern neoshamanic traditions, which, according to some of the leading shamans, dates back some 30,000 years, to a time when Sami and Norse paths had not yet diverged.

Although obviously not exhaustive, *Nordic Neoshamanism* indicates some of the diversity and breadth of the contemporary neoshamanistic setting, as well as important currents and currencies. Sami shamanism is the most complex and multifaceted shamanistic tradition thus far to emerge in Nordic landscapes, and has therefore been granted particular attention. Adding to its position as a "proper religion" and to the typical register of courses and workshops, Sami shamanism has entered experience and entertainment institutions such as museums, festivals, tourist locations, theaters, music, and films, and also comes in a cultural heritage-style version, as part of Sami nation-building and the ethno-political field of indigenous revival (Kraft 2009)

Outline of the Chapters

The book is divided into three parts: "Background," "Late Modern Shamanism in Nordic Countries," and "Neoshamanism in Secular Contexts." The first part begins with a chapter by Olav Hammer in which macro theories are brought into focus, providing readers with a background for the balance of the volume. In chapter 1, "Late Modern Shamanism: Central Texts and Issues," Hammer reasons about how such canonical texts as Mircea Eliade's *Shamanism: Archaic Techniques of Ecstasy* (1957) and Michael Harner's *The Way of the Shaman* (1980) mirror the Western postmodern context in which they were created. Both the ethnographic and neoshamanic image of shamanism have become part of the modern human mythical understanding of how humans and the world are constructed. Whether Eliade is considered a "better" scientist than Harner, they are comparable from a different perspective, Hammer argues.

Part 2, "Late Modern Shamanism in Nordic Countries," consists of seven case studies of particular persons, groups, and institutions, and indicates the variety of contemporary neoshamanism. In chapter 2, "The Rise of Nordic Neoshamanism in Norway: Local Structures—Global Currents," Trude Fonneland describes key contexts and events behind the rise of a Nordic neoshamanistic milieu in Norway. The article explores the dynamics through which abstract concepts and ideas find moorings in a local community and in participants' reality here and now, gradually generating distinct cultural fields.

Chapter 3, "The Way of the Teacher," explores Danish neoshamanic courses rooted in Michael Harner's teachings. Merete Demant Jacobsen shows how second- and third-generation course organizers create their own understanding, both of the shaman and of the spiritual needs of modern people. The chapter provides insight into ways in which the concept of shamanism is merging with other approaches to the spiritual and other belief systems, and how each teacher creates his or her own conglomerate of spiritual practices.

In chapter 4, "Shared Facilities: The Fabric of Shamanism, Spiritualism, and Therapy in a Nordic Setting," Anne Kalvig analyzes "shared facilities," represented by people using and creating spiritual reservoirs marked by neoshamanism(s), spiritualism, and alternative therapy. She describes how this unfolds within the contemporary spirituality scene in Norway, offering insights into the production, consumption, and mediation of contemporary spirituality, under the wide umbrella of Nordic shamanism.

Chapter 5, "Shamanism—a Spiritual Heritage? The Significance of the Past in Shamanic Discourses," discusses the importance of the past in supplying an anchor and authoritative foundations for spiritual ideas and practices. Torunn Selberg highlights descriptions and narratives relating shamanism to traditions from an ancient past and shows how interpretations of ideas about the past take on sacral and mythological dimensions.

Henno Eriksen Parks' (chapter 6) takes as his starting point Estonian sources, under the title "Metroshamanism: A Search for Shamanic Identity in Modern Estonia." A primary focus is on connections between local traditions of witches, healers, and shamans, all of which fall under the Estonian label of *nõid*. "Metroshamanism" is proposed as an alternative to the problems connected to the "shamanism" in contemporary ethnological and religious research—as it more accurately portrays the religioscape of modern shamanic practices.

In chapter 7, "New Age Medicine Men versus New Age *Noaidi*: Same Neoshamanism, Different Cultural-Political Situation," James R. Lewis analyzes the contrast between the contexts of New Age Sami shamanism and New Age Native American shamanism. Relating how the neoshamanism found in North America and the neoshamanism that has taken root in the Nordic region of Europe have come to embody different social significances, he emphasizes the importance of being aware of how new contexts supply new meanings, to avoid the error of essentialism.

Bente Gullveig Alver (chapter 8) tells the story of the Sami woman Ellen Mari Gaup Dunfjeld, and her career as a shaman. Among the issues at stake, as the title of the chapter indicates, are notions of "More or Less Genuine Shamans," in this case connected to complex negotiations of local traditions and traditions from outside; "The Believer in an Exchange between Antiquity and Modernity, between the Local and the Global."

Part 3 deals with neoshamanism in secular contexts—in films, festivals, museum displays, and music. Cato Christensen (chapter 9) discusses the relationship between Sami shamanism and Indigenous film, taking as his empirical starting point *The Pathfinder* (1987) and *The Kautokeino Rebellion* (2008), by the Sami filmmaker Nils Gaup. These films, Christensen argues, have contributed in important ways to perceptions of the Sami religious past, both inside and outside of Sami communities. They belong to a broader international tendency to use feature film to convey and (re)construct indigenous peoples' culture, identity, and history. Several such "indigenous films" promote spirituality as a marker of indigenous groups' ethnic and cultural particularity.

Stein R. Mathisen, in chapter 10, "Contextualizing Exhibited Versions of Sámi Noaidevuohta," investigates and contextualizes attempts to display Sami shamanism—the Sami shaman's drum (*goavddis*) being the most central exhibit, in museums, exhibitions, and other similar touristic displays. Mathisen further discusses how these versions relate to colonizing histories, aesthetic valorizations, and (ethno)political considerations, and not least how they connect to other prevailing (but conflicting) narratives of Sami religion, culture, and identity

Chapter 11, by Trude Fonneland, "The Festival Isogaisa: Neoshamanism in New Arenas," examines stories, products, and services that take shape as a Sami shaman festival opens its doors to the public for the first time. Fonneland asks what is included and what is excluded in the marketing of Isogaisa as an attractive happening. She further explores the role the past and Sami pre-Christian religion play in the production of the festival experience, and examines how what is distinctly local at Isogaisa is highlighted on the basis of global structures and organizations to create interest in a chosen product at a specific destination.

Finally, in chapter 12, Siv Ellen Kraft explores the relationship between music and shamanism through a case study of Mari Boine, a leading world music artist and one of Norway's most influential musicians. Titled "Mari Boine—World Music, Shamanism and Indigenous Soundscapes," the chapter explores Boine's connections to the neoshamanistic field and to notions of "indigenous music," as well as the shamanistic content of her texts and performances. A primary argument is that Boine has contributed to a cultural heritage-style version of shamanism, and has helped soften resistance toward shamanism in Sami circles.

Note

1. Estonia was part of medieval Denmark during the thirteenth–fourteenth and again in the sixteenth and the seventeenth centuries, and of Sweden from 1561 to 1721. There are also numerous links between the mythical cosmology of the Finno-Baltic and the Northern Teutonic peoples, with early contact influencing lexical exchanges, cultural phenomena, and some theological conceptions.

References

Christensen, Henrik Reintoft. 2010. *Religion and Authority in the Public Sphere Representations of Religion in Scandinavian Parliaments and Media*, PhD dissertation, The Graduate School of Theology and the Study of Religion Department of the Study of ReligionFaculty of Theology University of Aarhus.

Endsjø, Dag Øystein, and Liv Ingeborg Lied. 2011. *Det folk vil ha: Religion og populærkultur*. Oslo: Universitetsforlaget.

Fonneland, Trude. 2014. "Sjamanistisk Forbund: Ein ny religiøs organisasjon tek form," *Din. Tidsskrift for religion og kultur* 1: 93–112.

Frisk, Liselotte, and Peter Åkerbäck. 2013. *Den mediterande dalahästen: Religion på nya arenor i samtidens Sverige*. Stockholm: Dialogos Förlag.

Harner, Michael. 1980: *The Way of the Shaman: A Guide to Power and Healing*. San Francisco, Harper & Row.

Henriksen, Jan-Olav, and Kathrin Pabst. 2013. *Uventet og ubedt: Paranormale erfaringer i møte med tradisjonell tro*. Oslo: Universitetsforlaget.

Hornborg, Anne-Christine. 2012. *Coaching och lekmannaterapi—en modern väckelse*. Stockholm: Dialogos förlag.

Kalvig, Anne. 2013. *Åndelig helse: Livssyn og menneskesyn hos alternative terapeutar*. Oslo: Cappelen Damm Akademisk.

Kraft, Siv Ellen. 2009. "Sami Indigenous Spirituality: Religion and Nation Building in Norwegian Sápmi." *Temenos: Nordic Journal of Comparative Religion* 4: 179–206.

———. 2011. *Hva er nyreligiøsitet*. Oslo: Universitetsforlaget.

Lindquist, Galina. 1997. *Shamanic Performances on the Urban Scene: Neoshamanism in Contemporary Sweden*. Stockholm: Almqvist & Wiksell.

Pharo, Lars Kirkhusmo. 2011. "A Methodology for a Deconstruction and Reconstruction of the Concepts 'Shaman' and 'Shamanism,' *Numen* 58: 7–70.

Rydving, Håkan. 2011. "Le chamanisme aujourd'hui: constructions et déconstructions d'une illusion scientifique," *Études mongoles et sibériennes, centrasiatiques et tibétaines* 42 (DOI: 10.4000/emscat.1815).

Sorgenfrei, Simon (ed.). 2013. *Mystik och andlighet Kritiska perspektiv*. Stockholm: Dialogos.

Stuckrad, Kocku von. 2003. "Discursive Study of Religion: From States of the Mind to Communication and Action," *Method and Theory in the Study of Religion*, 15: 255–271.

———. 2002. "Reenchanting Nature: Modern Western Shamanism and Nineteenth-Century Thought." *Journal of the American Academy of Religion*, 70(4): 771–799.

Strmiska, M. F. (ed.). 2005. *Modern Paganism in World Cultures: Comparative Perspectives*. Santa Barbara: ABC Clio.

Svanberg, Jan 2003: Schamanantropologi i gränslandet mellan forskning och praktik: En studie av förhållandet mellan schamanismforskning och neoschamanism. Åbo: Åbo Akademis Förlag.

Znamenski, Andrei A. 2007: *The Beauty of the Primitive: Shamanism and the Western Imagination*. Oxford: Oxford University Press.

I

Background

1

Late Modern Shamanism: Central Texts and Issues

Olav Hammer

Shamans and the Modern World[1]

Shamans and their séances exert a striking fascination for people in the Western world. Thousands of articles and books—both academic and popular—have been written about the subject. The words *shaman* and *shamanism* no longer belong merely to the professional jargon of scholars of religion and anthropologists, but have become part of everyday language. Shamanism has even, as few other religious phenomena, inspired people in modern times to create their own innovative versions. There is a wide variety of neoshamanic rituals that one accesses through books and via courses of various lengths and costs. The experiential nature of much neoshamanism is apparent from such recent titles as Serge Kahili King's *Urban Shaman* (1990), Alberto Villoldo's *Shaman, Healer, Sage: How to Heal Yourself with the Energy Medicine of the Americas* (2000), Tony Samara's *Shaman's Wisdom: Reclaim Your Lost Connection with the Universe* (2012), and Sandra Ingerman's *The Shaman's Toolkit: Ancient Tools for Shaping the Life and World You Want to Live In* (2013). For readers of such volumes, it is clear that shamanism is not an exotic practice found among various indigenous peoples, but practices that can be sampled by anybody willing to buy a book and try out the methods found there.

Although neoshamanism belongs to the same cultic milieu in which New Age practices are offered, the Western world's fascination with shamanism is by no means a recent phenomenon; the historical background has been meticulously documented by Ronald Hutton (2001), Kocku von Stuckrad (2003), Andrei Znamenski (2007), and other researchers. Most of this earlier history is no doubt unknown territory for present-day practitioners of neoshamanism. Contemporary attitudes to shamanism outside academia are rooted in a very small number of widely read books. The classic of all classics, Mircea Eliade's *Shamanism: Archaic Techniques of Ecstasy*, first published in French in 1950, has been central to both the academic world's understanding of the phenomenon and to the popular imagination. Eliade's pioneering work came to define a concept and an often-implicit theory of how to approach that concept—something few other works have succeeded in accomplishing.

Another seminal text is Michael Harner's *The Way of the Shaman* (1980). For the academically trained reader, the juxtaposition of Eliade and Harner might seem absurd. The same research community that once hailed Eliade's book as a milestone has marginalized or scorned Harner's work. For many people outside academia, however, the concept of shamanism has become redefined so that it is effectively synonymous with Harner's neoshamanism. When in the autumn of 1997, Ma Oftedal was expelled from her position as a priest of the Church of Sweden, one of the main reasons was that she practiced shamanistic rituals with her confirmation candidates. The case was extensively covered in the Swedish media, but nobody seemed to pay attention to one of the most striking aspects of the case: no Siberian or Native American rituals took place in the Swedish confirmation camp, but rather so-called drum journeys, rituals that had been created by Harner.[2]

Together, these two books have been so influential that one might call them the canonical texts of Western neoshamanism. One can, of course, deal with texts of this nature in a variety of ways. Perhaps the most obvious perspective would be to evaluate them in relation to the ethnographic data we have on indigenous shamanisms. In this chapter, I will pursue a different approach and consider how such canonical texts mirror the Western context in which they were created. Regardless of whether Eliade is considered a "better" scholar and Harner an "inferior" one (or perhaps even no longer a scholar at all), they are comparable from a different perspective. Both have become instrumental in shaping modern people's understandings of the spiritual legacy of indigenous peoples.

Modern Religiosity in Three Stages

Sociologists of religion Rodney Stark and William Bainbridge have developed a tripartite typology of modern religious formations.[3] The least demanding, the *audience cult*, is based on access to information through books, magazines, and broadcast media, but also through personal contacts. The interested audience comes into contact with different religious options by passive consumption of information; active involvement is not required. A form with a somewhat higher degree of commitment, the *client cult*, is based on the same kind of market economy in which most other goods and services are offered. One participates in the religious activity by paying a fee and taking part in a course, or participating as a client in a therapeutic situation. Even in client cults involvement is frequently minimal. After completing a course, interested clients often move on to other religious alternatives, without immersing themselves in depth in any of them.

The third form, the *cult movement*, is an organization with members and a leader, in which the top echelon typically attempts to define the dogma, mythology, rituals, and other religious activities with which members are involved. Unsurprisingly, cult movements demand a considerably more stable commitment than the two other forms.

Loosely structured religious milieus like neoshamanism can take on any of Starks' and Bainbridge's three variants. Through books, large groups of people come into contact with a new imaginary world. The many people who have read and appreciated Carlos Castaneda's books on the mysterious Yaqui shaman Don Juan—or titles such as Olga Kharitidi's *Entering the Circle* and Harner's *The Way of the Shaman*—without actively carrying out the rituals described in them or fully accepting the cosmology they present, represent a very broad, but moderately engaged audience cult. The audience cult's only common interpretative framework would be that indigenous peoples possess superior knowledge, and possibly, also, that altered states of consciousness can impart insights that our everyday consciousness is unable to provide. For an audience cult of this kind, it does not really present a problem that Castaneda's books, and probably also Kharitidi's, are works of fiction. As it is sometimes said in New Age circles: the important thing is not whether something is true in any objective sense, but that it works in one's own life.

Both factual descriptions of shamanism like Eliade's and fictional depictions such as Castaneda's can serve as the basis for a wide audience to form opinions on the phenomenon of shamanism. A Google search will quickly reveal that Internet sites about shamanism can refer to Eliade and to neoshamanic literature side by side, as if they fall into the same category. Eliade's book has also met with the somewhat strange fate of being reprinted in paperback edition in Penguin Publishing's Arcana imprint, a series that otherwise consists of handbooks in astrology and cheap editions of *A Course in Miracles*. The categorization is less surprising than one might initially think. To this we will return.

In order for a client cult to be established, something more than reading experiences is required. Once a practice-based client cult arises, any remaining links to indigenous peoples are fully severed—probably because both creators and consumers of neoshamanistic courses are modern, often urban, people with a Western cultural background. Finally, for a much smaller group of people who have passed through the audience and client cult stages, neoshamanism becomes a fully organized cult movement. Such cult movements bear unmistakable traits of the late modern context within which they arise, as has been amply documented by Galina Lindquist.[4] This small core of firmly dedicated neoshamanic practitioners will not be discussed further in the present chapter.

Mircea Eliade on Shamanism

The bare essentials of Eliade's life can be summarized in a few sentences. Eliade was born in Bucharest in 1906. He started his university studies in philosophy in 1925 and became a disciple of and friend with the philosopher Nae Ionescu. Because Ionescu was actively involved in fascist politics, Eliade's contact with his mentor subsequently came to tarnish Eliade's reputation. Eliade's own political sympathies continue to be discussed in an often highly polemical literature, but this aspect of his legacy is not crucial for present purposes. After World War II, Eliade moved to Paris and taught history of religions at Sorbonne. In 1956, he was invited to the University of Chicago by then-professor of history of religions, Joachim Wach, and stayed there until his death in 1986.

Eliade was from an early age an academic with encyclopedic ambitions. Scholarly trends have gone in the direction of increasing specialization: many years of study are needed to master the languages, the sources, and the literature of any given religious tradition. Eliade's omnivorous interests belong to a largely bygone age. A Master's thesis on Italian Renaissance philosophy was followed by studies in Sanskrit at the University of Calcutta and a PhD on yoga. After finishing his studies, Eliade embarked on an amazingly prolific career as a writer on highly diverse topics, which—to quote one of Eliade's book titles—ranged from "primitives" to Zen. Some 20 monographs and no less than 1,500 texts of other kinds, from articles and novels to short stories and reviews, comprise his bibliography. Much of this written output continued to be characterized by an all-encompassing approach, with examples taken from all parts of the globe and all historical periods. The span of topics is also wide, from general surveys of the history of religions, to works on particular religious phenomena. Much of this oeuvre is characterized by a way of understanding religion that has been heavily criticized over the last decades. The point of summing up the main issues with his work is, however, not to engage in yet another unrewarding round of

Eliade-bashing, but to uncover some of the presuppositions underlying his work on shamanism, and to show that precisely the same characteristics of his approach that many academics have found rather hard to accept are the very same features that can appeal to spiritual seekers.

Nostalgic Hermeneutics

In his writings, Eliade creates a distinction between two modes of being. Archaic, religious man experienced a distinct difference between profane and sacred time, and between secular and sacred space. For modern people, however, both time and space have largely become experientially homogenous, a mode of being in the world that in Eliade's descriptions comes across as a state of loss. Thus Eliade's way of presenting the contrast between archaic and modern people can be roughly characterized as nostalgic antimodernism. Nevertheless, Eliade finds authentically religious human beings in most times and places, from the shamanic cultures of hunter-gatherers to medieval and renaissance alchemists. Even modern human beings are in a sense crypto-religious,[5] which leads to the strange and perhaps unintended consequence that the initially sharp distinction between the archaic *homo religiosus* and the profane modern human being dissolves as soon as it is established.

The Sacred

Writers like Eliade who had long careers and left extensive corpora of texts are often read in dramatically different ways. In Eliade's case, the picture is further complicated by his preference for presenting numerous brief concrete examples over extended discussions of theory, method, and definitional issues. What, precisely, did Eliade assert when he suggested that archaic, religious man was acutely aware of the sacred?

Perhaps Eliade understood the sacred as a category that members of a religious tradition ascribe to certain places, times, or objects. As in the work of Émile Durkheim, people are the agents who describe something as sacred. If so, the "sacred" is hardly more than a convenient label for things set apart, that is, for whatever triggers a certain form of behavior among the members of a tradition. However, if one interprets "the sacred" in Eliade's texts as a term denoting a distinct ontological category, as critical commentators have done, Eliade appears to construct a theology according to which the sacred actually exists and decides to manifest itself.[6]

The sacred and the profane are not just two categories; they also stand in a hierarchical relationship, in which "the sacred" is the superior term. To quote Eliade, "All history is in some measure a fall of the sacred, a limitation and a diminution."[7] As a consequence, only the profane can or should be understood in profane terms, that is, as something that can be truly explained by invoking sociological, psychological, or historical factors. The sacred, as Rudolf Otto would have said, is something completely different, it is sui generis.

Individualism and Elitism

Eliade's understanding of religion as a nonreducible or sui generis phenomenon pervades his way of writing about religious phenomena. All sociological reasoning, according to Eliade, misses the essence of religion; all historical depictions in the ordinary sense do as well. Since sociological perspectives are so inimical to the Eliadean approach, *Shamanism* has little to say about the social relations between the shaman and other members of his group, and focuses on the individual shaman and his heroic status. The archaic, religious person who is the ostensible main protagonist of much of Eliade's work is the deeply engaged religious virtuoso, and in this sense Eliade's approach is elitist.[8]

The shaman wields power even in Eliade's world, but this is power in a world of ideas, a power that is achieved in an initiatory crisis as the shaman strives to master the techniques for getting in touch with the sacred realm. Both the yogi's and the shaman's liminal status fascinated Eliade, who viewed his own life in terms of such initiations.[9] The shaman, the archaic initiate par excellence, seems partly to serve as Eliade's alter ego, a lone antimodernist culture hero.[10] The down-to-earth social and political power that shamans had in various cultures, by contrast, seem to have been of little interest to him.

On Constructing Typologies

If the reading of "the sacred" as a distinct ontological category is correct, some puzzling questions arise. Given that religious phenomena in Eliade's view are not social or cultural, historical or psychological, but something entirely distinct—how can observers who are inevitably culturally and historically situated know when they have encountered any particular religious phenomenon such as shamanism? What makes, for example, the Mongolian religious expert who uses a drum as a ritual means to contact various hierarchically ranked deities an example of the same phenomenon as the Kwakiutl religious specialist who cures diseases by enlisting the aid of various animal spirits and sucking out the illness from the patient?

If all of history, the entire set of events that can be observed in the world is merely a poor reflection of this utterly distinct category of the sacred, how can one know anything about what a religious phenomenon "really is"? The answer, it would seem, is close to that given by other authors with similar hierarchical, idealistically based views of religion. One knows because of an inner certitude, born perhaps of one's own spiritual maturity and development. *Shamanism: Archaic Techniques of Ecstasy* is one of Eliade's seemingly most empirically oriented studies. It plays a minor role in much of the secondary literature on Eliade. Bryan Rennie's rich review of Eliade's theoretical and methodological foundations mentions it only in passing.[11] This may be because the theoretical discussion of the nature of shamanism takes up a limited space compared to the many hundreds of examples given. However, Eliade's way of identifying shamanism and discussing its concrete manifestations is in line with his approach to religious phenomena as it appears in other works.

How is shamanism identified and defined? First and foremost, by being localized in a Central Asian core area. Although shamanism exists elsewhere, Eliade insists that "Shamanism in the *strict* sense is pre-eminently a religious phenomenon of Siberia and Central Asia,"[12] and that "this magico-religious phenomenon has had its most complete manifestation in North and Central Asia."[13] On what grounds does Eliade conclude that *strict* or *complete* shamanism is the Siberian and Central Asian form of shamanism, and not, say, the religious practices of the Sami of northern Scandinavia, the Amazonian Shipibo, or the circumpolar Inuit? Presumably this distinction between shamanism in a strict and a broad or loose sense of the word is connected to the historical coincidence that made the Tungus language of Siberia the source from which the word shaman was borrowed. The first attested instances of the word in a Western language date back to the 1660s (Znamenski 2007: 5–6). The derived forms *shamanism* and *chamanisme* are only attested much later: in English in 1780 and in French in 1801. At the time, the word shamanism still denoted a Siberian religious practice. But from the second half of the nineteenth century and onward, the word began to be used more and more frequently as a generic term for religious phenomena among other indigenous groups, such as Native Americans.

Rather paradoxically, for Eliade, even the Tungus with their strict and complete form of shamanism apparently only practice a distorted form of what shamanism *really* is: "Nowhere in the world or in history will a perfectly 'pure' and 'primordial' religious phenomenon be found."[14] The epistemological problem alluded to above recurs here: if all documented forms of shamanism are impure or even corrupt, how does one know that one has actually identified the phenomenon? Creating a definition of shamanism and setting boundaries around the concept come with problems of a different order of magnitude than, say, defining Islam. Since Islam is a self-designation, an empirically based definition could begin by observing discourses and practices of groups that describe themselves as Muslim, and gradually construct a chain of family resemblances that connect various versions of what these groups self-identify as Islamic. The work involved would, of course, be immense, but at least in theory it would be possible to proceed along those lines. Shamanism, on the other hand, is not a self-designation. Eliade just presents examples of local religious practices and declares that they denote variations of the same underlying phenomenon.

Although local specifics may be quite diverse, it does make sense to construct a scholarly terminology that encompasses a number of such local traditions. The alternative would be the rather fruitless exercise of using only indigenous terms and therefore of failing to address similarities between local concepts and practices. Such a terminology, however, denotes ideal types designed as such by the scholarly community. There is in no sense such thing as, for example, a "pure" or "original" creation myth, initiation ritual, or diviner, with all empirical instances identified in the historical record merely constituting a decline or a limited form. Eliade's problem is that he seems to conflate the activity of *constructing* a boundary around a heuristically useful concept such as shamanism, and that of *discovering* an already existing boundary around a natural category. Because all real, observable religious practices represent decayed forms from a supposed original, Eliade's concept of shamanism appears to belong in a Platonic realm not directly accessible to empirical observation.

Synonymization

A key element in Eliade's (and, as we will see, in Harner's) depiction of shamanism is the insistence that observable religious phenomena are basically superficial variations on the same underlying essence, and that it is therefore legitimate to compare practices from various traditions from different historical epochs and all parts of the globe. This way of reducing differences to shared essences, a discourse that we can call synonymization, has ancient roots and a long history, and it is impossible within the confines of a brief chapter even to sketch the development of the idea that the core elements of various religions are essentially all the same.[15] In a pretheoretical context, the idea of synonymization is found in concepts as diverse as the conviction in much of Graeco-Roman intellectual culture that various names of deities refer to the same gods, and in the later idea that much of what was of value in antique philosophy, Christian thought, and various other traditions could be traced back to a perennial philosophy. Structurally similar ideas were absorbed into the discipline history of religions. By allowing a considerable interpretive freedom when examining religious data from around the world, one could conclude that, for example, totemism was a well-defined religious practice common to a vast number of different indigenous peoples, regardless of where and when these people lived. Eliade's book *Shamanism* is permeated by synonymization. Already on page 4, the reader is told that a number of etymologically unrelated terms in the Tungus, Yakut, Mongolian, Buriat, and Tatar languages mean the same thing, namely shaman. Much of what constitutes the taxon "shaman" depends on other broad categories set up on equally synonymizing grounds. One of the shaman's primary functions is to undertake a ritual journey. His body may remain as in a coma, while a part of him embarks on a voyage through heavenly or underground realms. For this reason, as Eliade expresses it, "the shaman is the great specialist of the soul."[16] How is this soul constituted? Cross-culturally, conceptions vary greatly. Some people think that human beings have one soul, others that they possess between three and seven different souls. The soul, according to some local beliefs, dwells in birds after the human body's death. According to others the soul—or one of the souls—risks being eaten by demons. In some cultures, the soul is identical with the shadow, in others the soul is a life force that is located the blood, and in yet others the soul is equal to the breath. On what grounds are all of these beliefs examples of the same concept, and why is this concept usefully labeled by our word "soul" with all its Christian connotations? The reasons for adopting this term are never clearly explained, but depend on the same tacit assumption that similarities are important and differences trifling.

Ancient Wisdom

Outside of academia, the idea of a perennial philosophy has had a considerable attraction. Who are the carriers of the ancient wisdom? Over time, a range of different cultures has been identified as particularly wise. As intellectual fashions have changed, the prime candidate for this role has been ancient Egypt, a generalized Orient, sometimes specified as India, Tibet, or the Himalayas, or even imaginary cultures, the Atlantis myth being the best-known example of the latter.

Indigenous groups have on various occasions been identified as particularly wise people. Hence, when French explorers came in contact with Brazilian Indians in the late 1500s, an image of the Indian as a positive moral antithesis to the supposed decadence of the French upper class was created (Léry 1990). Representations of indigenous peoples as primitive and barbaric nevertheless remained staple fare over the following centuries. The contemporary surge of interest in, or rather projection of positive fantasies onto, indigenous groups is a late-twentieth-century phenomenon, which has been extensively surveyed in critical literature such as Berkhofer 1978, Deloria 1998, and Huhndorf 2001. Eliade's

Shamanism is certainly not an overt espousal of such projections, but can be read as an endorsement of indigenous spiritual wisdom by readers aware of his fascination with archaic *homo religiosus*.

The Allure of Shamanism

What appears from one perspective to be a series of complications or even unsolvable problems with Eliade's approach can, from another, be seen as active assets. For a person interested less in the ethnographic specifics of ritualism among one indigenous culture or another than in the appreciation of shamanism for the spiritual insights it might give us, the way Eliade describes shamanism has several attractions. Shamanism is not an umbrella term designating a range of quite distinct phenomena, but is part of the shared human heritage. It is no longer primarily linked to the specific social structure of, for example, a seminomadic group of reindeer herdsmen in Siberia, but is an individualistic quest for inner, spiritual power. Nor is it connected to, for us, exotic cosmologies and concepts of personhood, but is a technique that deals with well-known phenomena such as "the soul." At the same time as shamanism is made compatible with a modern, Western cultural context, it becomes an expression of a nostalgic sentiment of loss for an archaic mode of life, when people were supposedly in tune with the sacred. Finally, this sacred is (perhaps) not just a culturally postulated transempirical entity, but may really exist as an ontological domain of its own. As we will see, these are characteristics that also resonate with the way Harner describes shamanism in his canonical text.

Michael Harner and the Emergence of Core Shamanism

If Eliade's approach to shamanism can partly be understood as resulting from his personal background and his intellectual preferences, things are rather different with Harner and his version of neoshamanism. Harner has published rather sparingly, has not revealed much of his biography, and is not involved in academic debates on theoretical and methodological issues. The main features of Harner's understanding of shamanism can be found in his book *The Way of the Shaman*, and information on his method that can be obtained at first hand by participating in courses,[17] or at second hand via, for example, sources published by practitioners of Harnerian neoshamanism,[18] and from texts that advertise his courses.[19] Information on how Harnerian neoshamanism was created is harder to glean from published sources. In particular, *The Way of the*

Shaman presents the reader with a puzzling lacuna. The introductory chapter describes Harner's dramatic experiences as an anthropologist overwhelmed by a hallucinogen-induced altered state of consciousness. The rest of the book serves as a manual explaining how to perform a set of much less intense rituals. The difference between shamanism in Amazonian Peru and in the neoshamanic setting is immense, but nothing in the book explains how Harner made the transition from one to the other. How, when, and why Harner decided to create the drum journey and other rituals is left outside the discussion.

A few basic facts are clear enough from his publications. Harner studied the practice of Amazonian shamanism during field work conducted in 1961 and 1964. Around that time, he also began to experiment with the use of drum to provoke altered states of consciousness. In the 1970s, he began holding workshops for small groups of people. The first center for training in neoshamanic methods was founded by Harner and his wife, Sandra, in 1979, and was transformed into a foundation in 1987. Merely presenting such bare facts, however, says next to nothing about what must have been a fundamental transmutation for Harner himself, from academic researcher to spiritual teacher.

Fundamental Traits of Core Shamanism

The presuppositions that undergird Harner's approach to shamanism must be reconstructed from the end result, the neoshamanic method itself, and the social setting that Harner created in order to disseminate this method. Such a reconstruction reveals that all of the fundamental features of how Eliade presented shamanismits—quasi-independence of any particular ethnographic context, its heroic individualism, the potentially distinct ontological status of the "sacred" encountered by the religious hero figure, and so on—can also be found in Harner's *The Way of the Shaman*, but are here taken to the next level.

Firstly, the synonymization that characterizes Eliade's *Shamanism: Archaic Techniques of Ecstasy* is even more extensive in Harner's book. Rituals from three different continents are modified and merged into the ritual repertoire of the neoshamans. References to half a dozen different ethnographic traditions can coexist on the same page. Secondly, the social aspect of shamanism, the interaction between the local group and the shaman, that still plays some role, albeit a subdued one, in Eliade's depiction of shamanism, has disappeared completely. Neoshamanism in Harner's case is very much a story of a heroic journey of self-discovery into alternate worlds, but Eliade's elitism is here replaced by a characteristic oxymoron of contemporary spirituality: everybody can become a hero on a quest. Various forms of modern religiosity, from transpersonal psychology to Transcendental Meditation and from Scientology to New Age, revolve around a sacralization of each person's individual self.[20] Neoshamanism, too, is presented in similar terms, and the heroic quest is at least in part a journey of self-discovery. Conversely, and unlike shamanism in ethnographic contexts, there is no socially defined role that awaits the person who pursues this quest. What kind of objectives must be completed in order to be acknowledged as a successful neoshamanic practitioner? What broader purposes does one as a practitioner fulfill? One presumably needs a significant amount of entrepreneurial spirit in order to create a neoshamanic social role on one's own, highly personalized terms.

Thirdly, neoshamanism operates with a vaguely defined cosmology that leaves what is perhaps the most basic question a would-be practitioner might ask unanswered: in what sense does the visionary world that one visits on the drum journey "really exist"? Epistemologically, neoshamanism resembles Paganism and New Age in that it rarely demands an overt leap of faith. A form of mild skepticism is encouraged—at least rhetorically. For many people in the New Age milieu, the important thing is not to *believe* in reincarnation or angels, but just to be open to the idea that past lives or transcendent beings may exist. Harner presents neoshamanic cosmology in similar terms. *The Way of the Shaman* explains that there are two different forms of consciousness. Everyday consciousness is the way of perceiving the world what we all know. Shamanic consciousness is what we gain access to by learning to undertake drum journeys. At the start of the journey of discovery, one should not worry about whether the shamanic world "really" exists, or whether it is a product of one's own mind. Play with the fiction, be open to the possibility that the power animals and the different worlds you visit have their own existence, and see what results such an open attitude can lead to.

Fourthly—and here Harner goes well beyond anything Eliade suggests—the claim that shamanism is a form of generic ritualism practiced by members of very diverse societies means that modern, urban middle-class Westerners can also access the insights imparted by shamanism. The fact that Harner's book is a do-it-yourself manual for presumptive neoshamans in the West gives the text a distinct feeling. Particularly telling in this respect is the iconography in Harner's book, which by means of 15 illustrations describes neoshamanism as a practical project to be undertaken by any reader. Harner's suite of illustrations begins with a drawing made by a Shuar shaman. The caption explains how the head of another Shuar shaman, who is in an altered state of consciousness, is surrounded by a golden aura. The choice of starting out with this illustration anchors Harner's neoshamanism—a decidedly modern religious construction—in an indigenous context. At the same time, a subtle synonymization states that there is no essential difference between the reader of Harner's book, sitting in his living room chair at home, and the Shuar shaman in the rain forest. The concept of an *aura* (referred to in the caption) is a widespread component of modern alternative religiosity. Harner implicitly states that a contemporary concept with its most proximate roots in early twentieth- century Theosophy[21] is the "same" as an (unspecified) concept held by the Shuar.

The ethnographic anchorage continues in Figures 2 and 3 (from the Hopi Indians), Figure 4 (an Inuit mask), and Figure 5 (Tibetan). Then the context switches in Figure 6. We see a figure beating a drum, presumably embarking on a "shamanic journey." This is no Native American or Siberian shaman, but a balding, bespectacled middle-aged man facing away from the reader. The portrait, in fact, bears a striking resemblance to Harner himself. Most of the remaining illustrative material depicts Westerners. The sequence of images in *The Way of the Shaman* with its tacit switch from ethnographic materials to drawings of modern practitioners of drum journeys suggests that shamanic techniques and experiences anchored in archaic cultures are nevertheless universal, and thus available to any seeker from a Western background.

Other features of the book add to this presentation of neoshamanism as a culturally decontextualized form of do-it-yourself spirituality. Modern religiosity in Pagan or New Age versions is often vague on belief but highly ritualized. Many therapeutic methods that exist within the New Age milieu are based on the ritualized manipulation of a kind of vital force or "energy." Practitioners can have precise opinions as to what methods should be used, but little interest or ability in explaining the origin and nature of the "energies." Harnerian neoshamanism follows the same pattern. The central ritual, the "drum journey," is described in detail in *The Way of the Shaman*. Introductory courses provide hands-on instruction on precisely how the ritual should be performed. The point of the ritual is to access another dimension of reality, a shamanic reality populated by various beings. The precise geography of that realm and its ontological status are, as we have seen, left deliberately vague. There is a rhetorical purpose served by this vagueness: neoshamanism is presented as an utterly individualistic quest. Shamanic reality is open to virtually everybody, and anyone experimenting with the shamanic rituals learns of the new dimension of reality he or she is accessing through personal experience.

The claim that shamanic knowledge is available to everybody is, however, a truth with some important qualifiers. Courses in Harnerian drum journeys are promoted and sold on market premises. People who teach courses obviously need to receive an income that is sufficient to cover their living expenses and generate at least a modest surplus. Drum journeys and other neoshamanic rituals are therefore necessarily treated like any other goods—available for those able and willing to pay for the courses. These are priced roughly at the same level as New Age offerings of similar duration. At the time of this writing (2014), two-day workshops in topics such as shamanic healing and shamanic dreamwork were offered for roughly $250. As yet another sign of the commodification of shamanism, Harner's method has given rise to a series of spin-off products. Just as there is merchandise associated with most other spiritual alternatives in the marketplace, there is a Shamanic Store, where books, CDs, drums, and other products can be ordered online.

Religiosity and Bureaucratization

The New Age milieu is characterized by utterly fluid organizational forms. Readers of inspirational books and individuals with a more or less passing desire to try out one or another of the many products available on the religious market will form loose networks of friends with similar interests, but are only rarely willing to join forces in a more structured way. Therein certainly also lies a part of the allure: such forms of religiosity constitute an oasis of *Gemeinschaft* in a desert of *Gesellschaft*. Harnerian neoshamanism is a striking departure from this general picture of a large number of individuals doing their own thing in whatever way they please. The training as a shaman is not only structured on commercial principles but also exhibits a high degree of formalization. Whereas indigenous forms of shamanism tend to be reproduced by apprenticeship, that is, a relationship over a long period of time between individuals with strong personal ties, Harnerian neoshamanism is thoroughly bureaucratized. Given that thousands of people have participated in courses in neoshamanism, such a high degree of formalization is probably inevitable.

Harner's school of neoshamanism, the Foundation for Shamanic Studies (FSS) as presented on his website www.shamanism.org, is organized very much like other American private educational centers, that is, as a foundation governed by a board of trustees and a number of executive officers. For each step in the training there are formalized requirements, set dates, a schedule, and carefully specified learning goals. The introductory course, for instance, needs to be completed under the aegis of a certified FSS faculty member to provide the basis of subsequent studies. These include a range of courses, such as a Five-Day Harner Shamanic Counseling Training, a Two-Week Shamanic Healing Intensive, and at the top level, a Three-Year Program of Advanced Initiations in Shamanism and Shamanic Healing. Specific requirements can be waived by a review board that processes individual applications for participating in higher-level echelons of the training. The three-year program, it may be noted, is adapted to the realities of the employment situation of most people in the modern West, and in reality consists of six weeks distributed over the three years. Admission requirements for each course are carefully specified. Upon completion of a given number of such courses, a certificate is issued. A caveat on the website reminds potential participants that a certificate is not the same as being a bona fide shaman. Despite appearing to downplay the significance of these documents, the FSS website provides detailed information on how to qualify for, for example, a bronze, silver, or gold certificate. For a credential at the highest level, the gold certificate, a long list of individual steps is listed, and all the formalities and costs of receiving the desired document, including an online form to be filled out by the applicant, are explained in detail. At this point, the distance between the Siberian Tungus' local religious specialist and the neoshamanic foundation's bureaucratized method of training would-be shamans seems vast.

Notes

1. The present text is a reworked English-language version of an article originally published in Swedish as Hammer 2000. The tight publication schedule under which the original text was revised has unfortunately made it impossible to take newer sources into account. Michael Harner in 2013 published a book entitled *Cave and Cosmos: Shamanic Encounters with Another Reality*, which I was not able to consult for more recent information on his views.
2. A drum journey is a ritual in which participants, to the sound of a drum, visualize how they travel down through a hole in the ground and reach an alternate reality, often described as a landscape populated by animals.
3. Stark and Bainbridge 1985: 19–37.
4. Lindquist 1997
5. This idea is ubiquitous in Eliade's writings. See, e.g., Eliade 1961.
6. See, for example, Morris 1986: 174–181 and the sources referred to there.
7. Eliade 1964: xix.
8. Olson 1992: 4
9. Olson 1992: 169.
10. Regarding the shaman as Eliade's alter ego, see Olson 1992: 169.
11. Rennie 1996.
12. Eliade 1964: 4 (emphasis added).
13. Eliade 1964: 6.
14. Eliade 1972: 11.
15. The history of the twin ideas of a primeval theology (*prisca theologia*) and perennial philosophy (*philosophia perennis*), and of the belief that most or all religions are essentially the same, are extensively documented in Figl 1993 and Hanegraaff 2012.

16. Eliade 1964: 8.
17. Harner's courses illustrate a particularly difficult circumstance for the field-working researcher. Neo-shamanism as an audience cult is openly available through vast quantities of printed material. Neo-shamanism as a cult movement can be approached through traditional fieldwork of the kind Galina Lindqvist conducted (1997).

    With client cults, the situation is different. All training after the initial weekend course commands high fees—in order to achieve the highest levels of shamanic training, the expenses quickly add up. My own first-hand experience is limited to an introductory course held in Copenhagen by Jonathan Horowitz.
18. See, for example, Sørenssen 1990.
19. See www.shamanism.org.
20. See Heelas 1996.
21. The modern concept of aura, a colored light surrounding the physical body, which can be seen and interpreted by people with a special gift, was popularized by the Theosophist Charles Leadbeater in his book *Man Visible and Invisible*, published in 1903.

References

Berkhofer, Jr., Robert F. 1978. *The White Man's Indian*. New York: Knopf.

Deloria, Philip. 1998. *Playing Indian*. New Haven, CT: Yale University Press.

Eliade, Mircea. 1961. *The Sacred and the Profane: The Nature of Religion*. New York: Harper Torchbooks.

———. 1964. *Shamanism: Archaic Techniques of Ecstasy*. Princeton: Princeton University Press.

Figl, Johann. 1993. *Die Mitte der Religionen: Idee und Praxis universalreligiöser Bewegungen*. Darmstadt: Wissenschaftliche Buchgesellschaft.

Hammer, Olav. 2000. "Senmodern shamanism—om två kanoniska texter," in Thomas Larsson (ed.) *Schamaner: Essäer om religiösa mästare*. Falun: Nya Doxa, 211–226.

Hanegraaff, Wouter J. 2012. *Esotericism and the Academy: Rejected Knowledge in Western Culture*. Cambridge: Cambridge University Press.

Harner, Michael. 1980. *The Way of the Shaman: A Guide to Power and Healing*. San Francisco: Harper & Row.

Heelas, Paul. 1996. *The New Age Movement: The Celebration of the Self and the Sacralization of Modernity*. Oxford: Blackwell.

Huhndorf, Shari. 2001. *Going Native: Indians in the American Cultural Imagination*. Ithaca and London: Cornell University Press.

Hutton, Ronald. 2001. *Shamans: Siberian Spirituality and the Western Imagination*. London: Hambledon.

Kharitidi, Olga. 1996. *Entering the Circle: The Secrets of Ancient Siberian Wisdom Discovered by a Russian Psychiatrist*. San Francisco: HarperRow.

Léry, Jean de. 1990. *History of a Voyage to the Land of Brazil, Otherwise Called America*. Berkeley: University of California Press.

Lindquist, Galina. 1997. *Shamanic Performances on the Urban Scene: Neo-Shamanism in Contemporary Sweden*. Stockholm: Almqvist & Wiksell.

Morris, Brian. 1986. *Anthropological Studies of Religion: An Introductory Text*. Cambridge: Cambridge University Press.

Olson, Carl. 1992. *The Theology and Philosophy of Eliade*. London: Macmillan.

Rennie, Bryan. 1996. *Reconstructing Eliade: Making Sense of Religion*. Albany: SUNY Press.

Sørenssen, Arthur. 1990. *Den stora drömmen: en invigning i praktisk shamanism*. Stockholm: Vattumannens förlag.

Stark, Rodney, and William S. Bainbridge. 1985. *The Future of Religion: Secularization, Revival and Cult Formation*. Berkeley: University of California Press.

Von Stuckrad, Kocku. 2003. *Schamanismus und Esoterik: Kultur- und wissenschaftsgeschichtliche Betrachtungen*. Leuven: Peeters.

Znamenski, Andrei. 2007. *The Beauty of the Primitive: Shamanism and the Western Imagination*. Oxford: Oxford University Press.

II

Late Modern Shamanism in Nordic Countries

2

The Rise of Neoshamanism in Norway: Local Structures-Global Currents

Trude Fonneland

Prior to the late 1990s, neoshamanism in Norway differed little from neoshamanisms found elsewhere in the Western world. Since then, practitioners of neoshamanism in Norway have been increasingly engaged in working to recover the indigenous traditions of their country and ancestors. A Sami version of neoshamanism has been established, along with a new focus on Norse traditions as sources for the development of neoshamanistic practices, notions, and rituals.

As a manifestation of these trends, a local shamanic association concerned with the preservation of both Sami and Norse shamanic traditions was granted status as a separate religious community on March 13, 2012, by the County Governor of Troms, Northern Norway. This means, according to the laws regulating religion in Norway, that they may perform religious ceremonies like baptism, weddings, and funerals, and, additionally, obtain financial support relative to membership. Interestingly, this shamanic association appears to have been created in order to meet the criteria required for obtaining the rights of Norwegian religious communities; the national jurisdiction thus inspired a diverse group of professional entrepreneurs to join forces and organize themselves. It is, at the same time, likely that the Sami dimension of these endeavors contributed positively to the Governor's decision.

In a northern European context, this was the first time a neoshamanic movement was able to obtain the status of an official religious community (see Fonneland 2014a; 2014b). However, this association is but one of many examples of how shamanism is expressed in contemporary Norway. In addition to the approval of this association, the growing interest in shamanic practices is reflected in, among other things, the alternative fairs (*Alternativmesser*) that take place in cities all across the country.[1] At these fairs, neoshamans and other New Age entrepreneurs market their goods and services by highlighting the uniqueness of the Arctic North, and the general public's interest and attendance has risen annually. A growing number of Sami shamans offer their services on home pages on the Internet (Fonneland 2010), and yearly neoshaman gatherings are arranged. Not least, a Sami neoshamanic festival, *Isogaisa*, has been established that gathers neoshamanic practitioners from all over the world (see Fonneland, this volume).

The increasing eagerness to "recover" local traditions confirms what Jenny Blain argues in her article "Heathenry, The Past, and Sacred Sites in Today's Britain," namely that geographically and/or ethnically local paganisms are becoming more popular and distinguishable. These reconstructionist pagans, Blain points out, explore the traditions of a particular culture or region to which they trace their heritage or feel a strong affinity, believing that historical documents and artifacts hold valuable clues to ancient religious practices, relationships with deities and spirits, and pre-Christian people's worldviews (Blain 2005: 184).

It is these developments and increasing spiritual inventiveness that are the focus of this chapter. I am particularly interested in how and what happens when the global culture of neoshamanism interacts with a specific local culture—in this case, Norwegian society. Drawing on developments within the field of neoshamanism in Norway, the chapter ventures between the local and global, highlighting how American Indian symbolism might serve as a spark that prompts a spiritual seeker to step onto the path of spirituality, making what is perceived as local traditions the basis for a new global religious movement. The cultural creation developed by practitioners of shamanism in Norway is here referred to as Nordic neoshamanism. Nordic neoshamanism can be described as a religious innovation in which practitioners draw inspiration from what they perceive as Sami, as well as from Norse religious traditions. This merging of Sami and Norse traditions in turn provides insight into processes of religious creation and creativity.

My analyses draw on interviews with leading practitioners of neoshamanism in Norway, participant observation at seminars and in ritual performances, elucidating what neoshamans do, as well as on document analysis of neoshamans' and neoshamanic institutions' home pages on the Internet.[2] The chapter starts with locating the roots of what we today know as Sami neoshamanism. Further, the processes connected with the approval of SA are discussed. Finally, I highlight how these constructions have been contoured by the domestic media and the local milieu, and look at how these types of constructs can be said to be entangled in conceptions of a common past and Nordic heritage.[3]

Sami Neoshamanism in Norway

Precisely when the interest in and the revitalization of symbols and beliefs from the pre-Christian Sami religion began is unclear. Political upheaval and struggles in the Sami community in the late 1970s, such as the protests related to the expansion of the Alta-Kautokeino River, can nevertheless be highlighted as a spark for some of what today is expressed within the neoshamanic environment in Norway (see also Kraft and Alver, this volume). The "Alta affair" was triggered by the Norwegian Parliament's decision in November 1978 to approve a hydroelectric project that involved the damming of the Alta-Kautokeino River, which flows through central parts of Finnmark, Norway's northernmost county. After a prolonged period of acts of civil disobedience as well as hunger strikes, the decision was effectuated in January 1981, despite massive protests.

These demonstrations sparked a Sami ethnic revival, and are generally regarded as the beginning of the Sami cultural revival movement. They also served as premises for what neoshaman Ailo Gaup has referred to as the 78 generation—the Sami version of the 1968 generation (Klassekampen March 11–12, 2006).

At the same time as these protests and demonstrations were playing out, new cross-Atlantic religious ideas and trends were introduced into Norwegian society. Just a decade earlier, anthropologists Carlos Castaneda and Michael Harner had published books based on their fieldwork among Indians in Mexico, Peru, and Ecuador that provided the ground for a neoshamanic movement with an international scope. As Bente Gullveig Alver describes in her chapter in this volume, "More or Less Genuine Shamans," Harner also visited Finnmark to gain knowledge about the Sami culture and religion. Searching for traces of Sami shamanism, he visited the Sami Mikkel Gaup, known as Healing Fox. Harner's focus on a core shamanism free from all cultural and social contexts makes his religious practices easy to integrate into almost every sacred symbolic language (see Harner 1980). His presence, courses, and writings also came to influence the development of Ailo Gaup, recognized as the founder of the Norwegian neoshamanic movement and the first Sami neoshaman in Norway.

Gaup tells the story of his personal spiritual development—including studies of scholarly literature on the pre-Christian Sami religion—in his semiautobiographical *The Shamanic Zone* (2005). Gaup describes how he was sent from Kautokeino to a foster family in Oslo as an orphan, and thus lost access to the land of his birth. Searching for his Sami roots, not the least for traces of Sami shamanism, Gaup traveled back to northern Norway and took part in the demonstrations against the damming of the Alta Kautokeino River. The early phase of the ethnopolitical movement was concerned with rights and politics, as well as identity issues, but for Ailo they also served as a spark for a religious revival (see Fonneland 2010).

However, what Gaup found in Finnmark that could be related to the practice of shamanism had no apparent connection to the *noaidi* traditions for which he was searching. At a hotel in Kautokeino, Gaup met the Chilean refugee Ernesto, who both practiced drum journeys and was willing to teach him the art. This was also how Gaup's first shamanic trance journey came about: accompanied by an African djembe drum (Gaup 2005: 86–98).

The second step in Gaup's training took place through several extended stays at Harner's Foundation for Shamanic Studies in Esalen, California. Having thus been trained in the practice of neoshamanism, Gaup settled in Oslo and established himself as a professional shaman. During its first decade, the Norwegian shamanic movement was more or less a copy of the system developed by Harner in the United States. Similarly, the broader New Age scene in Norway differed little from its counterparts in the United States and elsewhere in the world (see Fonneland and Kraft 2013).

Fieldwork conducted by Bengt Ove Andreassen and Trude Fonneland on the New Age milieu in Tromsø in 2002 indicated that what was expressed in the local New Age milieu did not seem to be tainted by place-specific elements, and found few, if any, references to the pre-Christian Sami religion (Andreassen and Fonneland 2002/2003). In his study of articles and advertisements connected with indigenous spirituality in the Norwegian New Age magazine *Alternative Network*, Cato Christensen similarly concluded that the Sami were more or less absent from the otherwise extensive material on shamanism, paganism, and indigenous people (2005).

However, over the course of the first five years of the new millennium, the situation gradually changed. From this period forward, professional neoshamans were depicted as representing an ancient Sami shamanic tradition (Christensen 2007), and the Norwegian New Age scene was increasingly filled with Sami shamans, symbols, and traditions, along with a new focus on local- and place-specific characteristics unique to the northern region, particularly in terms of domestic geography (Fonneland 2010). Contemporary Sami shamanism has become a core subject within the field of neoshamanism in Norway. The most profiled shamans, Gaup, Eirik Myrhaug, Anita Biong, and Ronald Kvernmo, teach courses in Sami neoshamanism and, except for Biong, have all published books on the subject (see Gaup 2005; 2007; Kvernmo 2011; Brunvoll and Brynn 2013). Additionally, guided vision quests in the northern Norwegian region, as well as courses on the making of ritual drums (runebomme) have been added to the shamanistic offerings. The various products are available through shamans' home pages on the Internet, local media coverage, Facebook groups, alternative fairs, and through local shops. A variety of Sami ritual drums are, for instance, today offered in tourist shops, at the annual New Age market, as well as on the Internet home pages of Sami shamans (see Fonneland 2012).

The interest in seeking local roots can be seen in the context of a growing reaction against Harner's core shamanism. As early as the 1980s, the Swedish neoshaman Jørgen I. Eriksson, a proponent of northern and especially Sami shamanism, was already writing extensively in the Swedish neoshamanistic magazine, *Gimle*, pointing out that Harner's core shamanism stripped shamanic traditions of their cultural uniqueness (see Svanberg 1994: 30).[4] Eriksson comments,

> Nordic shamanism lives an independent life again without any need for crutches from the Turtle Island. This is a tradition that is in agreement with the ancestors' will and orientation, with one's own earth, landscape, climate, light and darkness, one's own plants and animals. Therefore, those who want to walk the way of the shaman do not need to carry coals to Newcastle any more. The necessary knowledge and teachers are here. (Eriksson, in Gimle N.o- 11 1986)

In the practice of neoshamanism, various religious entrepreneurs obtain legitimacy through adaptation to the local environment and local culture. Featured cultural expressions are enrolled in discourses connected to tradition and continuity that legitimate the entrepreneurs' products and services, and reaffirm a certain quality of life. By underscoring their connection to "local" religious traditions, some of the practitioners of Sami shamanism wish to distance themselves from their American origins and present their practices not as "core," but as locally inspired.

The Sami neoshamanic movement participates in the global by promoting the local. Global new religious currents are here painted with local traditions and cultures, and transformed into something that practitioners can present as local and particular—reshaping stories about the local landscape and local religious traditions so that they appear in the glow of authenticity. As such the Sami neoshamanic movement stands out as a resource in the encounter with the global New Age subculture by drawing boundaries between what is perceived as real and what is perceived as illegitimate, between the authentic and the commercialized, between the unique and the common.

Negotiations and resistance regarding the merging of local and global religious expressions are also a central concern within the newly approved SA. In what follows I will focus on how neoshamanism in Norway has developed from a loosely organized movement into an approved religious denomination reaping broad support both from individual religious seekers as well as on a political level.

Vision of a Shamanistic Association

The development of new religious organizations often starts with a vision. In the case of SA, this vision is linked to a single person's interaction with the world of his spirits and spiritual helpers—a world that generated a revelation. The person who received this revelation was Kyrre Gram Franck, also known as White Cougar, now a leader of SA on the national level. Franck has been involved in neoshamanism since the early 1990s and says that he has had shamanic teachers inspired by American Indian as well as Sami indigenous traditions. In Tromsø, Kyrre has been a well-known local shaman and healer for a long time. He is also the organizer behind "The World Drum Project," a shamanic nonprofit organization founded in Norway in October 2006 that focuses on peace and environmental issues.[5] Kyrre can be viewed as a soteriological entrepreneur. He is a founder, an organization builder, a role model, and a motivator. As the association's appointed leader, Kyrre's personal background, his interests, friendships, and networks allowed him to put his imprint on the rise and development of the association (see Lindquist 1997:189). Regarding his vision, Kyrre tells me,

> It is difficult to express these images and feelings in words, but the vision came to me in a dream. That is, not in an ordinary dream, but in a state of trance and communication with the spirits. One of my spiritual helpers, an old man, came to me and showed me a picture of Scandinavia. He then told me that I should start up something called the Norwegian Shamanic Association. I could see that there was a slight contradiction here, but the explanation is probably that it is not me who will be starting up shamanic associations in the other Scandinavian countries. The vision also brought images and feelings of people sharing spiritual knowledge and learning, and I was told to focus on the past. Even though the Shamanistic Association embraces shamanism in its many variations, it is at the same time important for us here in the north to protect the northern traditions associated with shamanism. So what we hope to accomplish in the long term is to develop the Shamanistic Association into a tradition keeper for the northern traditions. (my translation)

This story can also be seen as a "call" narrative. It emphasizes Kyrre's experience of being chosen, and is interpreted as an injunction to use his special abilities for his fellows. Like other "call" narratives, the story is based on a series of events that are connected and interpreted as a summons from "outside"—from divine powers (Alver and Selberg 1992, 72–74; Alver 2011, 137–138). According to Kyrre, the intention behind the establishment of SA is that the association will develop into a unifying force with the ability to strengthen individuals' and groups' rights to practice shamanism. Not least, he hopes that the association will develop into a true alternative for those who adhere to shamanistic belief systems, and that the construction of life-cycle ceremonies like baptisms, confirmations, weddings, and funerals will help increase people's interest in neoshamanism.

As a first step toward the recognition and formalization of a neoshamanic association, Kyrre shared his vision with his friends in the local neoshamanic milieu. One of them, Ronald Kvernmo, who had been engaged in the development of the Sami neoshamanic festival Isogaisa (see Fonneland chapter 11, this volume), urged Kyrre to drop the word "Norwegian" from the association's title. According to Kvernmo, this word could be offensive to neoshamans involved in and inspired by Sami neoshamanism.[6] After consulting the spirits about this potential amendment, the name of the association was changed to the Shamanistic Association.

Kyrre's central position is also reflected in the organization of SA, in which, in addition to being a leader, he also has the status of vision keeper. According to the board protocol, in cases in which decisions might lead to significant changes in the vision, the vision keeper retains veto power. The position of vision keeper will follow Kyrre for life. He will also choose the person who will take over as leader of the association when he resigns. Due to his role as both vision receiver and vision keeper, Kyrre is a central catalyst in terms of how SA is profiled, and what is to be emphasized and possibly omitted in the creation of the group's identity and community. This is also, as Galina Lindquist argues, what is striking in the world of neoshamanic performances: "an important condition of its existence, its performative expressions, hinges entirely on certain individuals" (1997: 189). At the same time, the leader nevertheless exerts no strict control in relation to what members want to highlight as sources of authority and authenticity. In SA, Kyrre points out, they strive for a flat organizational structure in which each member has a chance to take part in processes connected with developing the association. Dialogues reflecting interactions between members, leader, and board members are realized through discussions that take place on Facebook. Here members interact, ask questions, and take part in the process of decision-making. For example, a member of the Facebook group makes the comment that

> those who are actively involved and dedicate their time to the association are also helping to shape these visions, so the role of the Vision Keeper must not be to engage randomly in determining all the guidelines, January 16, 2012 at 12:20 p.m. (my translation)

Lone Ebeltoft, who is the leader of the local association in Tromsø, replies,

> Thanks for these fine comments :) I also imagine a Vision Keeper as a tradition keeper—one who only intervenes if the board considers changing the main paragraph (section 1.1) in SA, January 16, 2012 at 1:15 pm (my translation).

Further Kyrre comments,

> That's right. A Vision Keeper is not intended to cast a veto in everything. . . . As mentioned this is a vision that came to me about two years ago. Therefore it is important for me that the vision is adhered to, but the ability to veto takes effect only where it would lead to a substantial changes in the main paragraph where the vision is expressed, January 16, 2012 at 3:01 p.m. (my translation).

Nevertheless, there is great variety in terms of each member's level of activity and involvement. On Facebook, it is clear that some voices are expressed more frequently than others, and that some dominate in various dialogues. SA consists of a group of people who have highly divergent views of what creates power in terms of neoshamanistic practices and rituals, and whose dedication and engagement varies. These participants are also actors who, to varying degrees, put their imprint on and leave traces in the development of SA.[7]

At the same time as an interaction between the board and individual members is highlighted as central to the development of SA, the external forces of Norwegian governmental laws and regulations are also playing a role in shaping the association. Norwegian legislation and policy toward religious communities have direct consequences for SA's design and maneuverability. The Religious Communities Act that was introduced in 1969 provides a framework for religious organizations in Norway. The Act ensures virtually equal treatment of the Norwegian Church and other religious communities and denominations. No country provides the same level of financial support to religious communities as Norway, and by this arrangement the country represents an outer point where State and municipal grants form most of the resource base for the Norwegian Church, and where other religious communities receive similar public subsidies per member (see Askeland 2011).

Two years after receiving the initial vision, the application process for a neoshamanistic association began. In this process, governmental regulations were dealt with in many arenas. Initially, Franck applied to the County Governor for permission to start a neoshamanistic organization. But this proved difficult because of the bureaucratic system and the rules regulating freedom of belief. If SA was going to have a chance at getting approval to perform neoshamanistic life-cycle ceremonies, they first needed to establish themselves as a religious community.[8] Governmental regulations also impacted the design of these ceremonies. For a wedding to be considered legally binding, for instance, certain formulations needed to be included. SA, then, is a construct designed to meet the requirements for the recognition of religious communities, highlighting how religious practices are adapted, transformed, and changed to fit governmental regulations.

The Process Starts—the Letter to the County Governor

The letter Franck sent to the County Governor to establish both a national board located in Tromsø and a local neoshamanistic association is dated January 16, 2012. It contains information in a number of paragraphs that deal with everything from rules for membership, to objectives, to rules for leaders of local religious communities, to matters relating to the design of the Association's life-cycle ceremonies. Not least, the letter contains SA's confession of faith in the first section:

§1.

The power of creation expresses itself in all parts of life and human beings are interconnected with all living beings on a spiritual plane. Mother Earth is a living being and a particular responsibility rests on us for our fellow creatures and nature. All things living are an expression of the power of creation and therefore are our brothers and sisters.

A shamanistic faith means acknowledging that all things are animated and that they are our relatives. And that by using spiritual techniques, one can acquire knowledge through contacting the power of creation, natural forces and the spiritual world. A shamanistic faith involves a collective and individual responsibility for our fellow creatures, nature beings and Mother Earth. Mother Earth is regarded as a living being.

> Shamanistic practice means the use of shamanistic techniques both for one's own development and for helping our fellow humans and other creatures. This means that creation is sacred and one celebrates the unfolding of the life force. (my translation)[9]

This confession articulates, according to Kyrre, the main parts of his vision. It is with respect to this section that the vision keeper retains the power of veto. The main emphases here are the struggle to protect the environment, a holistic worldview, and Mother Earth as a key symbol for shamanistic practitioners. The symbolic values and ideals emphasized in this paragraph are not unique to Nordic neoshamanism, and can also be found in neoshamanic activities across the globe (see Beyer 1998, Stuckrad 2005). From the very beginning, Mother Earth has been a central touchstone in neoshamanic practices. She is an essential figure to which one attributes power as well as offers sacrifices. A broad statement like this serves to encompass the diversity of practitioners of neoshamanism, and excludes no one on the basis of their national or ethnic identity.

One of the other points highlighted in the letter is that the group will be divided into primary members and other members. Primary members are persons who are not members of another faith, while other members are those who want to support SA, but who are affiliated with another denomination. These persons cannot sit on the board, but otherwise have the same rights as primary members. The annual fee to participate in the Association was, for 2012, 150 Norwegian crowns per member (19.99 EUR). SA receives 500 Norwegian crowns (66.62 EUR) in governmental support every year for each primary member. Currently SA consists of 85 members from all over the country, 67 of whom are primary members. SA is also registered as its own group on Facebook, with 1,345 persons participating.

The letter to the County Governor further states that SA is to be a focal point for persons adhering to a neoshamanistic faith and that their goal is to designate and educate ceremonial leaders across the country. The ceremonial leaders' tasks are to hold regular gatherings for members and others who wish to participate, and this is especially important at the solstices, equinoxes, and full moons. According to the laws regulating religious bodies in Norway, as an approved religious community SA may also perform such religious ceremonies as baptism, confirmations, weddings, and funerals. A group of members is currently working on developing a ceremonial repertoire that will form the basis for the association's life-cycle rituals.[10] This work is organized through a closed group on Facebook, with 19 people taking part.[11] Drafts and ideas concerning the development of the association's main ceremonies are shared, evaluated, and discussed. Appropriate guidelines for the people who will be appointed ceremonial leaders have also been created. The candidate must be at least 23 years of age and have at least five years' experience with shamanistic practices. Ceremonial leaders will be appointed by the main board.

Its organization as a religious community gives SA a privileged role. The approval from the County Governor provides for SA to be a primary representative of the Norwegian neoshamanic milieu in public, although this does not necessarily reflect the situation within the community. Likewise, the State's accreditation implies an acceptance of shamans in the present, for their activities, attitudes, and conceptions, and it is further a means for SA to reach out to potential members and gain attention for themselves and their message.

Bridging Norse and Sami Traditions

Even though SA emphasizes shamanism as a universal phenomenon and embraces neoshamanism in its many variations, at the same time it promotes an agenda of emphasizing local roots and a local connection.[12] In his vision, Franck was told to focus on the past. This focus is also highlighted in SA's official statement, in which it is emphasized that their goal is to develop the organization into a tradition keeper for Nordic neoshamanic traditions.

According to(Franck and Ebeltoft), Nordic shamanism embraces both Norse and Sami pre-Christian traditions. By gathering Norse and Sami traditions under the same roof, they can be disseminated to a larger number of potential members. This is a strategy of inclusion that dissolves the taxonomies of insider and outsider and that is about who has privileged access to the traditions of the past. The term "Nordic neoshamanism" creates a common Nordic approach and a focus on shared traditions. In our conversation, Kyrre and Lone emphasize that the goal is to restore the original roots of Nordic shamanism, preferably back to 5,000 to 10,000 years ago when the differences between the "nature religion practices" of the various local tribes were minimal.

Neither Kyrre nor Lone are of Sami origin, although many of SA's members are. As mentioned, Sami neoshamanism has been marketed as an alternative to Harner's core shamanism in Norway since the early 2000s. This is a topic of contention, and there has been constant discussion about who has the right to take part in and practice what is perceived as Sami traditions (see Myrhaug 1997). The leader and board members of SA wish to avoid such tensions and not be accused of stealing traditions. The drawing of inspiration from a time when the boundaries between Sami and Norse traditions were supposedly blurred can be seen as an attempt to circumvent such tensions.

This desire to merge Norse and Sami traditions is expressed, for example, in the wedding ceremony that the association developed and that was approved by the County Governor. During the ritual, the bride and groom together hold a ring made of iron and copper. Iron in this context is meant to symbolize the Norse community, while copper is linked to the Sami past and Sami traditions. The first wedding ceremony organized by SA in Troms was held at Bjørnefjell, northern Norway, on June 24, 2013. According to the local newspaper *Fremover*, the ceremony took place just before midnight and lasted about 45 minutes. A photo in the news paper shows a bride and groom wearing blue wool clothes decorated with an Arctic symbol, encircled by family, friends, shamans, and not least, nature.[13] In a statement to *Fremover*, Kyrre highlights that the wedding ritual is reconstructed from both Norse and Sami shamanic traditions and that the main elements of the ritual include the reading of poems, the lighting of a sacred fire, and not least, the burial of a braid. This braid has been made in advance and consists of the couple's hair, silver threads, wool, and other assets of importance. The braid, according to Franck, is meant to symbolize the couple's fertility, and is buried as an offering to Mother Earth (*Fremover* July 10, 2013).

To bring Nordic shamanism into the present, SA's focus on northern traditions is also portrayed in their logo. Here Sami and Norse symbols are entwined in a joint expression.

In the logo, the Sami Sun symbol, *beaivi*, encircles Yggdrasil, known as the tree of life in Norse mythology, with a drumming shaman in the foreground. The logo expresses SA's desire to unite traditions, to find a model of a community in the past that all members can view as a resource for their practices in the present—a resource for identity and community. They seek to turn back time to a period when religious traditions formed the basis of community and were not (or so they imagine) identified with specific ethnic groups. The ideal is not to exclude anyone from taking part in a reconstruction of religious traditions. These different approaches to the past are undertaken as part of creating new practices, enacted and endowed with meaning, revealing how a distinctive new cultural milieu is gradually generated.

Parallels can also be drawn here to what Fredrik Gregorius describes as the basic notions of Nordic culture in Swedish Norse organizations—namely the notion of an authentic, organic Nordic culture living on in the guise of Christianity that is seen as more appropriate for people living in northern areas (2008:132). This is precisely what practitioners of both the Sami and the Norse traditions emphasize. Authenticity is localized to distant times and places, in a Nordic pre-Christian past that the detrimental influence of civilization has not yet touched. Embedded in this quest for

SJAMANISTISK FORBUND

Figure 2.1   SF Logo.

a Nordic past we can thus also trace a critique of civilization—a form of antimodernism and antiurbanism. What neoshamans seek, what is perceived as real and organic, is found in nature prior to the modern period.

Accessing the Past—Crafting Identities

To invoke "tradition" in order to legitimize one's religious beliefs and practices is central to Western religious history, from antiquity to the present. According to Lindquist, the types of "invented" traditions that take form in the neoshamanic milieu often refer to a past so distant that there are no living memories to challenge—or support—their images (1997:129). This then is a past far away in the mists of time, which can be touched only indirectly, through narratives, popular culture, myths, legends, and sagas, as well as through neoshamans' religious experiences. The quest for a Nordic neoshamanic heritage involves liberation from established discourses about the past, and opens the past for individual approaches and interpretations. But as Lindquist further states,

> For such a "constructed" past to be meaningful, it has to be helpful in understanding the present, and it must be anchored to people's current social concerns. Tradition becomes living only when it is projected on to, and enlivened with, the actualities of today's life. (129)

In SA as well as in Sami shamanistic practices outside of SA, local forms of neoshamanism are brought to life via the theme that these traditions correspond with our nature, our ancestors, roots, climate, and mind-set. These are traditions retained in our landscape, in old burial places and archeological sites, and thus are available to everyone inhabiting the northern latitudes.[14] The idea is that nature has the power to "release" ancient energy and knowledge. The Northern Lights as well as the midnight Sun are highlighted as domestic spiritual qualities that connect past to present. Similarly, the scenery with its plains, lakes, and mountains is interpreted as doors into the world of the ancestors. The landscape is interpreted as having the imprints and traces of the ancestors, and this crossover between time and space gives places a touch of mystery. As folklorist Anne Eriksen points out, "The past ceases to be a bygone age; it can be perceived as a now because it is related to a here—a here that is also part of contemporary man's own direct experiences" (1999: 92, my translation).

The longing for the past contains a creativeness in which people continually construct their traditions, values, and myths, and thus a connection in their own lives (see Selberg 1999 and Fjell 1998). History lies open for reinterpretation and can be adapted to the individual's desires and needs; it is optional rather than obligatory. This contributes to unsettling the overall authority that is no longer to be found in specific religious traditions, but is expressed in the individual seeker. Religious actors put the different parts together according to their own accounts, interpret with their own hearts, and replace parts when they find it appropriate to do so (see Eriksen 1999:149–151).

Key figures in the neoshamanic milieu are doing research to get closer to the sources of a Nordic shamanic heritage in order to further turn the diffused tradition of northern neoshamanism into a resource for contemporary practitioners of shamanism's shared community and identity. This research is distributed, popularized, commented upon, and embellished on shamans' home pages on the Internet and on Facebook, as well as conveyed in books authored by established neoshamans (see Gaup 2005, 2007; Kvernmo 2011; Brunvoll and Brynn 2011).

Ebeltoft has chosen to embark on this work, and emphasizes that she will especially focus on the traditions connected to the *Volve*, known as a sorceress in Norse traditions. Her quest for the past concretely illustrates the creativity that characterizes this type of historiography. As Lone points out, there are very few literary sources that document these traditions. To get closer to this tradition and to learn more, she seeks inspiration from women in the larger neoshamanic milieu who have been focusing on and marketing these types of traditions for years, including Anette Høst in Denmark and Runa Gudrun Bergman in Iceland. She hopes they can provide her with a deeper understanding, and help her anchor traditional practices in the present. Additionally, Lone seeks inspiration from popular culture, as well as from Celtic traditions, which she sees as enigmatic and open to interpretation.

Also the old Sami *siedi* (Sami pre-Christian sacrificial sites) hold a unique position within the neoshamanic milieu in Norway. Neoshamans use these sites to legitimize the indigenous roots of their contemporary pagan spirituality, and they are employed as symbols of an essentially local Sami neoshamanism. A parallel can be drawn here to how Kathryn Rountree describes Maltese pagans' use of local temples: "These are places of energy, prayer, communication with ancestors, and spontaneous insights about the ancient culture" (2010: 160).

In my interview with the Sami neoshaman Eirik Myrhaug, he describes rituals at the Sami *sieidi* Storsteinen/Rikkagallo, close to his hometown of Gratangen, Northern Norway. According to Myrhaug, the material place, Storsteinen, makes the magical tangible and shows that magic is located in a certain place, in a certain landscape. In a ritual realm of sound, scents, movements, and touch, the presence of magic and mystery is generated, bringing the ancestors back from oblivion and triggering a sense of power. At Storsteinen, Myrhaug points out, the magical is something the individual participant can experience by touching the *sieidi* and making a sacrifice. This ritual act recreates the past, and the past becomes part of the shaping of the present.

Same Content, New Wrapping?

Developing the field of Nordic neoshamanism, practitioners draw on a variety of different sources. As mentioned, practitioners look for inspiration through literature on pre-Christian religions as well as through popular culture, meditation, and various New Age courses. At his home page on the Internet, Gaup writes about some of the things that have inspired and shaped him as a Sami shaman:

> I have found inspiration and knowledge from many quarters. My first experience with shamanism I received from a Sami noaidi. Later I learned healing techniques that came from the Mapuche Indians of Chile. The first systematic training over time I got through Harner's courses on "Core Shamanism" in California. Later, I studied with Native Americans from North and South

America and the Huna shamans from Hawaii. I know shamans from all continents. (Gaup)[15]

Gaup's identity as a Sami shaman has developed through the exchange of knowledge derived from different cultures and traditions. It is also these different sources Gaup draws on when teaching his own courses. Subsequent to his stay at Esalen and his participation in Harner's "Foundation for Shamanic Studies," Gaup decided to develop his own shaman school based upon his newly acquired knowledge. This school is known as the Saivo Shaman school (Saivo being a Sami name for the underworld). Saivo shaman school is organized as a series of courses consisting of six gatherings that extend over three years. The courses are organized throughout the country. It is these shaman courses that have had the broadest resonance in Norway. All the established neoshamans in Norway whom I interviewed for my doctoral thesis in 2010 had been trained by Gaup and participated in one or more of his shaman gatherings. This also means that Gaup played a crucial role in designing the neoshamanic milieu in Norway.

The leader of SA, Kyrre, has also been trained in neoshamanism by teachers with different sources of inspiration. Like Gaup, he emphasizes that influences from other cultures can, to some extent, help develop Nordic shamanistic practices. Gaup and Kyrre here point to one of the core pillars within neoshamanism, namely perennialism. In *The Shamanic Zone* (2005), Gaup emphasizes this further:

> Shamanism has not been constructed in the same way as Christianity, Islam or Buddhism, created as they are by their own religious founders. The ancient practice has been with us all the time as an inborn potential in all humans. From ancient times a "shaman belt" meanders from Lapland and throughout Siberia. Immigrants from Asia brought shamanism with them to North and South America. From the beginning of time the phenomenon also existed in Australia and in the large island cultures of the Pacific and of course in Africa, the cradle of mankind. Set in historical context, shamanism is the first spiritual practice and the first major cultural subject. (2005: 9 my translation)

In terms of this juggling of different sources and the openness toward traditions from various cultures, how then does Nordic neoshamanism differ from its US origins? In the article "Sami Neo Shamanism and Indigenous Spirituality" (2013), Fonneland and Kraft claim that Gaup, as well as his colleagues in the Norwegian neoshamanic milieu have followed a route pointed out in Harner's teachings. Having identified what he considered to be the key ingredients of indigenous people's religious notions and practices, Harner urged indigenous people to trace their roots, and thereby to contribute to the reservoir of shamanic resources. This, one might claim, is precisely what Gaup and his colleagues have set out to achieve (Fonneland and Kraft 2013: 136). We have, as Stephen Prothero in a different empirical context has argued, a change of vocabulary, but continuity in terms of basic ideas, a Nordic lexicon built upon a neoshamanic grammar (1996).

The development of a neoshamanic movement concerned with the preservation and reconstruction of Norse and Sami traditions makes sense from the perspective of the broader ethnopolitical search for a Sami identity as well as the search for a Nordic heritage (see Kraft 2009). It also makes sense in economic and marketing terms. Nordic versions of shamanism are today presented and marketed as more authentic than the American Indian version, partly, some actors claim, due to the commercialization of the latter (Fonneland and Kraft 2013). The development of a local variant of neoshamanic practices can also be seen as a response to the criticisms leveled by Native American leaders against "plastic shamans" as appropriators of cultural traditions that do not belong to them (see Lewis, this volume). Even though it can be argued that core shamanism and other neoshamanic practices overlap in terms of basic ideas and practices, what is interesting is how these traditions are perceived precisely as different, and how the larger society responds to them—the media and the public sector. This leads us to a final question, the question of reception.

Reception—Concluding Remarks

Currently there seems to be an embracing of neoshamanistic practitioners by the general public in Norway, and this is in part due to positive media coverage. Historians of religion Cora Alexa Døving and Siv Ellen Kraft point out that the media is a central actor with regard to the development of religion, both in terms of internal conditions such as power and authority positions, and with regard to highlighting certain issues and perspectives as particularly relevant (2013:19). Thus religion is not only mediated through the media but also transformed and recreated through these processes of communication.

In the media coverage connected with the establishment of SA, the domestic media's stories are characterized by a positive attitude toward the newborn religious association. Both local and national media showed great interest in the rise and approval of SA. During the course of the Association's first year, papers carried such headlines as "Now Shamanism Is Officially Approved as a Religion in Norway" (Nordlys March 14, 2012), "Shamanism Finding Fertile Ground in Norway" (Dagen March 15, 2012), and "Shamans in from the Cold" (Bergens Tidende October 30, 2012). The Association's key figures, Kyrre and Lone, have been interviewed by local and national newspapers, radio, and television. TV2, one of Norway's largest national television channels, covered the initiation of a shamanistic association in Tromsø. In the program, it was emphasized that Lone welcomed the governor's decision and expressed her ambition to preserve and continue the shamanistic traditions and practices of the country. It was further highlighted that SA's goal is about understanding and respecting nature. Nor is Shamanism in any way mysterious. Shamanism is a world religion, and in the North people are committed to preserving the Sami and Norse (Arctic) traditions (TV2 March 14, 2012).

This positive attention stands in stark contrast to how the media in general has covered New Age events and entrepreneurs. According to Siv Ellen Kraft, the New Age movement does not hold a high position on the media's list of real religions and acceptable religiosity (Kraft 2011: 105). In the case of contemporary shamanism, however, we have media contributions that show a genuine interest in the phenomenon of Nordic neoshamanism. In the various reports, neoshamanism is not portrayed as a countercultural movement, characterized by oppositional attitudes and naïve as well as unreliable social actors, but rather as a positive contribution and a necessary alternative, embodying important attitudes concerning contemporary environmental issues and materialistic lifestyles. In line with what Anne Kalvig argues in her chapter in this volume, neo-shamans in Norway are portrayed as spiritually responsible, identifying with collective needs and the urges of environmentalism, bent upon reviving pre-Christian traditions (Kalvig 2014).

Additionally, "official" support of Sami and Norse shamanism has been rather extensive. Since 2006, the Sami People's organization (Samisk folkeforbund) and Norgga Sáráhkka (a Sami women's organization) have served as co-organizers of the aforementioned New Age festival in Tromsø, which has also been considered as the most crucial stage for the dissemination of Sami neoshamanism. In 2005, the mayor of Tromsø, in a speech at the opening of this same festival, praised it as "an alternative alternative fair, due to its location in a northern Norwegian city and its link to Sami traditions" (see Fonneland 2007, my translation). Also, the Sami shaman festival Isogaisa is annually assigned about half a million Norwegian kroner in financial support from the Sami Parliament, the Barents Secretariat, the Troms County Council, and the Nordic Culture Fund. The festival, in turn, hosts several co-arrangers, among which are the Spansdalen Sami Association (Spansdalen Sameforening) and the Costal Sami Association (Foreningen Kystsamene). Likewise, the State's approval of SA involves an acceptance of shamans in the present, their activities, attitudes, and conceptions, and is thus also a means for SA to reach out to potential members and gain attention.

The type of spirituality highlighted by the establishment of a religious practice claiming roots in Nordic cultures can be seen as a resource that provides a shine and an aura to surrounding social milieus. In this case, Nordic neoshamanism emerges as our common cultural heritage. According to Anne Eriksen, the concept of cultural heritage encompasses everything that is nice and (slightly) old and that generally has the status of being important and valuable and which is not imposed from the outside (2009: 478). Nordic neoshamanism is a religious community that can claim to be taking care of *our* traditions, *our* common Nordic religious roots. Even though Nordic neoshamanism first and foremost constitutes a spiritual community and is a venue for people committed to neoshamanistic practices, the milieu is not without social and economic implications, and, as such, neoshamanism in Norway is a cultural force.

Notes

1. Neo shamanism is ranked as one of the fastest-growing religions in contemporary Western society (Patridge 2004: 47, Wallis 2003: 140).
2. I have been conducting research on contemporary shamanism in Norway since 2004, and in 2010 I completed my doctoral thesis, "Samisk nysjamanisme: i dialog med (for)tid og stad" (Sami Neo Shamanism: In Dialog with the Past, Time and Place), which focuses on the development of the field of Sami neo shamanism in Norway.
3. This chapter draws on some of my previous work and articles (see Fonneland 2010, 2011, 2014a, 2014b).
4. Eriksson has published a variety of books that can be linked to the performance of contemporary shamanism (see, for instance, Eriksson 1987; 1988; 1990; 2012).
5. The core of this project is a shamanic drum, made by the Sami neo shaman Birger Mikkelsen. This drum has traveled and still travels to various destinations all over the world, and is intended to be a "wakeup call to humanity." According the project's home pages on the Internet, the intention behind the world drum is to bind people together across race, religion, borders, culture, ethnicity, color, and political conviction in a common struggle for humanity and Mother Earth. Internet site, http://www.theworlddrum.com/index.html. Accessed February 6, 2013.
6. Kvernmo is the driving force behind the development and organization of the neo-shaman festival Isogaisa. He has also published the semiautobiographical *Sjamanens hemmeligheter* (2011) (The shaman's secrets), which focus on neo shamanism in Norway and his own developments as a Sami neo shaman.
7. For the Shamanistic Association, with members and other devotees spread throughout the country, the Internet has become a key component in the organization of the larger Association because it allows widely separated individuals to communicate with each other and information to be disseminated more easily.
8. In Norwegian, the two terms are *livsynsorganisasjon* and *trudomssamfunn*.

9. The text is taken from the letter to the County Governor; Internet site, http://www.facebook.com/groups/291273094250547/files/#!/groups /291273094250547/doc/302374349807088/. Accessed January 29, 2013 (my translation).

10. The first shamanic wedding ritual was held at the Ireland Tysnes, outside of Bergen on July 27, 2012, with the shaman Arthur Sørenssen as ceremonial leader. This wedding was, however, held before the official shamanic wedding ceremony was approved by the County Governor. The local shamanic association in Tromsø is now preparing confirmation ceremonies for a group of youths that has expressed interest in a shamanic confirmation during the spring of 2014.

11. I have also been invited to take part in this group as a researcher, and all members have been informed of and accepted my participation.

12. The highlighting of shamanism as a universal phenomenon is inspired by the English translation of Romanian historian of religion Mircea Eliade's *Shamanism: Archaic Techniques of Ecstasy* (1961).

13. The wedding clothes were designed by Lone Ebeltoft, who runs the firm Alvedesign, which produces handmade wool garments with Arctic symbols.

14. According to Roy Wallis, neo shamanistic practitioners highlight archeological sites as places where ritual practices "work best" (2003: 141).

15. Ailo Gaup died on September 24, 2014, at age 70.

References

Alver, B. G. 2011. Fortælling, fortolkning, fortryllelse. Et kulturanalytisk perspektiv på fortælletraditionen om den kloge.—Din, tidsskrift for religion og kultur 1–2, pp. 132–154.

Alver, B. G., and T. Selberg. 1992. Det er mer mellom himmel og jord: Folks forståelse av virkeligheten ut fra forestillinger om sykdom og behandling. Sandvika: Vett & Viten AS.

Andreassen, B. O. and T. Fonneland. 2002/2003. "Mellom healing og blå energi. Nyreligiøsitet i Tromsø." *Din. Tidsskrift for religion og kultur* 4/2002 + 1/2003, 30–36.

Askeland, Ha. 2011: Hovedmodeller for relasjonen mellom stat og trossamfunn: Finansiering av majoritetskirker i Europa. KA-notat April 27, 2011. [Unpublished].

Beyer, P. 1998: "Globalization and the Religion of Nature," in J. Pearson and G. Samuel (eds.) *Nature Religion Today: Paganism in the Modern World.* Edinburgh: Edinburgh University Press, 11–21.

Blain, Jenny. 2005: "Heathenry, the Past, and Sacred Sites in Today's Britain," in Michael Strmiska (ed.) *Modern Paganism in World Cultures: Comparative Perspectives.* Santa Barbara, CA: ABC-CLIO, 181–208.

Brunvoll, Bente, and Grace Brynn. 2011: *Eirik Myrhaug: Sjaman for livet.* Oslo: Nova Forlag.

Christensen, C. 2005. "Urfolk på det nyreligiøse markedet—en analyse av Alternativt Nettverk," master's thesis in religious studies, University of Tromsø.

————. 2007. "Urfolksspiritualitet på det nyreligiøse markedet. En analyse av tidsskriftet Visjon/Alternativt Nettverk". *Din. Tidsskrift for religion og kultur* 1, 63–78.

Døving, Cora Alexa, and Siv Ellen Kraft. 2013: *Religion i pressen.* Oslo: Universitetsforlaget.

Eriksen, A. 1999. *Historie, Minne og Myte.* Oslo: Pax Forlag AS.

————. 2009. "Sideblikk. Kulturarv og kulturarvinger." *Nytt Norsk Tidsskrift* 3–4, 474–480.

Eriksson, J. I. 1988. *Sejd—en vägledning i nordlig shamanism.* Stockholm: Vattumannen Forlag.

————. 2012. *Rune Magic & Shamanism: Original Nordic Knowledge from Mother Earth.* Upplands Väsby: Norrshaman.

Eriksson, J. I. and A. Grimsson. 1990. *Runmagi och Shamanism 2.0.* Upplands Väsby: Norrshaman.

Eriksson, J. I. and L. Bäckman. 1987. *Samisk Shamanism.* Hägersten: Gimle.

Fjell, T. I. 1998. *Fødselens gjenfødelse: Fra teknologi til natur på fødearenaen.* Kristiansand: Høyskoleforlaget.

Fonneland, T. (forthcoming). "Approval of the Shamanistic Association: A Local Northern Norwegian Construct with Trans-Local Dynamics," in Lewis, J., and I. T. Bårdsen (eds.) *Nordic New Religions.* Leiden, Boston: Brill.

————. (2013. «Isogaisa: Samisk sjamanisme i festivaldrakt» *Aura* vol 5, 102–131.

————. 2014. "Sjamanistisk Forbund: Ei ny religiøs rørsle tek form." *Din. Tidskrift for religion og kultur,* 93–112.

————. 2012. "Spiritual Entrepreneurship in a Northern Landscape: Spirituality, Tourism and Politics." *Temenos* 48(2), 155–178.

————. 2010. *Samisk nysjamanisme: i dialog med (for)tid og stad.* Doctoral dissertation, University of Bergen.

Fonneland, T., and S. E. Kraft. 2013. "Sami Shamanism and Indigenous Spirituality," in I. Gilhus and S. Sutcliffe (eds.) *New Age Spirituality: Rethinking Religion.* Durham: Equinox Press, 132–145.

Frykman, J. 2002. "Place for Something Else: Analyzing a Cultural Imaginary," *Ethnologia Europea.* 32(2), 47–68.

Gaup, A. 2005. *The Shamanic Zone.* Oslo: Three Bear Company.

Gilhus, I. 2012. "Post- Secular Religion and the Therapeutic Turn: Three Norwegian Examples," in T. Ahlbäck (ed.) *Post-secular Religious Practices.* Åbo: Scripta Instituti Donneriani Aboensis, 62–75.

Gregorius, F. 2008. "Modern Asatro: Att konstruera etnisk och kulturell identitet." Doctoral dissertation, Centrum for Theology and Religious Studies, Lund University.

Harner, M. 1980. *The Way of the Shaman: A Guide to Power and Healing.* San Francisco: Harper & Row.

Heelas, P. 1996. *The New Age Movement.* Cambridge: Blackwell Publishers.

Kraft, S. E. 2011. *Hva er nyreligiøsitet.* Oslo: Universitetsforlaget.

————. 2009. *Sami Indigenous Spirituality: Religion and Nation Building in Norwegian Sápmi. Temenos: Nordic Journal of Comparative Religion* 45(2):179–206.

Kvernmo, R. 2011. *Sjamanens hemmeligheter.* Own Imprint.

Lindquist, G. 1997. "Shamanic Performances on the Urban Scene: Neo-Shamanism in Contemporary Sweden." Doctoral dissertation, Studies in Social Anthropologhy, 39. Gotab, Stockholm.

McCutcheon, R. T. 2000. "Myth," in W. Braun and R. T. McCutcheon (eds.) *Guide to the Study of Religion*, London, New York: Cassell, 190–208.

Myrhaug, M. L. 1997: *I Modergudinnens fotspor. Samisk religion med vekt på kvinnelige kultutøvere og gudinnekult*. Oslo: Pax Forlag AS.

Partridge, C. 2004. *The Re-Enchantment of the West*. London and New York: Continuum.

Prothero, S. 1996. *The White Buddhist: The Asian Odyssey of Henry Steel Olcott*. Bloomington: Indiana University Press.

Rountree, K. 2010. *Crafting Contemporary Pagan Identities in a Catholic Society*. London: Ashgate.

Selberg, T. 1999. "Magi og fortryllelse i populærkulturen," in B. G. Alver, I. Gilhus, L. Mikeaelsson, and T. Selberg (eds.) *Myte, Magi og Mirakel: I møte med det moderne*. Oslo: Pax Forlag AS, 122–133.

Stuckrad, K. V. 2005. *Western Esoterisicm. A Brief History of Secret Knowledge*. London: Equinox Publishers.

Svanberg, J. 1994. *Den skandinaviska nyschamanismen: En revitaliserande rörelse*. Unpublished master's thesis in Comparative Religion. Åbo, Akademi University.

Taira, T. 2010: "Religion as a Discursive Technique: The Politics of Classifying Wicca." *Journal of Contemporary Religion*, 25(3), 279–394.

Wallis, R. J. 2003. *Shamans/Neo-Shamans: Ecstasy, Alternative Archaeologies and Contemporary Pagans*. London: Routledge.

Newspapers

Bergens Tidende "Sjamaner inn fra kulden" (October 30, 2012)

Dagen "sjamanisme finner grobunn i Norge" (March 15/03, 2012)

Klassekampen "Sjamanen" (March 11–12, 2006)

Nordlys: "Sjamanisme offentlig godkjent som religion i Norge" (March 14, 2010)

Fremover "Narvikpar først i Nord-Norge. Nina og Per valgte sjamanistisk vielse" (July 10, 2013)

Internet Sites

http://sjamanforbundet.no/

http://www.theworlddrum.com/index.html

http://www.facebook.com/groups/291273094250547/files/#!/groups/291273094250547/doc/302374349807088/

http://www.sjaman.com/

http://www.livstreet.com/

3

The Way of the Teacher

Merete Demant Jakobsen

Shamanism is a term that has come to be used in contexts that often have little to do with the word's original meaning. This is a concern of mine, as it was a concern of S. M. Shirokogoroff, who conducted a fine study of shamanism in the early part of the last century in Siberia and Manchuria, titled *Psychomental Complex of the Tungus*. In this work, Shirokogoroff states that he hopes that it will be possible to preserve the term "shaman" without wearing it out "by the use in reference to very broad generalization, and at the same time clearing it from various malignant tumors—theories which associate shamanism with sorcery, witchcraft, the medicine man, etc." (1935: 271).

In 1980, Michael Harner's *The Way of the Shaman* was published and became the classic manual on the way to practice shamanism in modern Western society. As an anthropologist, Harner had studied shamanism among the Jívaro Indians in Ecuador and the Conibo Indians in the Peruvian Amazon in the 1950s and '60s. Inspired by his research, Harner created core shamanism, a contemporary version of shamanism built on his knowledge of traditional cultures. His aim was to make shamanism available to participants in the context of a course in a few days instead of the year-long training of shaman apprentices in traditional societies. He states in the preface, "At the same time, the classic shamanic methods work surprisingly quickly, with the result that most persons can achieve in a few hours experiences that might otherwise take them years of silent meditation, prayer, or chanting" (xii).

My interest in core- or neoshamanism was inspired in the spring of 1992 by an advertisement in the *Oxford Times*, in which such a course was offered. I participated in the course and, with my background in Greenlandic shamanism, decided to do a comparative study, undertaking fieldwork in core shamanic courses that was later published as *Shamanism: Traditional and Contemporary Approaches to the Mastery Spirits and Healing*. In this study, I raised several questions about the modern, Westernized version of the old belief system, some of which query the time scale of the training, the attitude toward evil spirits, and course participants' situation when, after four days of training, they return to "normal" life and so forth.

The Greenlandic shamans, the *angakkut*, were first and foremost dealing with the collective interests of society; they were, in the language of Shirokogoroff, masters of spirits, and they possessed great insight into the psycho-mental complex of their fellow human beings. Generally, they would only use their skills when life-threatening issues were at stake, as minor magic was available to everybody. They were, in other words, specialists in spirits and in communication with the invisible world. My conclusion when comparing these two attitudes regarding the role of the shaman, was that

> This very sense of the power of the specialist is what neoshamanism is attempting to eliminate. While trying to preserve the positive aspects of the interaction with the spirit world, in which the spirits first and foremost are allies and for the most part of good intention, the knowledge of the shaman is no longer of an esoteric character but instead available to all. There is no sense of a life-threatening tangible disaster instigated by Nature, which is instead perceived as the victim of human greed. Human suffering originates from a fragmented society whose value systems have collapsed into mere materialism and whose spiritual values are starved out of existence. (Jakobsen 1999: 217)

It was not the sole aim of the courses, however, to produce "shamans," and the course participants were not taught to master spirits, but instead just to use them as advisers and teachers in their own lives. The course organizer did not present him/herself as a shaman, but some participants did not make that distinction.

In Mircea Eliade's major work, *Shamanism: Archaic Techniques of Ecstasy*, he discusses the origin of the term "shaman" and proposes that it has come to the West through Russia from the Tungusic *saman* (1989: 4). He considers whether the term was ultimately derived from the Pali *samana* (Sanskrit *sramana*, referring to Shirokogoroff [1935:270]). Among the Tungus, *saman* describes "one who is excited, moved or raised" (Lewis 1971: 51), and Vilmos Diószegi refers to the root of *saman*, *sa-*, to know. In other words, the shaman in an excited state knows more than his fellow human beings about the world of the spirits, and therefore has unique insight.

This sense of a "being set apart," of having unique insight, is what led one of the course participants to continue studying the shamanic way and to become a teacher. A special knowledge experienced through the courses could be conveyed to new apprentices of core shamanism. In 2006, I therefore decided to interview him, and then followed this up in the spring of 2013.

This course organizer who is representative of the third "generation" lives in Jutland, Denmark. When I first interviewed him in 1995, he was new to shamanism. He explained that he had decided to participate in the course on Nordic Shamanism because he was inspired by North American Indian philosophy, as it connected human beings with all of the Earth and the Universe:

> Shamanism is new to me. I have been interested in many spiritual matters. In connection with the production of plant colours one is concerned with the basic processes. This is a natural approach for me towards a part of our world which we have forgotten to relate to: Nature.... We also have some roots. They are more or less destroyed after the introduction of Christianity. I am not a member of the church anymore. Are these roots here still? They must be part of me. (Jakobsen 1999: 178)

This search for roots earlier in human history than Christianity was important to several of the participants in the courses. Their relationship to the Christian Church was either nonexistent or strained, as the Church generally did not leave space for experiences of encounters with nature spirits, which many of the participants mentioned as one of their reasons for choosing shamanism. For these people, the core-shamanic method and its inclusion of Nature opened a door to experiences of nonordinary reality.

When I interviewed this man in 2006 and, later, one of his apprentices, it became clear that he was moving away from the "pure" Harner core shamanism, even though he had worked as the Foundations representative in Denmark since 2000. He had by 2006 started to incorporate other traditions into his teaching and added new concepts and rituals. This might be seen as a way of expressing a need to include a personal spiritual framework, which would also have been true of shamans in traditional cultures, but, according to this teacher, the Harner Foundation for Shamanic Studies did not approve of his deviation from the training they had provided, and there would be a point at which the deviation would transgress the boundaries for what could be termed core shamanism.

Through my own interviews, it was clear that most participants in core-shamanic courses in the 1990s did not generally seek to combine shamanism with other belief systems. But a decade later, this was happening frequently in non-core-shamanic courses, and a conglomerate of different beliefs might be presented in a single course. This teacher called himself a shaman even though it has been taught in the core-shamanic course of the '90s that this should not be done. He explained that this insight arose from an initiation into the spiritual world in which he had been tried on his morality. It was his own assessment that he was now a shaman. There had been no other persons involved in that decision.

In a course in London in the late '90s, Harner explained that he had made contact with shamans in Tuva, Siberia, and that his Foundation provided training for these shamans, for which they were very grateful. This teacher confirmed Harner's view after having visited Tuva himself.

Not only had this third-generation teacher included aspects of Buddhism in his teaching, he had also created his own four-module system. One aim was that during the courses the participants would realize whether or not they were meant to walk the shamanic way. He had also created a new healing method that no longer made use of the drum, but only the voice. Additionally, the concept of the tunnel as the route from ordinary to nonordinary reality was no longer part of the journey, as he believed that it could be frightening to travel through. Instead, he led the client to another level and lowered the person into a deeper state of mind of total darkness and peace.

These were major changes to core shamanism. The use of the drum as a travel instigator and the transformative tunnel journey preparing the traveler for the meeting with spirits at the end of the tunnel were no longer part of the teaching. Instead, he explored the nonordinary landscape together with the client. And when present there, while providing healing, he asked the client to put a hand on the areas of the body that seemed to be the sources of problems.

In his view, a shaman was an artist who gave the formless a form, color, and size. As a healer, he believed it was important to be led to the right tool and that disease might be viewed as a way of teaching a person. No evil or destructive spirits were mentioned. Instead, it was important for the healer to understand that the healing might have been successful even though the client died if it meant that the client had reached a higher level of insight.

As is clear from this description of the work of the third-generation teacher, he was inspired by Buddhism and combined this with some of the core-shamanic tools. The exchange between Buddhism, or Bon, and shamanism is not new. What is new, however, is the highly individualized version, which deviates from the system of the Foundation for Shamanic Studies.

There is generally among Danish healers a tendency to create their own system, with a "pick-and-choose" attitude toward existing approaches. This was also my conclusion when I looked at healing generally in the '90s, when teachers of core shamanism seemed to have a fairly consistent structure for their teaching.

The present-day spiritual smorgasbord creates a plethora of possible combinations of spiritual traditions in which the traditional starting point is less prominent and the creation of unique methods predominant. There is not one unified light to be seen at the end of the tunnel, but endless individual variations. Both the organizer and the client find themselves choosing among the methods on offer. According to Friedrich Nietzsche,

> The most characteristic quality of modern man: the remarkable antithesis between an interior which fails to correspond to any exterior and an exterior which fails to correspond to any interior—an antithesis unknown to people of other times. Knowledge...now no longer acts as an agent for transforming the outside world but remains concealed within a chaotic world which modern man describes with a curious pride as his uniquely characteristic "subjectivity"...for we moderns have nothing whatsoever of our own; only by replenishing and cramming ourselves with the ages, customs, arts, philosophy, religions, discoveries of others do we become anything worthy of notice. (1983: 78)

And it is no less important to become "worthy of notice" in a Western culture that focuses on "the relational self" as the center for meaning (Gergen 2009). Each individual creates his own spiritual universe, his own mythology, and the sharing of a belief system rests generally speaking on the teaching of "the other."

On the basis of this insight, it became relevant for me to interview someone from the fourth generation of teachers, an individual who had recently been trained by the aforementioned teacher, also in 2006. He showed me a pamphlet that he had put together and that offered several methods of healing, not just a Buddhist-inspired shamanism: healing therapy, Reiki healing, healing massage, Inka healing, and also drumming journeys. The latter was of core-shamanic origin; otherwise, he was taking a step yet further away from using only shamanic-inspired methods. He was still trained by the Danish course organizer, and his main focus was cooperation between the client and the healer. He did not believe that the healer alone would find the way for the client. The concept of mastery, of being the intermediary in charge of the communication with the spirit world, seemed to have been erased. He explained that he had observed that many people had begun to leave the responsibility for their lives in the hands of healers. Instead of being an authority on spirit communication and thereby of presenting solutions extracted from the spirit world, he would travel alongside the client. In his view, most clients had psychological problems, and his role was to assist them in giving these names.

A conglomerate of different approaches, and thereby an enlargement of the scope for the inclusion of new spiritual approaches with each new teacher, had clearly replaced the original core-shamanic method from which the teaching had sprung.

In the core-shamanic approach to the spirit world, the course participant was taught a method and then sent on his or her own journey to encounter the spirit world and to ask for assistance there. With the new teaching, the spirit world seemed to have retracted and been replaced by a "union" of teacher and client together undertaking the client's journey. Contrary to what this fourth-generation teacher believed, the actual role of the teacher seemed more intrusive and controlling. The traditional shaman was seen as a master of spirits and an intermediary, while the new "shaman" came across as a master of clients and their experiences.

Many questions therefore arise from the view expressed by these two teachers. One essential question is why the core-shamanic method is so readily watered down in the new millennium, thereby confirming the original fear of Shirokogoroff, that the word "shaman" should cover almost any spiritual approach.

One possible explanation is that it is not easy for one to uphold a genuine belief in the existence of a spirit world inhabited by wise animal spirits when one is outside the courses if there is no structure available in the "after course" life. Modern Western human beings do not live in such close relationship to nature as to feel the need to placate the wrath of spirits whose retaliation might lead to hunger, disease, and thereby death. Neither are the experiences of the course participants inspired by a common mythology upholding the mutual understanding of individual journeys and ultimately the universe.

Another explanation might be that core shamanism is taught in courses, in which within the frame of the four days a course lasts, it is natural so speak about these spirits, relating to them and communicating in a ritual language that is not easily transported into the outside world and introduced actively into the everyday life of the participants. In that respect it easier to talk about issues that are closer to the "myth" of psychology than that of nonordinary reality encounters with power animals.

Harner claims in *The Way of the Shaman* that core shamanism is a quick route to shamanic enlightenment:

> For this reason alone, shamanism is ideally suited to the contemporary life of busy people just as it was suited, for example, to the Eskimo (Inuit) people whose daily hours were filled with the task of the struggle of survival, but whose evenings could be used for shamanism. (1990: xii)

Shamanism is presented as the evening's "entertainment" in the cold and dark nights of the North. The struggle for survival and shamanism were not separated, however, and belief and life were united in the shamanic séance. In the shaman's hands was the survival of the community. In the hands of the facilitator of shamanic courses is the survival of the individual in a complex urban environment (Jakobsen 1999: 138).

Asked to contribute to this anthology, I interviewed the third-generation teacher for a third time in the spring of 2013, almost 20 years after our first encounter. I was interested in finding out how his method of teaching shamanism had developed. After I had seen him in 2006, he had, in 2007, founded a new Danish organization, The Shaman Society in Denmark. His website was called *The Meeting Point: The Way of the Shaman*, thereby preserving the term used originally by Harner. He had by now left The Foundation for Shamanic Studies. The reason for his choice was already in the making, when I met him in 2006.

In the description of a shaman on the website, he states that a shaman is a person who has undertaken an often long and thorough training. The teaching does not just take place in individual courses, but is a process of personal training. The basic apprenticeship lasts a minimum of five years, and thereafter requires a lifelong commitment to yearly training. This presentation of the shaman is then followed by a long list stipulating the content of the training, which includes the body and energy, psychosomatic insight to healing, and knowledge of the spirit world and of the world of plants and animals and so on.

As is clear from this training program, the teacher has come full circle, and is now presenting an approach to shamanism that adheres to that of traditional shamans, such as the *angakkut* in Greenland or those whom he met in Tuva. He is, however, at the same time utilizing words as "karma," "morality" and "ethics," "energy" and "matter"—words that makes sense to a modern Western person in search of his or her own spiritual approach, often in an urban environment.

The reason for this new development was his visits to Tuva, where he had later traveled on his own and not with the Foundation. There he befriended the leader of bear shamanism.

> The words are the same but the concept different....In the West we have another approach to good and evil, in the East they are clearly more able to be spiritual than we are.

There is no doubt that Christianity has had an impact on the version of shamanism often presented in the West, and angels are now mixing with the spirits of nature in some presentations of shamanism (Jakobsen 2006). This teacher is, however, trying to bring shamanic training back to its roots, but he is including Buddhism and his own "spiritual geography." He now sees core-shamanic training as an "unworthy" representation of shamanism and observes that in Western culture there is a lack of capacity to make a real commitment to the training involved. "We are not prepared to put in the effort that it takes to walk the spiritual way." On that basis, he sees the Harner method as "the pared down cheap version." He believes that the method has served its purpose in making shamanism popular. His own reason for separating from the Foundation was that core-shamanic courses were selling off shamanism "bit by bit" and supporting the "me, me, me" attitude of the West. In his opinion, as a consequence of his travels to Tuva, this approach differed profoundly from that of the shamans he met there.

In his revised training of the apprentice, he has now introduced an assessment period of half a year. In this a daily training is necessary, and his experience is that most people "run away" when they realize that they have to get rid of their own laziness. As a teacher, he daily spends hours on his own personal training, exploring three main areas:

1. the flow of consciousness
2. the capacity of being present
3. the shaman's route—shape shifting into either the wind, a crow, or a wood spirit and observing the area that he walks mentally from the specific angle that he has chosen

Buddhism is an active part of this approach and, combined with his knowledge of shamanism, he mentions the Bon religion as the link. He underlines that he has created his own system so as to adjust the method to Danish culture. In this connection he uses *Yggdrasil*, the tree of life, the immense tree that is central to Norse mythology.

Around this tree he has built his own spiritual geography, which has much in common with other cultures as it consists of four corners and four levels in which you can travel. West is the seat of substance, South of emotions and images, North consists of mathematical thought processes, and East of light and meaning. An area that he explains in detail is the relationship between the present and the future. The present is the future verbalized and thereby taking shape. In this context, he describes the experience of death and how it is possible to travel to one's own death and to acknowledge the geography of it. It is, however, never the same journey as time changes.

The image used for this emptiness of the future is another concept from Norse mythology: *Ginnungagap*, the big empty space in the middle of the Earth. The real self lies in the future, and the task is to travel into the light, into absolute nothingness and meet the self. The tunnel travel of core shamanism is criticized as this method takes the form of images of already existing emotions. He sees himself as an explorer of reality through his system of spiritual geography. In his cosmology, he knows what he is going to face and that differs from that of the core-shamanic tunnel journey to nonordinary reality. He clarifies that he is not only a teacher of methods for travel, he also participates in the journey of the client and communicates en route.

There is mastery at play, that of the client's journey. In core shamanism the course participant left through the tunnel for his or her own version of non ordinary reality. This teacher travels with the clients to their world, including other lives, and has a continuous dialogue with the clients so as to synchronize their journey. The client is typically one who has problems with finding a way through this life and with understanding the meaning of it. During this journey dialogue, the teacher creates images that take the client from a source of water into a cave and then to the inside of the body. In this way, they can detect cancer tumors: what do they look like, what is the shape and size? The patient can start to work on the tumors, but the shaman undertakes the extraction. If the client, however, is capable of doing this alone, it will be more effective and the tumors can be removed temporarily. But it is necessary to get to the source of the problem. The images of water and the roots of plants are used to illustrate this. It is important not to tear the roots. The core of this treatment is to make images of the places of the disease and the feelings connected to it. If the feeling is not transformed into a form, then the disease will eat the client.

This is not a new technique in a shamanic sense. The creation of an image that the person can relate too, to name the nameless, is partly what the séance is all about. The mythology justifying the action of the shaman and that of the spirit world is an important tool.

Joseph Campbell describes the role of the myth:

1. To create and sustain a sense of awe in the individual in connection with the secret dimension of the universe, not so that human beings will live in fear of it, but so that they realise that they are a part of it. The mystery of existence is as much the deep mystery of the individual.
2. To create a concept of the universe that agrees with the knowledge of the present time and the areas of life that the mythology is addressing.
3. To support the norms of a given moral code, that which rules in the society where the individual lives.
4. To support the individual step by step in connection with health, strength and harmony of spirit through a profitable life. (1972: 184)

Together with the client, the teacher creates an insight into the secret dimension of the universe and of the body through a narrative that is connected to and arises from the life of the client, and thereby a personalized myth through which knowledge of self arises. Such knowledge is an important tool in the healing process, and should lead to strength and harmony of the body and mind. Naming and giving a disease a form takes the threat away.

At the moment, the teacher is not teaching anybody as he has reserved the present time to do something for his own development. He states that "It is tough, it is really difficult, they (the clients) do not understand. They want it all immediately." To him it is possible to read a whole library full of books on shamanism with only confusion as the outcome. You can speak about shamanism without having experienced its essence. It is the experience of the individual that is the interesting part, and there is so much to be explored. He ends the interview by revealing his reasons for finding shamanism interesting: it takes its starting point in your own experiences and that is a fantastic and exciting world.

For this teacher, seen from the perspective of Christianity as the state religion of Denmark, the gospel of Christ has been replaced by the gospel of the individual, the holy spirit by the shaman as the mediator, and the image of an eternal God by the image of an eternal future in which the self rests and from which the present takes form.

Looking back over more than 30 years since Harner first published *The Way of the Shaman*, it becomes clear that a considerable change has taken place to the method of teaching shamanism to Westerners who predominantly live in an urban environment, and thereby to the concept of shamanism. The inclusion of Buddhism, of the concept of self, of the focus on the individual and not the society of which the individual is part, reflects a general development both in the concepts of the smorgasbord of spirituality and in the role of the individual in society.

The anthropologist Margaret Mead's classification of three forms of society springs to mind as a way of approaching this development (1970):

1) *The postfigurative society* in which the individual is born into a clearly defined social structure in which fitting into his or her preestablished role is the main task. The former hunting society of Greenland would serve as an example.

   Here the apprentice is born into his or her role either as an orphan, or chosen by the spirits or by a shaman, who is the master of the communication with the spirit world.

2) *The cofigurative society* in which the individual identifies with peers. To a certain degree it is possible to choose one's role with the focus on "who am I?" and "where am I going?" The choice of route is important, and as the answers are found through interaction with others, it might lead to identity crises, estrangement, and a sense of a decentered self, which characterizes postmodern society.

Core shamanism would be a fine example of a way of dealing with this kind social challenge. The journey to nonordinary reality is undertaken by the individual, but later shared with the group in a circle and creating the sense of participating in a mutual spiritual experience. The group's support is crucial to the individual. The focus is on participation. Here the course organizer is the master of the group's shamanic experiences.

3) *The prefigurative society* in which identification is now taking place in a constantly fluctuating social structure with no fixed roles, as relationships are changing quickly and the individual continuously has to adapt to new rules of play.

In this kind of society, according to the methods mentioned by the third generation teacher, shamanism will have to be internalized to make sense to the individual. Sharing with others is not at center of focus, and there is no common mythology and no common spirituality, as each person is left to his or her own version, which is shared with the teacher as a master of methods.

Western urban dwellers might be deeply fascinated by the mysterious spirit world of the shaman and find a sounding board for their own spiritual search. There has, however, been a progressive change in the role of the spirits. The mastery of communication with these often destructive entities that was crucial to traditional shamanism, has been watered down through core shamanism to the point where the spirits are mostly friendly advisers situated in nature, to the latest version in which the spirits are almost nonexistent and the focus is on the power of the individual and is thereby internalized. The mastery of spirits seems to have become the mastery of "my body and mind."

So why this constant search for spirituality, when it is clear that there is no common mythology or even no common language? To Émile Durkheim the answer is clear: it is human nature.

> A man does not recognise himself; he feels himself transformed and consequently he transforms the environment which surrounds him. In order to account for the very particular impression which he receives, he attributes to the things with which he is most directly in contact properties which they have not, exceptional powers and virtues which the objects of everyday life does not possess. In a word, above the real world where his profane life passes he places another which, in one sense, does not exist except in thought, but to which he attributes a higher sort of dignity than to the first. Thus from a double point of view it is an ideal world. (1976: 422)

In an ideal world the individual has control over the uncontrollable forces of nature, of society, of disease, and of self. The latest twig on the *Yggdrassil* of spirituality is mindfulness, which is focused on the internalized control of self in a prefigurative unpredictable urban environment. Equally, the latest version of the teaching of shamanism is, although adhering to the traditional shamanism, also internalizing what in traditional culture was external: the mastery of spirits has become the mastery of the mind. However, what has become clear from this research is that the way neoshamanism is taught by this third-generation teacher is equally true to the structure of the surrounding society and to that of traditional shamanic traditions. The way of the teacher is governed by the way of the spiritual expectations in a quickly changing environment. If the teacher, however, in an attempt to reflect traditional culture, asks too much commitment of the apprentices, "they run away."

References

Campbell, Joseph. 1960. *The Masks of God: Primitive Mythology*. London: Secker and Warburg.

Diózegi, Vilmos. 1968. *Tracing Shamans in Siberia*. Oosterhout, Holland: Anthropological Publications.

Durkheim, Emile. 1976; 1915, *The Elementary Forms of Religious Life*. London: George Allen and Unwin.

Eliade, Mircea. 1989; 1951. *Shamanism: Archaic Techniques of Ecstasy*. London: Arkanar.

Gergen, Kenneth J. 2009. *Relational Being: Beyond Self and Community*. Oxford: Oxford University Press.

Harner, Michael. 1973. *Hallucinogens and Shamanism*. Oxford: Oxford University Press.

———. 1990; 1980. *The Way of the Shaman*. San Francisco: Harper.

———. 1988. "What Is a Shaman?" on *Shaman's Path*, Garry Doore (ed.). London: Shamanbala.

Jakobsen, Merete Demant. 1999. *Shamanism: Traditional and Contemporary Approaches to the Mastery of Spirits and Healing*. Oxford: Berghahn Books.

———. 2003. "Researcher or Searcher: Studying Shamanic Behaviour in the New Millenium," *Shaman*, 11(2): 17–28.

———. 2006. "Power of Spirits: Spirituality in Denmark," *Shaman*, 14(2): 9–17.

Lewis, I. M. 2004. *Ecstatic Religion: A Study of Shamanism and Spirit Possession*. London and New York: Routledge.

Mead, Margaret. 1970. *Culture and Commitment*. London: Natural History Press

Nietzsche, F. 1983. "On the Uses and Disadvantages of History for Life," *Untimely Meditations*. Cambridge: Cambridge University Press.

Shirokogoroff, S. M. 1982; 1935. *Psychomental Complex of the Tungus*. London: Kegan Paul, Trench, Trubner & Co.

4

Shared Facilities: The Fabric of Shamanism, Spiritualism, and Therapy in a Nordic Setting

Anne Kalvig

In the fall of 2013, a spiritualist Medium Congress was held in Norway. The aim was to assemble the business sector of mediums and clairvoyants in order to achieve mutual understanding of the present situation and discuss a vision for the future.[1] In addition to numerous mediums, both Norwegian and foreign, who attended as speakers, the chief physician of the Norwegian alternative spirituality scene, Audun Myskja, gave a speech on the "Dying Process." Additionally, the Swede Lars Magnar Enoksen was invited to address the congress. A resident of Norway and a master of the Old Norse fighting tradition of Glima,[2] as well as a chanter of Old Norse runic songs known as *galdr*, he was introduced by the congress chairperson in the following way: "Today a lot of people turn to the Sami shaman tradition, acknowledging the Sami people's spiritual knowledge and guidance. They thus forget that we have our own Viking tradition to explore and utilize." Given this rather ethnocentric framing, Enoksen's task in the congress was to teach the mediums the secret lore of runic galdr, that is, the chanting of magical words following the metrics of the Old Norse *Edda*. He did this in a leather Viking suit, his long hair flowing and his voice resounding in the conference room, with all the attendees trying to howl the galdrs in a manner similar to Enoksen's. Galdr-chanting mediums illustrate the "shared facilities" of contemporary, Nordic spirituality. Here shamanism, spiritualism, and therapy comprise a fermenting blend that appeals to far more people than those attending a specialized business meeting.

Nordic shamanism is often delineated as the invention and/or revival of Sami religious traditions, with the *noaidi* understood as a core representative of a form of shamanism conceived of as perennial. However, shamanism as an element of Nordic paganism, understood as the invention and/or revival of the non-Sami traditions of the Vikings, can also be included in the concept "Nordic Shamanism." The "tension" between Sami and Viking shamanism constitutes a fertile ground for contemporary religious creativity and production. Implicit in much writing on shamanism is the understanding that neoshamanisms may have much or little reference to the practices of icons like Carlos Castaneda and Michael Harner. Additionally, an interesting development we may note is the intersection of spiritualism and neoshamanism, both in Nordic settings and elsewhere. Practitioners who primarily identify as alternative therapists also make use of neoshamanism in various ways, adding to the multicolored fabric of contemporary spirituality with a shamanistic twist. In this chapter I will analyze the "shared facilities" represented by people employing and creating spiritual reservoirs marked by neoshamanism(s), spiritualism, and mediumship-based activities, and alternative therapies. I ask how the fabric of shamanism, spiritualism, and therapy unfolds within the contemporary spirituality scene in Norway (and Nordic countries more generally), with a primary focus on insights into its production and consumption as a mediatized, religious/spiritual practice. The notions of "facilities" and "fabric" are meant to highlight contemporary spirituality as something taking place and evolving within spaces and areas that can be perceived as both concrete and abstract/virtual. When spirituality is likened to connotations and metaphorical meanings of facility and fabric, both its dynamic and more static aspects come to mind, while a constructionist, human creativity notion forms the basis for my analysis and understanding. What tales and exegeses are offered, and by whom, when the production and consumption of neoshamanism is mediated and remediated to wider audiences? How are ethnic issues pertaining to neoshamanism dealt with? This approach is informed by writings on the discursive study of religion (especially von Stuckrad 2013) and on medialization and mediatization theory in relation to religion (Lundby 2009, Hjarvard 2008, 2013). Following Stäheli (2000: 73, cited in von Stuckrad 2013: 15), I define discourse analysis as addressing the relationship among communication practices and the (re)production of systems of meaning, or orders of knowledge, the social agents that are involved, and the rules, resources, and material conditions underlying these processes, as well as their impact on social collectives. Mediatization theory, which presents religion and religious expressions as not only mediated by various, modern channels of communication but also transformed by these processes of communication/mediation, means that part of the focus will be on how neoshamanisms and adjacent practices are communicated in various media, and how this affects what is being thought, said, and done among the practitioners in this field of "shared facilities."

My material consists of field reports, meetings, and interviews with various practitioners, and textual sources, both printed and online, gathered from 2006 and onward. I have been conducting research in the fields of contemporary spirituality and alternative therapy during this period covering various thematic issues within the scope of Western culture, whereas ethnographic field work has been carried out mainly in Norway, but also Britain (Kalvig 2011). In what follows, I examine in more detail the aspects that appear central and illuminative for the main hypothesis of neoshamanism(s) that appear as warps in a sociocultural fabric woven by people drawing their threads from various places, traditions, and situations, where spiritualism and therapy merit special mention, and where the perceived ethnicities of neoshamanism surface and color the fabric in various ways.[3]

Studying and Categorizing Shamanism, Spiritualism, and Therapy

The academic literature on neoshamanism is to a notable degree written by people sympathetic toward it, and/or involved in it or in adjacent practices (see, for example, Blain 2002, Wallis 2003, Tedloch 2005, Foltz 2006, Tramacchi 2006, Greenwood 2005, 2009, Sanson 2009. See also Davidsen 2012). Although this situation is sometimes likened to that of gender or queer studies, the message it gives is that neoshamanism (and paganism) is something different from other religious or spiritual practices, as a detached, "neutral" position is generally encouraged within most academic traditions gathered under the umbrella of religious studies—as opposed to, for example, theology. The challenges of participant fieldwork, of insider-outsider problematics, and of studying religious-spiritual traditions with few or no sacred texts, are well known within the study of contemporary spirituality, and give clues to understanding some of the professional drives of the neoshamanistic academic. However, a different situation appears when considering ethnographic work on contemporary spiritualism and mediumship, where less research has been conducted, and with an imperceptible portion of academics "going native." The former practice obviously has a personal appeal to several academics, but the latter not. The reasons for this point to the subject matter of this chapter, namely, the discourse of neo spirituality, and thus the different positions of different spiritual practices within a sociocultural hegemony, of which academia is also a part. Whereas mediumship generally scores low, "plastic neoshamanism" (the so-called

New Age-diluted variant) ranges perhaps a little higher. And indigenous, tribal and/or "dedicated" neoshamanism clearly has a higher ascribed status. Studies of the intersections of shamanism and mediumship thus might be affected by the relatively low position of New Age bricoleurs and entrepreneurs, who are viewed as shallow shoppers and merchants in a market, as opposed to (the perception of) the more spiritually responsible paganists identifying with collective needs and the urges of environmentalists bent upon reviving pre-Christian traditions.

In Norway as in other Western countries, both neoshamanism[4] and spiritualism are in vogue as forms of contemporary spirituality. To begin with, one might expect these two categories of spirituality to be fairly distinct, even if one acknowledges that many people pick and mix concepts and practices freely—for example, from both the above-mentioned and various other traditions, in what has been labeled a "New Age buffet" or "smorgasbord" kind of spirituality. However, more than neoshamanism and spiritualism being possible preferences within one and the same spiritual seeker, my claim is that we witness a certain conflating of neoshamanism with spiritualism (and the other way round). This should perhaps not be too surprising, as both forms or traditions, variegated and categorically diffuse as they might be, center around a *practitioner communicating with spirits*, with the aim of bringing therapeutic relief and/or spiritual insight or enlightenment to the practitioner him/herself, a client, or a community. Still, talking to the dead and spirits "on the other side" and talking to the spirits of the ancestors, of power animals, or spirits of the underworld, has traditionally been conducted with different conceptual, sociocultural and historical references in spiritist and neoshamanistic settings. One tendency, from both academic and popular perspectives, has been to relate neoshamanism to ancient, indigenous traditions, threatened or suppressed by colonial forces. Spiritualism, on the other hand, has been related to nineteenth-century pioneers like Andrew Jackson Davies, the Fox sisters, Robert Owen, Emma Hardinge Britten, and Allan Kardec (spiritism), or perhaps the older Swedenborgianism, Mesmerism, or likened to the very "foundation of religion" as being communication with spirits, and thus the roots and history of spiritualism as well. Both spiritualism and shamanism, then, are often understood as "original" or "core elements" of religion or spirituality. More often, however, popular spiritualism is not being legitimized by historical, ethnical, or postcolonial claims, but simply by experience and belief.[5] In "classic" spiritualism as well as contemporary spiritualism, women dominate, both as practitioners and as clients/sitters/audiences. But this trait has not given rise to a particular "self-identity" of spiritualism as a feminist or womanist movement, although to some extent it was thought of in such terms in its heydays of the nineteenth and the early twentieth century (Braude 1989, Owen 1989, Mehren 2011, Kalvig 2012a). The gender issue with respect to shamanism is even more complex, as traditional or historical shamanism is known to involve "gender bending," a "third" gender, and the like, whereas contemporary investigations into the gendered notions and practices of both shamanism and neoshamanism must deal with the highly variegated forms and impact areas of these phenomena and practices where gender comes into play. Very generally speaking, however, (neo) shamanism seems to involve male participants to a larger degree than does spiritualism, and the less feminized perception of (neo) shamanism among the public, may explain some of the fluctuations in the field of spiritualism and shamanism.[6]

Additionally, the therapeutic side of both shamanistic practices and spiritist practices must be kept in mind when studying these phenomena and the discourses (both emic and etic) of which they are part, as this further blurs or complicates the categories of worthy/unworthy religion or spirituality in more traditional senses. The therapeutic side of contemporary spirituality is a large field of study within the history of religions, but it is often subsumed under other aspects of New Age or alternative spirituality.[7] Reasons for this may be seen in traditional definitions of our study object, religion, which is perceived as something less immanent, material, bodily, and relational than is the case, resulting in a perception of that what people do with their bodies and sense with and in their bodies may be less religiously and scholarly relevant. However, contributions have been made here concerning contemporary spirituality, and anthropological works have also traditionally had an interest in the embodiment of religion, upon which ethnographic studies within the history of religion heavily rely. In what follows, the therapeutic and/or bodily aspects of contemporary spirituality are included by employing a certain definition of religion that intends to cover also sensuous aspects, and including material on religion/spirituality that may have as its starting point healing practices without explicit, religious ambitions. Religion is thus in this chapter defined as "experiences, concepts and practices, in various combinations, referring to a spiritual dimension of relevance for men and their relation to all other things existing."

Traits of Nordic Spiritist-Shamanism

Norway's primary celebrity medium, Gro-Helen Tørum, launched an autobiography in 2012 entitled *Shaman in High Heels*, thus illustrating the conflation of the fields of spiritualism and shamanism. Tørum has gained her fame from appearing on the highly popular Norwegian television series, *The Power of the Spirits*, a house cleansing/exorcist kind of reality show, in which she costars with three other mediums. This series began in 2006, and as of 2014 it is still the producing television channel's (TVNorge) flagship program, with approximately half a million viewers each week (in a country of five million inhabitants). *The Power of the Spirits* sparked Tørum's national fame, but she initially entered television as cohost of an alternative spirituality talk show called *The Other Side* in 2009. Additionally, she had her own mediumship series called *From Soul to Soul* (2010–2011), a tear-jerking show in which people were put into contact with their beloved dead through Tørum, and filmed during the séance. In her autobiography, she claims to be first and foremost a shaman, in addition to being a medium, a light worker, and a "dancer between the dimensions." Her shamanic identity is related to North and South American shamanism, though, not Sami shamanism: "(T)he Inca culture is the closest shaman identity I know [*sic*]. While my Atlantic conscious-ness is water, my Inca-shamanic consciousness is earth" (Tørum 2012: 195). According to Tørum, she was trained by a female, Norway-based neoshaman between 2005 and 2007. In addition to this earthly master, she has a spiritual, non-earthly guide called Metatron. He is described as Tørum herself, in another dimension, as her contact with her own divinity (11). The North American Indian references to Tørum's version of shamanism come from dreams and signs urging her to take the name "Black Eagle Medicine Woman," which was partly channeled through a dreamcatcher she received as a gift from her closest girlfriends.

The intersections between spiritualism, mediumship, neoshamanism, and also Sami neoshamanism in a mediatized setting were initially obvi-ous in an episode of *The Other Side* in 2009. In this program, Tørum described her abilities to uncover and neutralize black magic as a sha-man. The same skills were demonstrated by the Sami neoshaman/*noaidi* Eirik Myrhaug, who appeared as a guest on the program. Using his drum, he released one of the talk show hosts from an alleged *gand* from which she claimed to be suffering—gand being a Sami word that is also used in Norwegian to describe an evil spell or curse.[8] However, what Tørum and other participants on the program discussed as gand or black magic, Myrhaug instead identified as a "darkness" stemming from the self-proclaimed cursed host's experiences as a little child while under house arrest with her family in Teheran, Iran (that is, in real life, rather than as a former life experience) (Kalvig 2009: 51–54). The skills of the Sami noaidi (and healer, as he notably refers to himself) impressed the host panel of the program so much that they were all crying by the end of the show. Although Tørum loudly proclaims her shaman identity, her sha-manistic performances are less well known than her mediumistic practice and her work as a life coach and lecturer. Actually, when she describes her shamanistic work in more detail in her autobiography, "chakra balancing" seems to be the central "rite." We never hear of drums or chanting, but one client story in the book is retold, of a more "typical" guided journey of the soul, with a jaguar as the accompanying power animal (Tørum 2012: 127–130).

Quite the opposite seems to be the case with another shaman medium, Lilli Bendriss, who is more easily recognized as practicing what is thought of as shamanism. Bendriss is one of Tørum's most famous costars on *The Power of the Spirits*. Unlike Tørum, she is more reluctant to promote herself as a shaman, preferring to talk about "employing shamanistic techniques." She reveals in an interview that she was "opened" as a medium by an old shaman called Wounded Eagle, who is with her all the time. "When I teach [shamanic] courses, I stand on the floor with the drum and feel the energy start flowing. And then the shaman enters my system. I shiver, my heart beats, I feel my throat is squeezed, and then I start singing. But it's not Lilli singing. It's a Native Indian song, and the voice is fierce." Beating the drum, she becomes an instrument for the old shaman's consciousness, Bendriss explains.[9] Bendriss is accordingly described in the following way in Tørum's autobiography (Tørum 2012: 195): "When Lilli Bendriss...bangs her shaman drum and chants and cries from the depth of her soul, I'm fiercely affected. Lilli, the elegant, west-end lady, possesses a tremendous power. She breathes herself into a trance and surrenders herself completely to the primitive force." Bendriss says: "It is as if the sound of the drum activates cellular memories of a past life as a Native American" (Tørum 2012: 196). Bendriss laments that Tørum does not dare to join her drum courses, called "The Primitive Force" (ibid.). Comparing the two prominent shaman mediums, then, we learn that the person who is most "apparently" a shaman, Bendriss, legitimates her shamanism by referring to soul/spirit possession; it is the old Native American, not herself, who "is" this tremendous force. In contrast, Tørum, more vague in her performance as a shaman, is definitely the shaman herself in her self-representations—and has been so, throughout distant past lives as well.

Discourses of the Culturally and Geographically Imminent or Distant Spiritual Resources

Both "The Primitive Force" course and another one called "Dream Journey" are promoted on Bendriss' homepage with photos of herself with a shaman's drum.[10] Following the presentation of "The Primitive Force" course are seven YouTube video clips. Of these, five have North American Indian content or references, one displays South American Native Indian content, and one has mixed content, with "The Universal

Mother" revealed as the "answer" toward the end of the clip. No Sami shaman or Sami pagan identification or references are given in either Tørum's or Bendriss' tales of their shamanic journeys as mediums.

The reason for the mediumistic "reluctance" toward a shamanism that is geographically more imminent as a possible tradition of identification and inspiration in Norway (the Sami tradition) is probably exactly this— imminence. In Norway, Norwegians can meet Sami people in various arenas, secular, Christian/pietistic, or New Age/pagan. Native Indian people, on the other hand, can probably be met at spiritual conferences, journeys, and meetings dealing with shamanism, paganism, or the New Age, in Norway or abroad. This kind of meeting will then probably take place within frames of mutual spiritual understanding and interest: if a spiritual seeker and student of shamanism in Norway ever met a person of Native Indian heritage, he or she would likely be someone who had already entered a spiritual (New Age) discourse in which communal interests and values may be found.[11] When, for example, Norwegian spiritual tour operator John Gursli offers tours to Arizona, Bolivia, and Peru through his bureau Total Helse AS, meetings with and initiations by shamans are thus provided. Although meetings with "locals" might also be included, they would not be promoted as "spiritual highlights" of the journey.[12] In striking contrast, when in 2011 Gursli arranged a spiritual tour in Norway (The Great Journey through Norway) from Oslo, ending in the North of Norway, no Sami encounters were included—only "energy work" at specific places of Sami heritage and other traditional significance.[13] Notably, Gursli's tours generally deal with the participants' own "energy work" in specific, spiritually outstanding places worldwide, but we note here what could be the same "reluctance" toward "utilizing" the neighboring spirituality of different ethnicities, as demonstrated by Tørum and Bendriss.

This apparent reluctance—which might also be called respect— toward the Sami tradition by Norwegians on the alternative spirituality scene could further be explained as an anticipated attitude toward what appears to be less exotic: exploring and utilizing what is thought to be Native American shamanistic traditions and techniques does not affect one's daily obligations in a political or social way concerning issues of indigenous people and indigenous rights. In the Sami case, the situation is obviously different: in Norway, one does not just don a Sami suit and claim heritage to Sami spiritual ancestors unless one actually has such a lineage. Some leather garment and feathers understood as North American Native Indian cultural markers seem legitimate (refer to Bendriss' homepage, for instance), but South American Native Indian references are far less commonly utilized by ethnic Norwegian spiritual actors. This might be due to the fact that North American Native Indian culture is to a much larger extent part of our medialized "cultural reservoir," or part of a "universal" ideational reservoir, with the United States being a dominant producer of popular culture (including images of the Native American). Also, quite a few Norwegians still have family bonds with the States, due to the great emigration of the nineteenth century, which provided a cultural imminence toward the North of America that is not the case for the South of the continent. The "white" perception of the United States in a Norwegian setting, as well as linguistic accessibility, is also not the case for the South American continent.

Nordic Paganism and Varieties of Shamanism

Wallis (2003: 33) notes the somewhat paradoxical situation in which paganism has become the popular generic term for different traditions like Wicca, Druidism, and Goddess spirituality—all are considered as employing neoshamanic techniques—whereas paganism is originally associated with classical antiquity. This unsettled conceptual situation also accounts for research like Galina Lindquist's (1997), which documents and analyzes what could well be labeled modern Àsatru (Nordic heathenry/paganism) as neoshamanism, in accordance with notable (emic) voices within the field in question, such as the Swede Jörgen I. Eriksson (2012). Eriksson also categorizes the healers and wise people of Nordic and other traditions as shamans, and states: "I do not adhere to the old Aesir faith [Nordic heathenry, the religion of the Vikings] but I have meticulously researched the shamanic elements inherent in the spiritual views of that time" (2012: 12). Jenny Blain (2002), anthropologist and neoshaman, also asserts that the shamanic element of the Norse tradition was "at the heart of pagan religions of Northern Europe," although she holds that the "Norse culture of 1,000 years ago was not obviously 'shamanic' in the sense in which Tungus or Sámi or Déné culture is said to be or have been shamanic" (2002: 47). Blain finds that the Norse material on *seid*, the name of the shamanistic-like practice of the seeress, or *volva*, and *seidmenn* (sorcerers), becomes particularly interesting because it is not supported by the entire community (49). Rune magic (Eriksson) and the practice of *seid* or spá (divination) (Blain) are central in the construction of Norse-identified neoshamanism, in addition to relating to the mythological universe of the Viking sagas.

The utilizations and understandings of the shamanic elements of the Norse tradition (and other pagan traditions) are highly variegated and expressed through diverse media. Anette Høst, a leading urban shaman in Copenhagen, Denmark, focuses particularly on the Norse tradition, with seidr, galdr, and runic song as her specialty, but her intention is not to revive Viking tradition, as she states on her website that "Tradition is about keeping the fire alive, not worshiping the ashes."[14] At the core of Høst's shamanic understanding lies the knowledge that "Without spirits, no shaman." This saying points to what has been shown as the close connections between the mediumship of spiritualism and shamanism. The Sami Ailo Gaup provides, like Høst and Eriksson, courses in and texts on (neo-) shamanism.[15] All of these Scandinavian representatives of neoshamanism, have been students of Harner—author of *The Way of the Shaman* (1980), several other books and texts on shamanism, and founder of the Foundation for Shamanic Studies in California. This center focuses not on academic studies, but on training programs for promoting neoshamanism to the late-modern citizen, understood as a perennial "core shamanism."[16] In 2013, in his 84th year, Harner published a book called *Cave and Cosmos*. In this book, he approaches the spirit world in great detail and gives numerous accounts of who the spirits are and how they communicate, providing ample cases from his own fieldwork between 1952 and 2009. He describes spirit possession in which various people, including himself, are able to speak in foreign languages of which they have no previous knowledge (2013: 23–30). Harner also refers to the natural scientist Alfred Russell Wallace and his 1874 book, *Miracles and Modern Spiritualism*, as providing a historical context for the ongoing gulf between science and spirit (198). Harner laments that Wallace's book had a hostile reception, and holds that Wallace, through the scientific principle of parsimony, offers an explanation for parapsychological phenomena like Near Death Experiences (NDE) and spirit possession that otherwise remain unexplained (199). Harner finds that the hypothesis of the spirit world is supported by shamans worldwide, throughout the millennia.

Jörgen I. Eriksson considers the Harner turn toward a more personalized spirit conception and focus somewhat disturbing, stating that it reminds him of Rudolf Steiner spiritualism. Core shamanism is to him disappointingly smug and with insufficient regard and reverence for Mother Earth, the living creatures, and the richness of various indigenous traditions. Eriksson dismisses his critical review as some kind of a patricide, but he clearly illuminates a development within the field of neoshamanism that corresponds with a theme addressed in this chapter, namely, the conflating of and attention to the fields of neoshamanism and spiritualism, both within the empirical field and academia. Lars Magnar Enoksen, the galdr-howling "Viking" of the Medium Congress mentioned in the beginning of this chapter, holds that the maintenance and the mastering of the combat sport *glima* is a bodily practice with a deep, spiritual meaning, although a revival of Viking religion per se is futile.[17] Enoksen was taught the glima in Iceland in the 1980s by men then in their eighties and nineties. For them, the glima was a spiritual, pagan practice, but since 1916, Icelandic authorities have held that glima should be considered a modern marital art. Icelanders born after the 1920s were less inclined to regard glima as spiritual practice, but Enoksen has reintroduced this aspect of the sport (2004, 2012). Being of both Sami and Nordic descent, Enoksen is certain that shamanism is not a part of the Norse tradition. He says that "it is not found in the textual sources," which he knows as an expert on Old Norse and runic writing (1998, 2000, 2003, 2004), in addition to being a writer on Norse religion. A former punk musician, he now participates in galdr howling on tours with the Viking pagan music group Wardruna, who use music as a way of "spiritual travelling," as Enoksen explains. Generally, he holds that many pagans employ and teach rituals too soon, resulting in people actually conducting inconvenient rituals. He further dismisses core shamanism as a "cozy," undemanding variant of spirituality.

Individual and Organizational Maneuvering between Sami and Native American Shamanism

Jorunn, a practitioner in the Western Norwegian alternative therapy scene, illustrates the apparent imminence of the Native American shaman and the distance of the Sami shaman for some ethnic Norwegians, without referring either to Harnerian core shamanism or to the Viking/Norse tradition. A coach, healer, and shaman, in addition to being a medium, she is married to a Sami man who is also an alternative spiritual therapist. In most public appearances he dresses in Sami clothes that clearly signal his Sami identity. From the married couple's web page, we learn that he gained his skills in "energy balancing" from his Sami shaman heritage, as well as his innate Sami "connection with nature." Jorunn, on the other hand, is an ethnic Norwegian raised in a west coast village with clear home mission dominance. Delving into Christianity for some time, she gradually turned to shamanistically oriented alternative spiritualities after significant experiences in nature and with communications with the dead:

> I used to be so much alone in nature, communicating with the plants and animals, these experiences were very strong. Once, sleeping outside in a snow storm, a raven came and sat down at my head, this trigged a lot of things. I've always been drawn towards the graveyards, sleeping in the graveyards always caused things to happen. (Kalvig 2012b: 55)

This narrative can be compared with Jorunn's story from childhood, when as a clairvoyant she "saw" the location of her drowned uncle in the sea, a memory awakened in a later past life regression in India (54). These narratives may be said to have both a mediumistic and a shamanistic character, but the shamanic identity became clearest when she started exploring this "way" as an adult: She was then "possessed" by a Native Indian spirit, causing her to speak a language unknown to her, but which was said to be a Native Indian idiom by people who heard her. It was a demanding task to learn how to control this spiritual force, but Jorunn eventually managed to let herself go into shamanistic trance journeying without becoming uncontrollably possessed or exhausted. In a passing remark Jorunn says she had been practicing as a shaman for ten years, before ever reading about it and learning the term "shamanism." Employing a whole range of spiritual and therapeutic techniques today, Jorunn calls her shamanistic work "shamanistic healing." She and her husband offer courses in "Soul Fetching" as well as "Shamanistic Education"—both of which are further described as "alchemistic practices" (neither Sami nor Native American). In Jorunn's own reflections on shamanism, she clearly relates her practice to Native Indian shamanism, not Sami shamanism, although she obviously is familiar with the latter through her Sami husband. He, on the other hand, stresses on their web pages his mastery of various Eastern therapeutic techniques, such as reiki, just as much as his Sami shamanist heritage. The couple's activities succinctly represent the multicolored fabric of contemporary neoshamanism, informed by a broad range of impulses, identities, experiences, and education.

Another therapist, healer, and clairvoyant representing the folk healing tradition of Norway, Bergit Loen Hatlenes, shows a more atypical ethnic Norwegian embracing of Sami shamanic and healing traditions. In her biography, *Bergit: Healing Hands* (Strøm 2013), Bergit, now in her eighties, describes her meeting with the Sami shaman and healer Mikkel Gaup in 1975 as a turning point in her life:

> I remember when shaking his hands, I felt a tremendous power. He had an extraordinary energy field surrounding him. I had no doubt that he was a shaman, psychic and healer. When we had met, he embraced my shoulders and said: "Use your forces carefully!" (Strøm 2013: 99)

After this meeting, the "Selje-woman," as she is called, and "Miracle-Mikkel," which was his nickname ("Healing Fox" was his international nickname),[18] collaborated for the rest of his life: he and his wife Brita visited Bergit and her husband, Anders, in the small village of Selje on the west coast, and they frequently visited the Sami couple in Finnmark. He taught her the tradition of Sami shamanism and healing, and gave Loen Hatlenes the confidence to develop her own natural healing abilities. In Bergit's account of her relationship with Miracle-Mikkel, their mutual understanding of the kinship between Sami and Native American culture is a recurring theme:

> We sat around the open fire at night, and Mikkel recounted the stories of his ancestors, of shamanism, of holy stones and of how nature teams up with us humans. He held that the Sami culture had a strong kinship with the North American Native culture....He in a way pursued everything that had been important to me as a child....Especially, we shared the sympathy for and fascination of the Native Americans. I had known this fascination ever since I was a little child, when we at home spoke of my uncles who had migrated to America. (Strøm 2013: 100–102)

Loen Hatlenes represents non-Sami folk healing in Norway, but unlike many such healers (especially in geographic areas where Sami culture is not traditionally found), she openly embraces and identifies with the Sami tradition. Such an embracing is more common in neoshamanic environments where Harnerian core shamanism is central, although there is still a notable reluctance toward "illegitimate" Sami posing in which one cannot display Sami descent, as previously discussed.[19] Among people advanced in age, operating on the fringes of the neospiritual and alternative trends of culture and following a folk healing tradition that is older than the contemporary resacralization of culture, ethnicity has also been a divisive issue.[20] The most famous Norwegian folk healer, Joralf Gjerstad, now nearly 90 years old, lives in what is one of the southernmost Sami communities of Norway, Snåsa/Snåase, and is known as the "Snåsa-man." In numerous publications about him and his healing practice, including several biographies and autobiographies, he alludes very little to Sami shamanistic and healing traditions in accordance with Christian tradition both within Sami and Norwegian culture. In the most popular biography on him (Kolloen 2008), he refers to a meeting with an old German fortune-teller as a turning point (when serving his conscription in 1947 in the German Brigade), and also his memories as a young man on a journey in the mountains with the old Norwegian folk healer "Great Sofie." He was told of his future good fortune as a famous healer by both of these women. The only—and probably unintended—reference to Sami tradition, imminent though it was and is in Snåsa, is in the following passage:

> This late summer night in 1948 Great Sofie told me what my life would be like...she described it as it has become, now sixty years later. She said the same as did the woman in Germany the year before, and more. But there was one crucial difference: There, by the *Finnkjerringfjellet* ["The Mountain of the Sami Crone"] I couldn't escape, as I did in the German market. (Kolloen 2008: 58)

The narratives of Loen Hatlenes and Gjerstad are thus quite different when it comes to Sami shamanism and healing practices, and also when it comes to the wider field of alternativity in culture. Loen Hatlenes demonstrates a sympathetic attitude, and in recent years confirmed to the medium Bendriss that she has channeled messages from Miracle-Mikkel to her. The Christian and religiously active Gjerstad, on the other hand, is bent on proving his healing abilities to be both God-sent and scientifically explicable, and states on the cover of his blockbuster biography: "Call me whatever you like, but not a [New Age] healer. A fellow man is what I try to be."[21] Loen Hatlenes, on the other hand, discredited Gjerstad's account in her biography. As an underlying theme, she compares Gjerstad to Miracle-Mikkel (and her own tradition), and the Christian, ethnic Norwegian male healer is clearly overshadowed and surpassed by the memory and tradition of the Sami shaman's aligning himself (and Loen Hatlenes) with Native Americans.

Yet another warp in the fabric of Nordic neoshamanism is provided by the Norwegian Shamanistic Association (SA), in which the effort to synthesize various traditions held to be shamanistic has been explicit. Here the claim is to represent a spiritual practice that goes back 30,000 years, and that "what binds all the different faces of shamanism is the belief that everything is animated and that all creatures of Mother Earth are kindred creatures."[22] SA was approved by Norwegian authorities in 2012 as a belief community with the right to offer rites of passage. Board member of SA Lone Ebeltoft stresses both the Sami and the Norse tradition as the group's heritage: "Shamanism is a world religion where we here up north are bent on preserving the Sami and Norse (artic) tradition," she tells the northern Norwegian newspaper *Nordlys* (Tårnesvik 2012).[23] Actually, on their web pages, one sees that Norse elements are absent, whereas Native (North) American references and resources are abundant, in addition to Sami ones. In the interview in *Nordlys*, Ebeltoft also says the shamanistic practitioner is mostly concerned with conserving and continuing a tradition almost forgotten by modern man. The reporter describes her in a "pagan" context as serving homemade chaga (bracket fungus) tea and crafting her own woolen clothing collection, adorned with "Arctic" symbols. In the Norwegian alternative magazine *Magic Magazine* (Halling 2013), Ebeltoft is portrayed once again in several photos displaying natural, Northern surroundings, including one in which she hugs a wolf in the "Polarzoo." The main photo shows Ebeltoft holding a drum and dressed in her colorful, handcrafted clothes, with a caption talking about shared facilities: "Lone is a great representative of Norse and Sami tradition, here dressed in her self-made elf-dress with shaman motifs." Ebeltoft says nature is holy and that she feels a strong affinity with animals. Even though she has a leading position the congregation, she does not refer to herself as a shaman. Being a shaman is more like a profession—to be likened to the difference between a Christian and a Christian priest. "If you tread the natural religious, shamanistic path, you're not automatically a shaman," Ebeltoft holds (Halling 2013: 17). At present, what it means to be a shaman, and what it means to build a shamanic organization, is debated on the SA's open Facebook page. The Norse preferences of some of the members are more clearly displayed here, and Sami identification by non-Sami people is criticized by a few. The use of magic and spells, like gand, is commented and frowned upon. The lively debate reflected in the Facebook version of SA is probably more representative of the organization as such, as compared with the rather sparse information on their web pages. The board even suggests taking down the regular SA web pages, since "no one uses them," as Ebeltoft comments (there is a member forum at this site that has obviously been ousted from Facebook's facilities—a situation common in many groups and organizations).[24]

In the same magazine that presented Ebeltoft, a subsequent interview portrays Sami Anneli Guttorm (Halling 2013b), known from her participation in the television series and competition *The 6th Sense*, on the same channel that broadcasts *The Power of the Spirits*. Both these interviews are presented under the heading "Shamanism in the North." Guttorm is also shown in natural surroundings in northern Norway, dressed in Sami traditional festive clothes. "With her Sami, colorful outfit she looks like a true shaman, but she doesn't address herself so," Halling writes (2013b: 19), making a not-so-subtle equation between any traditionally adorned Sami person and a shaman. Guttorm says she holds the ancestors and old traditions in too high esteem to call herself a shaman, preferring to talk about drum healing, clairvoyance, mediumship, and Bach flower therapy. She employs the Sami song tradition of *joik*, though, and says, "The power of the joik, the Sami culture, the use and understanding of nature, is natural and important to me. It has its own 'rhythm' that makes me whole and enables me to pass this on to others and to help them" (Halling 2013b: 19).

Whereas Guttorm, radiant in her Sami attire, refrains from being called a shaman, another Sami woman, Astrid Ingebjørg Johnsen, calls herself a shaman and is pictured in "ordinary" clothes when performing what she sees as a Sami shamanistic house cleansing, in an article in the alternative magazine *Medium*.[25] However, when promoting her Sami beauty salon, Sarahkkas Beauty,[26] she is beautifully seated in the snow, with a drum and Sami festive clothes, actually offering "shamanic healing" as a skin beauty product. With or without Sami descent, people who adhere to neoshamanism and/or (folk) healing in Norway thus seem to employ a whole range of strategies concerning how to make their own position(s) meaningful.

Conclusion: The Width of the Neoshamanistic Fabric

The practices and strategies pertaining to neoshamanism are mediated through various channels such as books, both emic and academic, manuals, and do-it-yourself literature, and biographies and autobiographies, through interviews and reports in magazines, through television and visual media, through various communications in online resources, such as organizational websites, personal websites, and social media such as Facebook. Additionally, there are "real-life" communications in rituals, at gatherings, in therapeutic relations, and in alternative and pagan fairs. I will conclude this chapter by pointing to what might be, for now, the limits of this kind of communication, namely when neoshamanism is mediated to children in a secular context, as in the Disney children's comic *Donald Duck*.

The character Donald Duck is well known as a global product of the Disney Corporation. In recent years, Nordic cartoonists and scriptwriters have been allowed to put a regional stamp on the Donald stories, in order to give readers more culturally relevant or familiar stories with which to relate.[27] The present story, "A Coin for Two" (*"Tiøring for to"*), is written and drawn by the Finn Kari Korhonen[28] and translated into Norwegian. The issue is number 51/52 of 2013, that is, the popular Christmas issue of *Donald Duck*. The plot takes place in Finnish Lapland, with Uncle Scrooge, Donald, and his nephews arriving by plane, asserting that "everybody knows Santa Claus has moved from the North Pole to Finnish Lapland." The Duck family's mission is to find out why Scrooge's enterprise Nisseland ("Santa-land") is not making money. It turns out that tourists are leaving in anger because the attractions of Nisseland are outdated and overpriced. When Scrooge pulls out his lucky charm coin to remind his family of his capitalist ethos, the reindeer in the area react strongly. This is where the Sami shaman enters the story: the Sami herders (depicted in Sami clothes) of the animals note that they have seen this behavior from the reindeers only once before, and that was when a shaman came to town to cast a spell. The story continues by shifting to a cabin in the countryside, where the drum of the Sami shaman Elmeri comes to life, with a bone stick drumming, by itself, on the Sami symbols of its drumhead. The reason is that, in the past, Elmeri has placed a spell on the lucky charm. The shaman is thus awakened, and shown lying in his bed fully dressed in Sami clothes, as well as with a wand. He is black bearded, but otherwise drawn like a duck, like Donald and the rest. Summarizing the story, it turns out that Elmeri is a black magician like the witch Magica de Spell, with whom he has a fight—the story's main dramatic event—over Scrooge's lucky coin. Both Elmeri and Magica are defeated by Santa Claus, who at the end of the story lectures Elmeri: "Don't you realize what happens to witches and wizards who become obsessed with material goods? Remember that you have lived a peaceful life until now; you don't want to end up like Magica, do you?" to which the remorseful Elmeri responds, "Absolutely not."

Before judging this story as a mediation of a racist, Nordic majority perception of Sami cultural and spiritual key figures, redeemed by a god-like Santa Claus ("go, and sin no more"), we could ask if this story reflects a new, cultural acknowledgment of diverse practices and traditions in the Nordic countries. In the *Donald Duck* universe there is a reluctance to deal with overt religious themes, but there is a wholehearted embracing of *magical* and certain *folk religious* themes (predating the mediatization thesis' claim of the contemporary media's love for banal religion—as in the popular 1952 Disney movie and print version *Trick or Treat*, as one example). Young readers in Nordic countries are given a dramatic story about two figures with extraordinary powers, of which Elmeri is a novelty, controlling animals (weasel and owl) and the weather with his drum. One sympathizes with him, because it is actually his weakness for ice cream that repeatedly gets him into trouble. Thus children will probably identify more with him, than with Scrooge's blatant materialism or Magica's "continental" sorcery (she is a resident of Vesuvio, Napoli). A theme integrated into this story is modern media as a way of achieving magical results, possibly resonating with children's reality: both Magica and Elmeri use the Internet in their endeavors, and Donald manages to alert Santa Claus by phoning him on his cellular phone.

As an unexpected and unprecedented mediation of Sami shamanism in the Donald universe, this story is clearly part of the cultural reservoir of spiritual ideas and practices, and could well be many children's first encounter with Sami shamanism. As such, the story, under the wide umbrella of Disney's political and moral correctness, is somewhat grating, depending on how one judges the figure of Elmeri: he is a bad Sami shaman, but perhaps that is better than no Sami shaman? If the figure of the shaman or *noaidi* in the public gains a role as a prominent religious figure, it is unlikely that *Donald Duck* will include a story like this again—just as priests, imams, or traditional believers are hardly represented in this comic. However, such a shaman role is unlikely, and a result of the present weaving of *Donald Duck* into the fabric of neoshamanism is that children are presented with a caricature of Sami spiritual practices that will add to their knowledge of aspects of Nordic neoshamanism.

This is similar to other examples of enchanted children and youth culture in which something actually "takes place," although not in circles we traditionally think of as religiously or spiritually relevant. Gilhus (2013: 47) categorizes this kind of "mediatized New Age...as *religion every-where*" (emphasis in original). Since Western culture is more prone to identify and cherish "religion there" (following Smith's spatial model of religion, which refers to traditional, institutional religion [2003: 27–30]), what is actually thought, said, and done by people in other places often goes under the radar, as when Sami shamanism enters *Donald Duck*. For the student and the consumer-producer of contemporary spirituality, however, Elmeri is one of many figures residing at the fringes of the fabric of Nordic neoshamanism. The fictional figure of Elmeri at one end and the historical figure of Miracle-Mikkel at the other, in a succinct way sum up the complex and ever-shifting relationship between the secular and the sacred: *religion everywhere* does not wipe out the *nonreligious everywhere*, but claims attention and space in ways rather new to late modernity.

Notes

1. The annual congress was held for the second time in 2013, and is an initiative from the Norwegian Spiritualist Union. On the congress (in Norwegian), see: http://mediumkongressen.no/om-kongressen/. The author attended on the September 13, 2013.
2. The Viking Glima Federation: http://www.viking-glima.com/.
3. When referring to textual sources and to people who are famous or on other aspects impossible to anonymize, real names are used. Otherwise, interviews with practitioners follow standards of anonymizing according to Norwegian, public academic ethical standards: http://www.etikkom.no/Forskningsetikk/ Etiske-retningslinjer/Samfunnsvitenskap-jus-og-humaniora/. All translations from Norwegian to English are mine.
4. In what follows, I do not distinguish between different types of shaman-isms with regard to the followers' alleged level of involvement, dedication, or sociopolitical evaluation of the role of shamanistic practice, as opposed to the aforementioned, possible hierarchical (both emic and etic) evalua-tion. Variants of shamanistic engagement will be commented upon when rel-evant, but not within an essentialist understanding of religion and religious commitment.
5. This holds for the popular version of spiritualism that is the focus of this chapter. For the more organized versions of (Norwegian) spiritualism, it is more correct to refer to this as spiritualism (for example, The Norwegian Spiritualist Union), and here the historical roots and predecessors are given ample attention. However, French/Brazilian Kardecism is often denoted as spiritualism as opposed to (British/American) spiritualism, pointing to the

former's focus on the reincarnation and evolution of the soul. As ideas of reincarnation and spiritual evolvement have a common-sense status in today's occulture/resacralized culture, I prefer the notion of (popular) spiritualism, but the conceptual situation of the study of this field is unsettled.

6. This is explored in more detail in Kalvig 2013.

7. Note, for example, that within a standard publication of close to 500 pages like Brill's *Handbook of New Age* from 2007, only one chapter of 20 pages is dedicated to issues of holistic health and therapeutic practices (Tighe and Butler 2007).

8. See Kalvig 2009 for a more detailed analysis of this show, the role of the television channel as promoter of alternative spirituality, and a consideration of the handling of the problem of evil in this program.

9. From an interview in the alternative magazine *Magic Magasin,* available here: http://magic.no/magic-magasin/reportasjer/narkontakt-med-andeverdenen?tlf=79000450.

10. http://www.lillibendriss.com/urkraft.html and http://www.lillibendriss.com/dream-journey.html.

11. A few Latin American Native Indian Norwegian residents provide spiritual products that could be put in the "Native Indian Spirituality/Paganism/Shamanism" category (like the spiritual shop "Pachamama" in Oslo, run by a Peruvian Indian), but I know of no North American equivalents.

12. See http://www.totalhelse.no/?page=26.

13. See http://www.totalhelse.no/?menu=67&page=81.

14. http://www.shamanism.dk/whoah.htm.

15. http://www.sjaman.com/.

16. Harner's "core shamanism" promotes the idea that the central features of shamanism from tribal people all over the world were and are the same, and can be learned and practiced by following Harner's courses and methods.

17. Personal communication, December 2013.

18. Confer also the memory of Miracle-Mikkel/Healing Fox on this site by Sami (neo) shaman Ailo Gaup : http://www.sjaman.com/om-sjamanisme/utfordringen-mainmenu-57/127-sjamansonen-ett-pett.html.

19. Bente Brunvoll, the Norwegian wife of Sami shaman Eirik Myrhaug, wears a costume of semi-Sami traits in this photo from their web page—without the traditional colors, it is not mistaken for a proper, Sami costume: http://www.livstreet.com/default.asp?pageid=3695.

20. An example of a notable Norwegian-Sami bridge-builder from the past in this field is the South Norwegian Ole Olsen Sangesand (1779–1858), who established the present stock of reindeer in the mountains of Ryfylke, by bringing the animals from Finnmark to this southern county, together with Sami shepherds. He also stayed in Finnmark for periods of time. He was taught Sami traditions, and was said to be able to shape shift into a bear and snake, and to cast spells (gand). See Kalvig 2012b.

21. "Healer" is in Norwegian synonymous with New Age healer, whereas a healer of folk tradition has been known by other names, like *kloke, handspåleggar, helbredar*—meaning "wise people," "layer of hands," "healer."

22. http://sjamanforbundet.no/blog/archives/53.

23. http://www.nordlys.no/nyheter/article5970091.ece.
24. https://www.facebook.com/groups/291273094250547/?fref=ts.
    The Nordic Pagan Union (*Nordisk Paganistforbund*) was disbanded in the
    summer of 2013, 20 years after it was founded, due to lack of activity/adher-
    ence (information from Geir Uldal, one of the central participants, personal
    communication January 2014). With the loss of this eclectic/universal pagan
    organization, shamanistic association will perhaps by some be understood
    as an umbrella organization filling the void after The Nordic Pagan Union.
25. http://mediumforlag.no/article/2011/6/23/astrid-ingebjrg-johnsen-er
    -sjaman-og-renser-hus-hrer-stemmer-som-hvisker/.
26. http://www.sarahkkasbeauty.com/v2/?project=test.
27. Local/national formulations of *Donald Duck* have been handled differently
    in various regions. In 2008, the Nordic distributor of Disney cartoons, the
    Danish media corporation Egmont, launched a Norwegian staff of new
    cartoonists and scriptwriters, and the story starting it all off was a Viking
    adventure called "The Raven of Odin" http://www.aftenposten.no/kultur
    /article2759738.ece#.UvNdUfl5P7M. See also http://www.dn.no/d2/article
    2529463.ece.
28. http://www.perunamaa.net/ankistit/korhonen.htm. The Finnish *Donald
    Duck—Aku Ankka*—has the largest edition per capita in the world for a
    Donald Duck magazine, with 320,000 copies weekly. http://en.wikipedia
    .org/wiki/Aku_Ankka.

References

Blain, Jenny. 2002. *Nine Worlds of Seid-Magic: Ecstasy and Neo-Shamanism in North European Paganism*. London: Routledge.
Braude, Ann. 1989. *Radical Spirits: Spiritualism and Women's Rights in Nineteenth-Century America*.
Bloomington: Indiana University Press.
Davidsen, Markus Altena. 2012. "Review Essay: What Is Wrong with Pagan Studies?" *Method and Theory in the Study of Religion* 24: 183–199.
Enoksen, Lars Magnar. 1998. *Runor. Historia, tydning, tolkning*. Lund: Historiska media.
———. 2000. *Fornnordisk mytologi enligt Eddans lärdomsdikter*. Lund: Historiska media.
———. 2003. *Vikingarnas egna ord*. Lund: Historiska media.
———. 2004. *Vikingarnas stridskonst*. Lund: Historiska media.
———. 2012. *The Secret Art of Glima: An Introduction to Viking Martial Arts*. Malmö:Scandinavian Heritage Publications.
Eriksson, Jörgen I. 2012. *Rune Magic & Shamanism: Original Nordic Knowledge from Mother Earth*. Umeå: Norrshaman.
Fedele, Anna and Kim E. Knibbe. 2013. *Gender and Power in Contemporary Spirituality: Ethnographic Approaches*. New York: Routledge.

Gilhus, Ingvild S. 2013. "'All over the place': The Contribution of New Age to a Spatial Model of Religion," in Steven Sutcliffe and Ingvild S. Gilhus (eds.) *New Age Spirituality: Rethinking Religion.* Durham: Acumen, 35–49.

Greenwood, Susan 2005. *The Nature of Magic. An Anthropology of Consciousness.* Oxford: Berg.

———. 2009. *The Anthropology of Magic.* Oxford: Berg.

Halling, Kari Flaata. 2013a. "Sjamanisme har alltid ligget mitt hjerte nær." *Magic Magasin* no. 1: 16–18.

———. 2013b. "Jeg har stor respekt for mine forfedre og de gamle tradisjoner." *Magic Magasin* no. 1: 19–21.

Harner, Michael. 1980. *The Way of the Shaman.* San Francisco: Harper & Row.

———. 2013. *Cave and Cosmos. Shamanic Encounters with Another Reality.* Berkeley: North Atlantic Books.

Hjarvard, Stig. 2008. *En verden af medier: medialiseringen af politik, sprog, religion og leg.* Fredriksberg: Samfundslitteratur.

———. 2013. *The Mediatization of Culture and Society.* Abingdon: Routledge.

Kalvig, Anne 2009. "TV Norge og Kanal FEM—den nye tids bodbringarar." *Din—tidsskrift for religion og kultur* 4: 45–63.

———. 2011. "Kornsirkler og spirituell turisme: Fra åker til internett." *Aura: Tidskrift för akademiska studier av nyreligiositet* 3: 33–70.

———. 2012a. "Seansar og minnet om dei døde." *Kirke og kultur* 2: 128–141.

———. 2012b. "Alternativ folkemedisin? Om røter og nye skot på det søvestlaqndske, holistiske helsefeltet." *Tidsskrift for kulturforskning* 2: 45–62.

———. 2013. "Shamans on High Heels." *Alternative Spirituality and Religion Review* 2: 201–217.

Kolloen, Ingar Sletten. 2008. *Snåsamannen. Kraften som helbreder.* Oslo: Gyldendal.

Lewis, James R. and Daren Kemp (eds.). 2007. *Handbook of New Age: Brill Handbooks on Contemporary Religion*, Volume 1. Leiden: Brill.

Lindquist, Galina. 1997. *Shamanic Performances on the Urban Scene: Neo-shamanism in Contemporary Sweden.* Stockholm Department of Social Anthropology, Stockholm University.

Lundby, Knut (ed.). 2009. *Mediatization: Concept, Changes, Consequences.* New York: Peter Lang.

Mehren, Tonje. 2011. "Engler mer enn en rapport fra jenterommet? Kvinner og spiritisme i Norge." *Kirke og kultur* 2: 114–130.

Noegel, Scott B., Joel T. Walker, and Brannon Wheeler (eds.). *Prayer, Magic and the Stars in the Ancient and Late Antique World.* University Park: Pennsylvania State University Press.

Owen, Alex. 1989. *The Darkened Room: Women, Power, and Spiritualism in Late Victorian England.* London: Virago Press.

Pizza, Murphy and James R. Lewis (eds.). 2009. *Handbook of Contemporary Paganism.* Leiden: Brill.

Sanson, Dawne. 2009. "New/Old Spiritualities in the West: Neo-Shamans and Neo-Shamanism," in Murphy Pizza and James R. Lewis (eds.). *Handbook of Contemporary Paganism*. Leiden: Brill, 433–462.

Smith, Jonathan Z. 2003. "Here, There, and Anywhere," in Scott B. Noegel, Joel T. Walker, and Brannon Wheeler (eds.). *Prayer, Magic and the Stars in the Ancient and Late Antique World*. University Park: Pennsylvania State University Press, 21–36.

Sointu, Eeva and Linda Woodhead. 2008. «Spirituality, Gender, and Expressive Selfhood». *Journal for the Scientific Study of Religion* 47 (2): 259–276.

Strøm, Anne-Karine. 2013. *Bergit: Helbredende hender.* Oslo: Orfeus Publishing.

Stuckrad, Kocku von. 2013. "Discursive Study of Religion: Approaches, Definitions, Implications." *Method and Theory in the Study of Religion* 25: 5–25.

Sutcliffe, Steven and Ingvild S. Gilhus (eds.). 2013. *New Age Spirituality: Rethinking Religion*. Durham: Acumen.

Tårnesvik, Geir. 2012. "Nå er sjamanisme offentlig godkjent religion," in *Nordlys*, http://www.nordlys.no/nyheter/article5970091.ece.

Tedlock, Barbara. 2005. *The Woman in the Shaman's Body: Reclaiming the Feminine in Religion and Medicine*. New York: Bantam Books.

Tighe, Maria and Jenny Butler. 2007. "Holistic Health and New Age in Britain and the Republic of Ireland," in Lewis, James R. and Daren Kemp (eds.) *Handbook of New Age: Brill Handbooks on Contemporary Religion*, Volume 1. Leiden: Brill, 415–434.

Tørum, Gro-Helen. 2012. *Sjaman på høye hæler: Min reise i ukjent landskap*. Oslo: Cappelen Damm.

Tramacchi, Des. 2006. "Entheogens, Elves and Other Entities: Encountering the Spirits of Shamanic Plants and Substances," in Lynne Hume and Kathleen McPhillips (eds.) *Popular Spiritualities: The Politics of Contemporary Enchantment*. Aldershot: Ashgate, 91–104.

Wallis, Roy. 2003. *Shamans/Neo-Shamans: Ecstasy, Alternative Archeologies, and Contemporary Pagans*. London: Routledge.

5

Shamanism—A Spiritual Heritage?: The Significance of the Past in Shamanic Discourses

Torunn Selberg

In *Yakutia Today*, under the headline "Shamanism—the Heritage of the Past," we are told,

> Shamanism is one of the most ancient systems of philosophy. The history of its existence extends back over many thousands years. Traditions, practices, customs and laws of this oldest form of religion are different in every region. The situation in Yakutia is unique: the latest technologies go side by side with ancient ideas about the world. Here pagan traditions are respected even by those who have lived all their life in a city.[1]

Yakutia is a region in Siberia, also known as *Sahka*, a region well known for shamanistic culture. Despite widespread persecution during the period of Soviet state atheism, shamanism is today undergoing a revival in this region.[2]

The above passage contains core notions connected to ideas and discourses about shamanism in late modern society. Concepts like "ancient," "tradition," "oldest form of religion" and so on are emphasized as qualities essential to "modern" shamanism. On the other hand, it is said that shamanism lives side by side with the most modern technology. Although shamanism is described as something descended from ancient times, it has something to offer humans who "have lived all their life in a city." An oft-repeated idea is that modernity and technology will wipe out traditional phenomena; tradition and modernity have been considered opposites. In the above passage, shamanism is described as something premodern that also has a place in late modern society. Modern technology is not wiping out tradition; there are many examples of modern technology supporting traditional communications and ways of life.[3]

In this chapter, I will discuss narratives that relate shamanism to traditions from an ancient past, ideas tied to Mircea Eliade's 1951 study of shamanism.[4] He described shamanism as humanity's oldest religion. And although his work has been criticized, it has also been a source of inspiration for new religiosities.[5] In today's society, it is a common idea that the past and history hold great value and significance for the present. It is also said that history contributes to our identity, both on an individual and at the social level.[6] History can be used to legitimize certain rights, and also as the basis for arguments in various other arenas. It is even said that people have a *right* to history, and thus that it is a problem for people to be *without* history.[7] In my opinion, discourses about the relation between shamanism and the ancient past can be seen as variations of late modern discourses about the value and meaning of history.

Additionally, modern shamanism is part of the increasing religious diversity expressed outside traditional religious institutions, delimited groups, doctrines, and canonical scriptures.[8] Paganism (and shamanism) is "fast developing as the new religion of the twenty-first century, a religion based on Nature worship and ancient indigenous traditions," as Charlotte Hardman writes in the introduction to *Paganism Today*.[9] The borderline between emergent religious diversity and other currents and discourses in culture in general is vague. In Paul Heelas' words, "the religious has become less obviously religious, the secular less obviously secular."[10] There has been much talk about the reenchantment of culture because religious images and meanings have acquired increasing significance in society.[11] But we may also talk about the ways in which nonreligious discourses and trends have continuities with modern religiosity and how they are interpreted and understood in such a context.

In his book, *The New Age Movement*, Heelas writes,

> More generally, the new Age is a spirituality of modernity in the sense that it (variously) provides a sacralized rendering of widely-held values (freedom, authenticity, self-responsibility, self-reliance, self-determination, equality, dignity, tranquility, harmony, love, peace, creative expressivity, being positive and, above all, 'the self' as a value in and of itself).[12]

Heelas is interested in New Age as a religion of the self. This is not my concern here, but I am inspired by his idea that modern religions and spiritualities can be understood as interpretations—yes, sacralizations—of values and trends in modern society. Expressed in several connections and in many ways, the past is perceived as a resource and used as an argument. The positive evaluation of the past is often articulated in the popular concepts and processes to which we refer as cultural heritage and tradition. I will analyze how this relationship is being discussed and interpreted. The examples I use are from the late 1990s up to the present, representing a period of 15 years. Shamanism—as well as contemporary religious diversity more generally—has become increasingly more visible. It is no longer limited to indigenous peoples in inaccessible areas untouched by modernity, although such pasts and places do continue to play a role in some stories. Currently the concept is also applied to urban shamans: practitioners within various therapeutic, spiritual, and cultural movements in the West.[13] The shamans discussed in this chapter are (by chance) all female. The narratives discussed are both personal experiences and general statements about shamanism, but they have in common the utilization of the past as a resource for their stories.

The Past as Resource and Mythology

One of the most renowned shamans in contemporary Norway is Gro-Helen Tørum, well known from successful television productions like *Åndenes hus* (The House of the Spirits). She is clairvoyant and can speak to the dead. She also gives talks about spirituality and the good life. Some years ago she probably would have been referred to as a wise woman or a healer, but today she is one of an increasing number of urban shamans involved in therapeutic and spiritual circles. Her 2012 autobiography is entitled *Sjaman på høye hæler* (Shaman in high heels), an apparently paradoxical title that highlights shamanism as a modern, urban phenomenon.

The book relates Tørum's inward and outward journey toward the realization that she is a shaman. She talks about several past lives. She claims that she lived among the Cathars and was burned at the stake. She lived another lifetime as one of Genghis Khan's horsemen[14] (91–92). Through contact with a shaman who had received messages that she should become Tørum's teacher, she finally learned through several soul journeys that she had been shaman in earlier lives among the Incas, "several hundreds of years ago." She says that this experience "was as real as life here and now."[15]

"Comprehending that I was shaman made me humble, because being a shaman is not something you can learn, it is something you *are*," she says. "And I knew that I *was* a shaman....Finally I had a name for the powers I had inside me, a name for the feeling of being different that I had felt my whole life, a name for the longing I had always felt inside me. I understood that what I had tried to hide could be my strength." Further, she says, "I had spent seven years of my life travelling inwards. I had now found my identity and would dare to show who I am! I was once 'Black Eagle Medicine Woman.' The time was now ripe to turn the journey outwards." [16]Her present task is "to collect old knowledge and wisdom and translate this information into valuable insights in the present life."[17]

Gro-Helen Tørum's story has much in common with "Inger"'s personal narrative about being a shaman. I interviewed Inger around the end of the 1990s. She lives in one of the larger cities in Norway, and when I met her she had begun "the long, hard way of the shaman." And why was she—a journalist and mother to a five-year-old son —on "the way of the shaman"? She recounts,

> I attended a course in shamanism, and during this course I experienced that I already *knew* the things that were being taught in the course. And I could not understand where I had learned these things. Then it turned out that I also knew how to go further and do things we had not yet talked about. I became steadily more aware that I knew and remembered things, but that I had no idea from where this knowledge had come.

After a while, Inger understood that she already had advanced understanding about shamanism because she had been a shaman in several earlier lives among the Hopi Indians. She also remembers being a shaman in Siberia. She states that her duty here and now is to collect information from earlier lives, especially knowledge about our relation to nature, and to share and communicate such knowledge to people here and now. To be able to do this, one has to live one's present life according to knowledge gained in earlier lives. Inger felt a strong relation to the Hopi, and she has also visited them. She is of the opinion that the Hopi are the last authentic Indians because they have preserved their old religion. She feels she has actually visited and experienced the past to which she feels tied.

The notion of reincarnation forms the foundation for a personal relationship with the past, both for Gro-Helen Tørum and Inger. They claim that their knowledge of shamanism and their identity as shamans are from former lives. Tørum links her wisdom to the Incas—"several hundred years ago"—and Inger to the American Hopi Indians without any specification of time. As Tørum states, the experience of former lives as a shaman is a proof that she is a shaman, because that is something you cannot learn to be. The idea of reincarnation can be understood as a key symbol within the alternative spiritual subculture.[18] Modern conceptions of reincarnation are a strong expression of how history and the past are evaluated in our own time.[19] Certain pasts have distinctive value within this discourse, for instance, ancient civilizations like Egypt, Rome, Greece, and India. In later times, however, the increasing interest in and knowledge about indigenous people have extended this universe,[20] as both Inger's and Tørum's narratives demonstrate.

The two narratives also indicate that being a shaman is not something they have chosen; rather, it is something they *are*. They have brought this vocation with them from earlier lives. They have been chosen independently of their own volition. These past lives are seen as evidence that it is their destiny to be shamans and their duty to bring the wisdom from earlier lifetimes into the present.

In January 1997, the book *Entering the Circle: Ancient Secrets of Siberian Wisdom discovered by a Russian Psychiatrist*, by Olga Kharitidi, was "book of the month" in the book club *Energica*, aimed at people interested in alternative spirituality. In the club's magazine, the book was introduced in the following way:

> Have you ever dreamed about a journey with the Trans-Siberian railway? The book of the month will give you the chance to undertake a trans-Siberian journey of transformation. We shall travel to the legendary Altaj Mountains. You can expect an unusual meeting—with age old, mystical traditions and forceful shamanistic rituals, with the origin of religion itself—the spiritual civilization (high culture) of the holy land Belovodja.[21]

In this short description we find many concepts indicating the antiquity of shamanism: age old, tradition, origin, and also legendary. The book contains Olga's personal narrative. Together with a patient, Nikolaj, she travels to the Altaj Mountains in Siberia, a fateful journey for Olga. The Altaj Mountains have a prominent place within the neoshamanistic universe, and are a destination for neoshamans seeking gurus and Shambala.[22] Olga meets the female shaman Umai, a meeting that changes her personal and professional life forever. Umai wants to transmit her powers to Olga, and she is introduced to a world that is simultaneously threatening and miraculous. After Olga's return to the hospital and her practice as a psychiatrist, Umai is spiritually present—speaking to her and giving her advice—the result of which is that Olga is able to heal a patient whom she had earlier tried to help without success. In this way we are told that ancient shamanistic wisdom has much to contribute to modern psychiatry, and that there is no opposition between ancient shamanism and modern science. At the same time as we follow Olga into a shamanistic world, we also follow her on a spiritual journey that reveals the holy land Belovodja to us. Belovodja is "the Siberian homeland of a long forgotten, advanced, esoteric civilization," we are told. [23] The magazine asks, "Has it ever existed? Was this the spiritual cradle of our culture?" And it provides the answer: "Many things indicate that the world religions as we know them today are just dim shadows of a spiritual greatness the world once knew."[24]

The kingdom of Belovodja is part of narratives about mythical kingdoms. In this context, however, Belovodja is conceived of as a real place in the Siberian mountains. Olga's story is a version of a narrative tradition about lost civilizations, a "stock in trade of Western occultism."[25] Olga's story indicates that ancient wisdom has been hidden in the inaccessible Siberian mountains. We are told that in a community untouched by modern times, so to speak, ageless wisdom and knowledge have been preserved. This wisdom exceeds modern knowledge in such areas as, for instance, the nature of the human psyche. The story indicates that in remote places of the world, age-old traditions have been preserved in unchanged forms. The past takes on a mythological dimension when it is recounted that ancient wisdom is superior to our own knowledge and that it will provide a new dimension to modern life and understanding. In this story and in the review of the book, it is asserted that modern people need ancient wisdom to be able to manage life in the here and now more successfully. In these narratives, *time* is also *place*; they illustrate the saying, "The past is a foreign country." They indicate that ancient times have been preserved in certain places where the past can be found, for instance, among the Hopi Indians or in inaccessible places in the Siberian Mountains. We are told that various pasts still exist in distant and far-off places.

The Past as Authority and Authenticity

The following story was published in the newspaper *Dagbladet* in August 1998. The story's headline was "Drum Fight in a Sami Village," and it related the experience of a female Sami shaman in a small village in *Finnmarksvidda*, on the Finnmark plateau. The drama in the story is a conflict between the shaman and the village's Christian inhabitants, but implicitly the story concerns the place of shamanism—and alternative religion—in modern culture. The story includes a picture of the shaman in traditional Sami costume with a decorated drum—a *runebomme*—with a fire in the background. The lead-in to the article states,

> She believes in the power of drums and is accused of being the Devil's representative.—"But it was the Christians who brought God and the Devil to the Sami, not I," the female shaman Biret Maret Kallio chuckles.

The story further relates that the people in Tana call Biret Maret *noaidi,* the Sami name for shaman, and that the drum constituted a central part of the Sami pre-Christian religion. We are told that Christian missionaries burned the pagan drums, and that most people then believed that Christianity had triumphed over paganism once and for all. So it is highly controversial that Biret Maret assembles her group—which is called *Noaidi*—and sacrifices to and worships the old gods. The newspaper further states that the villagers are fighting over the soul of the Sami village, and that Biret Maret is surprised that she encounters so much fear and antagonism from Christians. She believes that the drum is a healing instrument. The newspaper story also relates that she demonstrates some of the old rituals for them.

The story ends with a statement from the shaman:

> Biret herself knows that she is carrying on a highly controversial tradition. "Had I lived a few generations ago, I would have been burnt at the stake," she states. "My work has nothing to do with New Age—this is Old Age. The drum is a vehicle for contact with one's inner self, with nature, with the forefathers, and the spirits."

The newspaper story is formulated as a news story about a conflict in a local community, which has materialized in the form of something as exotic as a shaman's drum. But the ramifications of the article are more than just one local conflict. What makes the narrative thought provoking is the implied larger conflict between deviant religiosity and traditional Christianity. Additionally, it is a minority group that practices a religion said to have its roots in pagan times. Ideas about the past, about tradition and continuity, are prominent in the story, in which terms are used such as "pre-Christian religion," the "times of our forefathers" and, not least, "old age." The image of Biret Marit is quite different from Gro-Helen Tørum's urban shaman in high heels. The article in *Dagbladet* presents a traditional shaman in a traditional context, part of a group practicing the old religion and depicted with a traditional drum in a traditional Sami costume. The two stories—and the two female shamans—together present a wide-ranging image of contemporary shamanism.

Similar to Olga's story, the narrative about Biret provokes ideas about old traditions preserved in isolated areas and kept alive in the shadow of a dominant ideology. In older folkloristic theory, this was referred to as relict areas, places where old traditions were preserved, unaffected by modernization. The stories about Olga and Biret Maret incorporate this theme. Those ideas are still alive. Both the newspaper story and the Khartidis book embody ideas about the preservation of cultural practices—almost unchanged—through time. When Biret distances herself from the New Age by stating that her beliefs and practices are *Old* Age, and claims that her beliefs are older than Christianity, she describes her religion as ancient, although preserved through generations. When she connects her own activity to a past that, to her way of thinking, is also more congruent with Sami culture than with Christianity, shamanism is positioned within tradition and continuity. She is *traditionalizing* her activities and ideas, which makes them meaningful and authoritative.[26]

She is authenticating a religion that is looked down upon, both in the local community and in the outside world.

However, age and tradition can also be used in arguments *against* the authenticity of modern shamanism. In 1995, a Norwegian writer and journalist, Bjørg Vindsetmo, published a book entitled *Sjelen som turist* (Spiritual tourism). From a Catholic standpoint, she throws a critical light on the innumerable forms and mixtures of religions and therapies found within the New Age. She writes, "Typical of the new religiosity of our times is its *therapeutic* essence. Therapy has become religion, and even worse, religion has become therapy."[27]

One of the chapters focuses on neoshamanism—in the writer's view, one of the four most important modern "alternative therapies." The title of the chapter poses the question "Are Shamanistic Journeys Therapy?" The chapter begins with a description of a female Swedish shaman, whom the writer nicknames "Little Hiawatha." By using a name from the Disney universe, the writer invokes ideas of a superficial, trivial, commercial, and thus an *inauthentic* world.

The shaman is described as "super elegant" as a "wandering fashion show for indigenous people," as Vindsetmo ironically puts it. And we are told that Little Hiawatha teaches modern businessmen creativity and self-development as part of her practice.[28]

After describing Little Hiawatha, Vindsetmo describes "real" or genuine shamanism. She refers to it as the world's oldest religion and asks, "How can our earliest forefathers' religious life become something that, in a modern woman's world view, is a new form of therapy she may perhaps be trying? And what makes Little Hiawatha believe that she is a shaman?"[29]

By arguing that shamanism is our earliest ancestors' religion, Vindsetmo intends to create a distance between current shamans and ancient shamans. She is of the opinion that significant elements of the traditional shaman's universe have been lost in modern versions. To her, neoshamanism is not authentic: she describes it as a *break* with tradition, a remnant or a shadow of the true version. She characterizes the new version as a bleak forgery, lacking continuity with the original forms.

The foregoing narratives are about personal experiences. In most of the stories, the teller is also personally involved in various pasts and has opinions about the significance of the past. In more general descriptions of modern shamanism, such as the one that introduces this chapter, the connection of shamanism with ancient times is even more explicitly expressed.

In an article from the Scandinavian Centre for Shamanic Studies, we are told that "Shamanism is an ancient spiritual tradition and magical craft, used the world over for healing, for solving problems and for maintaining the balance between man and nature."[30] In an interview in *Sjamansonen* (The Shaman zone),[31] Ailo Gaup[32] claims that "if we go back to the time before the great religions, we will see that the highest spiritual tradition was what we now call shamanism." He claims that shamanism is found throughout the entire world, and "that shamanism is really our [universal] spiritual heritage."[33]

Here shamanism is described as a form of spirituality so old that it belongs to humanity's common past, before the time of the founders of the great religions. "Shamanism has been there the whole time as a possibility within us," says Gaup.[34] He claims that it is a heritage from "Neolithic" times, "when humans lived in tribes without private rights of ownership, without social classes and the social structures that are characteristic of later periods. From the dawn of time the shaman has wandered through history..."[35]

The Rhetoric of Tradition and Old Age

The stories, narratives, and statements recounted here are drawn from different levels of communication and contexts, but the different speakers are part of a larger dialogue in which the meaning and significance of ancient times are discussed. Their utterances can also be understood as answers to critical comments or disagreements about modern shamanism, and as arguments over the authenticity of current shamanistic ideas and practices. There is an intertextual quality produced by the juxtaposition of these various utterances. In Richard Bauman's words, "speakers...align their words to the words of others." The production of intertextuality can be understood as a web extending over time,[36] in this case using various interpretations of and expressions for "pastness."

In Vindsetmo's story, neoshamanism represents a break with the shamanism of the past, and is described as a weak echo of a genuine tradition. She sees shamanism as humanity's oldest religion, and, in her eyes, modern shamanism represents spiritual decline. The story about the shaman in the Sami village in northern Norway, and the story about a Russian psychiatrist's encounter with Siberian shamanism share the theme of continuity with old traditions. The stories say that this tradition and wisdom from the past can help modern people achieve better lives for themselves. Inger and Gro Helen Tørum relate how former lives as shamans give them the opportunity and also the duty to bring their knowledge from earlier times into the present.

Vindsetmo describes contemporary ideas about shamanism in terms of spiritual decline, while the other stories describe ways of using ideas from the past to improve the present. The stories contain shared ideas about the past, representing more consistent traditions and greater wisdom. Also common to these stories is the theme that the past is not merely a context for the narrative but is also both a certain quality as well as an authenticating argument for the practices in the stories. The past and tradition are arguments for the value of various beliefs and ideas, and traditionalizing these beliefs creates meaning in the present. Ancient times are sacralized in discourses about shamanism, which is perceived as containing wisdom and spirituality beyond the scope of contemporary society. When—in the various stories—the symbolic power of the past is transferred into the present, it creates an atmosphere of enchantment.

In modern popular religiosity—and especially within modern paganism—the value of the past is expressed in ideas about superior wisdom and spiritualities. In that sense, we can talk about a mythologization and sacralization of the past within modern religiosity, both on an individual and a collective level. The past is lost, but narratively reproduced in stories about earlier wisdom and spirituality that exceed modern knowledge and represent wisdoms that modern man needs.

Within contemporary paganism, Peter Beyer claims, ancient myths, rituals, and symbols in pre-Christian religion and pretechnical civilizations are interpreted as the source for a growing spiritual knowledge, and also as countercurrents against the ills of modern civilization. The idea is that the wisdom of the ancient religions is as valuable as modern technology, and as stated in the introductory citation from *Yakutia Today*, Paganism and modern technology can live side by side; they are not competitors. Pagans see themselves as representatives of forgotten or suppressed religions of the marginal, the weak, and the suppressed, as Beyer says. But, he further states, there are also intricate connections between paganism and the values of the dominating structures of global society.[37] On the one side, shamanism and paganism are seen as countercultural to modernity; on the other side, as parallel to modernity—simultaneously antimodern and very modern. Thomas Ziehe has asserted that to opt for premodernity is an act of late modernity,[38] and that shamanism is a kind of spirituality said to stem from premodern times that appeals to modern people.

Cultural Heritage and Heritagization

A point of departure in this chapter was that trends and discourses in society can develop into constructions within modern religious diversity and there take on a sacred dimension. My assertion is that in late modern society the past is of special significance, and that there is a connection between valuations of history in general and the discourses that have developed about shamanism in contemporary society. Today, we find a popular, diverse, and steadily increasing production of "history" expressed in, for instance, numerous festivals, pageants, and jubilees that refer to historical happenings of both local and national interest. Scholarly research into history is just part of the current production of history; we also find popular books—widely read—describing the past in attractive terms. People engage in writing local histories and in genealogical studies. Celebrations and uses of the past are increasingly present in various ways. The value of the past is currently expressed in an increasing use and interest in *cultural heritage*. A popular understanding of heritage is that it ensures continuity between those who have produced it and ourselves, who become heirs as we receive it.[39]

In contemporary society we can talk about *heritagization*, a concept referring to processes of cultural production by which cultural or natural elements are selected and reworked for new social uses; it is *reinterpretations* of the past based on contemporary issues.[40] The concept also refers to how increasing numbers and types of material—and immaterial—structures and phenomena are continuously being incorporated and turned into heritage objects. Although heritage indicates history and old things, it is, as American folklorist Barbara Kirshenblatt-Gimblett has noted, "a new mode of cultural production in the present that has recourse to the past."[41] She claims that "heritage adds value to existing assets that have either ceased to be viable (subsistence, lifestyles, obsolete technologies, abandoned mines etc.), or that never were economically productive....Heritage...ensure[s] that (such assets) will survive."[42] Although it is a new cultural production, the age of heritage is central and adds value to selected phenomena designated as heritage. Thus, cultural heritage is not about things or expressions, but more about our *relation* to things and expressions, and not least to their "pastness" and age. Heritage and interpretations of the past are as much about our present needs as about the past itself. History and the past give meaning to the present, and heritage is about reclamation and cultivation of the past. In discourses about shamanism, heritage is about worship of the past.

Heritage is not lost or found; rather, it is produced in contemporary society. It gives new life to old things. It is old in a modern way. Our approach to heritage indicates that it had a prior existence before it was identified, valuated, and "celebrated" as such. Heritage produces something new that has recourse to the past and to the process of protection, of "adding value." It speaks in and to the present even if it does so in terms of the past.[43]

Shamanism is also discussed as heritage. If we look back at the interview with Gaup,[44] he claims that "if we go back to the time before the large religions, we will see that our greatest spiritual heritage was what we now call shamanism." He asserts that shamanism is found in the whole world and "that shamanism is really a spiritual heritage."

In www.sjaman.com, it is stated that "Shamanism is really a spiritual world heritage." But as with heritage, shamanism—in its present form—is a new cultural production with recourse to the past, a past that is creating identity, authenticity, and meaning.

Peter Beyer says that religion is like a mirror that makes possible a critical reflection of normal reality by creating a virtual, reverse, and thus spiritual image of that reality, but this generation of a spiritual image is only possible in terms of the normal world that is being reflected. I agree with Beyer in his portrayal of the relation between the "normal" world and paganism. But I would rather say that paganism is an interpretation of ideas about the past circulating in current society than a reflection of the ideas of the past in contemporary society. Whereas within the larger society the past is being cultivated, within shamanistic circles it is being worshipped and has taken on sacred and mythological dimensions.

Notes

1. www.Yatoday.ru/culture/92 (Yakutia today. Lest 19122013)
2. Harvey and Wallis 2007: 186.
3. See, for example, Blank 2009.
4. Mircea Eliade, 1998: *Sjamanisme. Henrykkelsens og ekstasens eldgamle kunst* (orig. 1951). Oslo, Pax forlag.
5. Fonneland 2009: 11.
6. Eriksen 1999, Lowenthal 1985, 1998, Kirshenblatt-Gimblett 1998, Fonneland 2009.
7. Eriksen 1999: 9.
8. Christensen 2013: 36.
9. Hardman 1996.
10. Heelas 1998: 3.
11. Gilhus and Mikaelsson 1998: 5.
12. Heelas 1996: 169.
13. Harvey 2003: 1.
14. Tørum 2012: 91–92.
15. Ibid.: 108.
16. Ibid.: 110.
17. Ibid.: 109.
18. Gilhus 1999.
19. Ibid., Kraft 2011.
20. Ibid., 1999.
21. Energica januar 1997.
22. Harvey and Wallis 2007: 17.
23. Harvey and Wallis 2007: 121.
24. Energica januar 1997.
25. Haanegraaff 1998: 309.
26. Bauman 2004.

27. Vindsetmo 1995: 15.
28. Ibid.: 18.
29. Ibid.: 22.
30. www.shamanism.dk Scandinavian Center for Shamanic Studies. Lastet ned 19122013.
31. www.sjaman.com visited19.12.2013.
32. The name is not mentioned in the article
33. Ibid.
34. Ibid.
35. Ibid.
36. Bauman 2004: 128.
37. Beyer 1998: 18–19.
38. Ziehe 1986.
39. Roigé and Frigolé 2010: 11.
40. Ibid.: 12.
41. Kirshenblatt-Gimblett 1998: 149.
42. Ibid.: 150.
43. Ibid.: 149–150.
44. The name is not mentioned in the article.

References

Bauman, Richard. 2004. *A World of Others' Words: Cross-Cultural Perspectives on Intertextuality*. Oxford: Blackwell.

Beyer, Peter. 1998. "Globalisation and the Religion of Nature," in Joanne Pearson, Richard H. Roberts and Geoffrey Samuel (eds.) *Nature Religion Today*. Edinburgh: Edinburgh University Press, 11–21.

Blank, Trevor (ed.). 2009. *Folklore and the Internet: Vernacular Expression in a Digital World*. Logan, Utah: Utah University Press.

Christensen, Cato. 2013. *Religion som samisk identitetsmarkør. Fire studier av film*. Akad.avh, Universitetet i Tromsø Eriksen, Anne 1999: *Historie, minne og myte*. Oslo: Pax.

Fonneland, Trude. 2009. *Samisk nysjamanisme: i dialog med (for)tid og stad. Ein kulturanalytisk studie av nysjamaner sine erfaringsforteljingar—identietsforhandlingar og verdiskaping*. Akad.avh: Bergen.

Gilhus, Ingvild. 1999. "Sjelevandring—et nytt nøkkelsymbol," in Alver. Bente Gullveig e.a. (eds.) *Myte, magi og mirakel i møte med det moderne*. Oslo: Pax forlag, 31–42.

Gilhus, Ingvild and Lisbeth Mikaelsson. 1998. *Kulturens refortrylling*. Oslo: Universitetsforlaget.

Hanegraaff, Wouter J. 1998. *New Age Religion and Western Culture: Esotericism in the Mirror of Secular Thought*. Albany: State University of New York Press.

Hardman, Charlotte. 1996. Introduction, in Graham Harvey and Charlotte Hardman (eds.) *Paganism Today: Wiccans, Druids, the Goddess and Ancient Earth Tradition for the Twenty-First Century*. London, Thorsons, ix–xix.

Harvey, Graham. 2003. General introduction, in Graham Harvey (ed.) *Shamanism: A Reader*. London: Routledge, 1–24.

Harvey, Graham and Robert J. Wallis. 2007. *Historical Dictionary of Shamanism*. Lanham, MD: Scarecrow Press.

Heelas, Paul. 1996. *The New Age Movement: The Celebration of the Self and the Sacralization of Modernity*. Oxford, Blackwell.

———. 1998. Introduction: "On Differentiation and Dedifferentiation," in Paul Hellas (ed.) *Religion, Modernity and Postmodernity*. Oxford: Blackwell Publishers, 1–18.

Kirshenblatt-Gimblett, Barbara. 1998. *Destination Culture: Tourism, Museums, and Heritage*. Berkeley: University of California Press.

Kraft, Siv Ellen. 2011. *Hva er nyreligiøsitet?* Oslo: Universitetsforlaget.

Lowenthal, David. 1985. *The Past Is a Foreign Country*. Cambridge: Cambridge University Press.

———. 1998. *The Heritage Crusade and the Spills of History*. Cambridge: Cambridge University Press.

Roigé, Xavier, and Joan Frigolé. 2010. Introduction, in Xavier Roigé and Joan Frigolé (eds.) *Constructing Cultural and Natural Heritage: Parks, Museums and Rural Heritage*. Girona: ICRPC (Institut Catalá de Receres en Patrimonial Cultural, 9–27.

Tørum, Gro-Helen (samarbeid med Tove Skagestad). 2012. *Sjaman på høye hæler: Min reise i ukjent landskap*. Oslo: Cappelen Damm.

Vindsetmo, Bjørg. 1995. *Sjelen som turist: Om religion, terapi og magi*. Oslo: Gyldendal.

Ziehe, Thomas. 1986. "Inför avmystifieringen av världen: Ungdom och kulturell modernisering," in Mikael Löfgren and Anders Molander (ed.) *Postmoderne tider*. Stockholm: Norstedt, 345–361.

6

Metroshamanism: A Search for Shamanic Identity in Modern Estonia

Henno Erikson Parks

In a survey conducted in 2011, only 20 percent of Estonians responded that religion played an important role in their life, suggesting that, statistically, it is the least religious country in the world. A combination of Estonian religious history, linguistic barriers, and 60 years of Soviet occupation has undoubtedly contributed to such statistics, however, it belies the real spiritual landscape of the country. Despite such surveys, it would seem that Estonians do believe in something, with over half the population claiming that they believe in an unspecified spirit or life force, often taking a pagan form of one kind or another, whether it be through nature worship, ancient runic calendars, or shamanism (Esslemont 2011). It is this final category of shamanism on which this chapter will focus, while at the same time attempting to tackle the complex and problematic issue of how to define that term within an Estonian, or even Northern European, context. Because the term "shaman" has become an all-encompassing category in contemporary ethnological and religious research—and has come to represent so much more than its original native Siberian meaning, which describes a specialized type of wise person—it does not take into account the various forms of existing shamanic practices and beliefs, nor how specific cultures interpret them.[1] In order to better define what Estonian shamanism is, we will look at the central works of Michael Harner, Andrei Znamenski, Annette Høst, and Jøn Asbjørn, who discuss shamanisms in a wider sense; we will examine videographic evidence from Harry Johansen and Torill Olsen, and Lennart Meri; and, finally, we will review some of the personal interviews made with key figures in Estonia today, among them Sven-Erik Soosaar, Thule Lee, Mikk Sarv, and Mare Kõiva.

Finding a Solution

We should begin by asking whether it is possible to apply only one specific label, shamanism, to a plethora of practices and beliefs found in different countries and regions, which have experienced such different histories, environments, and cultural influences,

There are, of course, some basic core elements that can be found in the shamanisms practiced worldwide; however, this does not take into account how the above-mentioned considerations impact those practices. Indeed, attempts have been made to do so since Harner[2] introduced his concept of *Core Shamanism* some 30 years ago, or Mircea Eliade[3] before him. Ultimately, the term shaman became an academic and social construct used to try and fit various specialized roles and types of practices from different cultures under the umbrella of shamanism so that they could be compared with apparently similar roles and practices in other cultures. Amazonian cultures have many different categories of shaman, and are typically named after the plants in which they specialize. The same differentiation holds true for Estonian shamanism, which traditionally has used the term *nõid* to describe those engaged in this type of work. This is similar to the Finnish *noita* and the Sami *noaidi*, although the latter term more closely represents the actual practice of shamanism in a Siberian sense. With the advent of Christianity in Estonia—which was quite late in the European context, extending well into the fifteenth century—these terms acquired a more negative connotation. Practitioners were generally categorized as *witches* or *sorcerers*, although nowadays Estonians continue to use the term nõid to label anyone practicing healing or magic, including shamans. The Sami author and historian Aage Solbakk presents a very clear picture of how shamanism fit into the worldview of the Sami people, and how the introduction of Christianity changed the roles and even the titles of shamans in order to accommodate the new order of religious life in the north. He states that

> The Sámi people had our world as we all see it with our own eyes. Then there was the other world that only the Noaidi, or Sámi shaman could comprehend— the unseen. There were two worlds. In the old days, this knowledge, the power to heal, belonged to the shamans; but when Christianity came to our land, they started to call the shaman the devil's disciple. What did they do then? Well, they started to use other terms, terms like helpers and so on. And by changing the terms, this tradition survived until today.[4]

I assume that this same process of integration and adaptation went on, to a lesser or greater degree, among many indigenous populations, Estonia included. For the most part, the word shaman is a relatively new term in Estonia, even though the practice is considered to be endemic. The actual practice of shamanism in Estonia can be traced throughout its history, under the commonly used term nõid, who was a person who basically performed similar tasks to shamans in rural communities. It was only during the Soviet period (1940–1991) that the word shaman came into the Estonian vocabulary, along with the compulsory learning of the Russian language and the corpus of literature that came with it. However, at that time, it was never used to describe local practitioners, but rather those of cultures outside of the country, and Siberian shamanism in particular. Currently, the term shaman has become interchangeable with the word nõid in Estonia. We can see from the etymological map in Figure 6.1 that the word nõid occurs in all of the various dialects throughout Estonia[5] (see Figure 6.1).

There are, however, many titles used to reflect the different types of shamanism practiced in Estonia. As mentioned above, the term nõid, which could be broadly defined in Estonia as a person who is able to affect the world and control power through their knowledge, abilities, and various skills, and receive their power and its characteristics from different sources, shares commonalities with other labels given to practitioners of similar arts. Some of the other common terms used are *Šamaan* (described more as a primitive witch or priest[ess]), *Manatark* (an exorcist or conjuror), *Lausuja* (spellbinder, speaker of words of power or *loitsud*—incantations or spells), *Võlur* (sorcerer[ess], or enchanter[ess]), *Posija* (charmer—again having to do with speaking words of power or charms), *Tark* (wise man [woman]), *Teadmamees* (also wise man), *Ravitseja* (healer), *Ennustaja* (fortuneteller), and *Meedium* (medium).

As one can see, all these different categories that represent the paranormal abilities and skills of the practitioner no longer precisely fit under the universal label of shamanism. "Neoshamanism" is another commonly used term, which is defined as signaling a "new" form or a revival of an old form of shamanism. Annette Høst discusses the dilemma this term creates in modern shamanic circles, because she feels that the label has a critical and pejorative undertone that separates present-day shamanic practices from the so-called "real" shamanism practiced in traditional settings (2014). Furthermore, she dismisses the term "urban shamanism" outright, as promoting a complete break with the vital core of shamanism as a nature-based practice. Nevertheless, for many practicing shamans, urban life is a reality with which they must deal, as well as discover new ways to relate to and work with the natural world and their spirit helpers, which are so essential to the worldview of classical shamanism. These terms struggle to address the multiplicity of the word shamanism within a modern context.

The question then becomes, what term(s) would appropriately reflect the landscape of shamanic practices culturally, geographically, and conceptually in modern society today, and is it even feasible to accurately

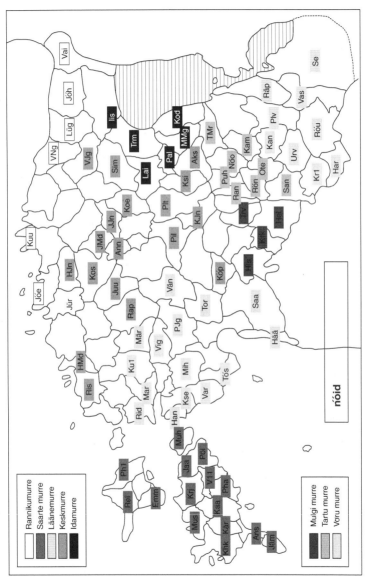

Figure 6.1 Map of Estonia.

portray them? This also creates a certain dilemma as to whether we are using the term shaman in an etic sense, emphasizing the way scholars might interpret and understand the practice, or whether we are approaching it from an emic point of view regarding how shamans themselves perceive and interpret their own practices and beliefs. In many cases, the two approaches merge, especially when the scholar and the practitioner are one and the same. A good example of this would be Høst, cofounder of the Scandinavian Center for Shamanic Studies and a key contributor to the development of Norse neoshamanism, who argues for terms such as "modern Western shamanism" or even "modern European shamanism." She defines it as "modern and it is Western/European shamanism meaning that its form, its practice, is rooted in and shaped by our own (modern) time and our North European culture, with its spiritual, material, political conditions and traits" (2014). These terms are undoubtedly an improvement in the sense of clarifying this aspect of regional phenomena, and certainly might suffice when trying to characterize local practices within a larger complex whole. However, because it is intrinsically influenced by cultural variables and exists on a continuum of multiple titles and roles, it still does not fully justify the label shamanism. Furthermore, the term "Western" would exclude Estonian shamanism, since it could be considered as Eastern European, even though the society is very much western, and most certainly culturally northern. Krippner posits that indigenous terms should be used where possible when discussing specific types of shamanism or practitioners, and to only use the broader label of shaman or shamanism in a general sense (Webb 2013). However, I feel that even these broader and more generalized terms are not sufficiently accurate and do not include the historical, cultural, environmental, and spiritual elements from which the label shamanism is invariably composed.

It is not merely a question of defining the region in which shamanism is practiced, but also fully qualifying the meaning and connotations that the word itself embodies, while at the same time allowing for variation and specification. Perhaps there is no one label or definition that clearly works for this overused word, and we could look at it more as a methodological description or specific point of view from which to classify the various shamanisms that exist. I would suggest that a methodological term such as "metroshamansim" could be used, loosely based on the linguistic concept, and which perhaps would better reflect a modern interpretation of the practice. It can be defined as encompassing inherently creative shamanic practices that extend across the borders of culture, history, time, and politics.[6] The new shamanisms that are being constructed and reconstructed are a product of modern interaction, describing the ways in which people from different backgrounds use, experiment with, and negotiate identities, titles, and concepts through a variety of shamanic practices and beliefs. Furthermore, the term also incorporates the characterization that many neoshamanic movements have arisen in a primarily urban setting, a drastic departure from past practices that were more rural and often solitary, and certainly a phenomenon seen in Northern Europe. To a degree, then, the focus shifts from the complexity of shamanic belief systems in natural environments to shamanism emerging from urban interaction and modern interpretations and implementations of practice. The notion of metroshamanism would give us ways of moving beyond the common frameworks of shamanism, providing insights into contemporary practices and beliefs as emerging from these contexts of interaction and, at the same time, accommodating the multifarious nature the term shamanism has acquired. Certainly, there has been movement in the opposite direction in recent years, in attempts to reconnect with the natural forces central to shamanic belief and practices; however, the reality is that the great majority of practitioners cannot live solely on shamanism as a profession in modern society. Likewise, a term such as contemporary shamanism might serve the same purpose, since we are speaking of the shamanisms practiced today and not attempting to tackle the complexities of past descriptions of the practice.

So, how can we describe the different phases of metroshamanism in modern Estonia? Beyond the labels described earlier regarding the various roles into which practitioners fall, metroshamanism in Estonia can be divided into four general categories that are by no means static, and that tend to overlap frequently. They are *homegrown, experiential, extraneous appropriations*, and *fusional*. They can be defined as follows: (1) homegrown—practitioners and practices that rely on archeological, historical, and traditional records, ethnographic literature and data, and popular culture. This form of practice would address the issue of how shamanism can be defined as a religious movement—whether through the use of indigenous ethnographic literature and data, history, archeology, popular culture, its underlying philosophical premises, or the practices and beliefs of the communities that are constituted or drawn together by shamanic activities in the context of modern Estonian society. This category can be further divided into an aspect labeled *traditional*—which are the local circumstances and background from which shamanic practice develops. Within the traditional part there are also three other possible subdivisions: *familial*, meaning that the abilities and skills are passed down from one generation to another; *positional*, in which the practitioner undergoes an apprenticeship or the passing of knowledge by a senior member; and *archival*, in which the practitioner learns from archival material relating to previous historical figures, or from cultural memory. (2) experiential—having to do with individuals and their personal experiences, for example, through inspiration, revelations within the practice of shamanic trance and ritual dance, hallucinogens, prophetic dreams, and premonitions. This category also contains an aspect that can be described as *transcendental*—which relates to the unlimited experiences of nonreality with or without the aid of hallucinogens. (3) extraneous appropriations—a concept related to the various foreign practices and systems of belief borrowed and incorporated into the practitioners' own modus operandi. In many cases, this begs the question of how appropriate the appropriation is, or, in other words, how much borrowing from other indigenous belief systems and practices is acceptable or even necessary? This category likewise contains two separate parts: *elemental influences*—in which practitioners choose specific elements from a foreign shamanic practice that best fit their own purpose and aims, and incorporate them into their practice and/or belief system; and *comprehensive influences*—in which entire belief systems, rituals, and ceremonies are appropriated and incorporated, with little alteration from the original. And finally (4) fusional—which can be almost synonymous with the methodological term for metroshamansim, and most likely reflects the current situation of most shamanic practices in the world due to globalization and modern social media, in which a practitioner uses the resources he or she has and combines them with other internal or external sources. This category also examines regional influences on local shamanism, such as Eastern, Western, Northern, Native American, and South American.

Fusion and Its Influence on Shamanism in Estonia

For the purpose of this chapter, I will examine only the last category of fusional influences on metroshamanic practices in Estonia. Perhaps a good indication of early external influences on Estonian shamanism can be found in the cosmological constructions of its mythology and epic poetry that have clear connections and parallels to its immediate neighbors in Northern and Eastern Europe. Some of these associations can be traced to the pantheon of deities found in Scandinavian and Finno-Baltic cultures, demonstrating early contact between them through trade and colonial expansion. Asbjørn states that

> Wide ranging lexical exchange between Finno-Baltic and Northern Teutonic peoples during the main composition period of Finno-Baltic magic and shamanic epic poetry (ca 200 B.C.-550 A.D.) is now largely accepted by scholars, and has in most cases been attributed to such early contacts. Therefore, it is also highly possible that some theological conceptions were also exchanged between the Teutonic and Finno-Baltic peoples during such early meetings. (1999: para. 2)

The idea that certain divine characters from Northern Teutonic peoples have had a strong influence in defining the role and worldview of the Finno-Baltic pagan traditions in general, and shamanism in particular, is an interesting one. Certainly, we can see clear connections between Finnish and Estonian cosmological constructs, especially through their epic poetry, folk tales, and songs, and so, perhaps, it is also possible that Scandinavian religious concepts and practices might have had a great deal of influence on the pre-Christian communities of these areas.

During the period of awakening national identity in the nineteenth century, the creation of such epic poems as the Finnish *Kalevala* and the Estonian *Kalevipoeg* became synonymous with the creation of a nation. Indeed, both were direct products of this period in history, and have been vital in providing a wealth of ethnographic and folkloric data that has since been used by emerging pagan movements in both countries. How much of the material was authentic and provided an accurate picture of pre-Christian Estonia is debatable, although certainly a good portion of what was collected and used in their creation was based on genuine cultural memory.[7] Nevertheless, the epic poems serve as a broad template and as a source of inspiration and information for many practicing shamans and other contemporary pagans.

There are numerous other clear analogies that point to a Scandinavian or Finnish influence on Estonian practices and beliefs. The island of Saaremaa, off the coast of mainland Estonia was recently in the news in June 2013, when two intact Viking ships and their slain crews were discovered during routine power line excavations. This archeological find has shaken previous notions of when the Viking age began and how their culture evolved.

> The archaeologists believe the men died in a battle some time between 700 and 750, perhaps almost as much as a century before the Viking Age officially began. This was an era scholars call the Vendel period, a transitional time not previously known for far-reaching voyages—or even for sails. The two boats themselves bear witness to the tremendous technological transformations in the eighth-century Baltic. (Curry, 2013)

Saaremaa developed its own homegrown Viking culture, and it can be assumed that they were influenced and impacted by trade, warfare, and the exchange of human hostages as part of the spoils of battle. Physical evidence of these interactions still exists to this day in the form of inscriptions on Scandinavian runic stones, the sagas (notably the Icelandic Njáls saga and the Olav Tryggvasons saga), and various chronicles.[8] There is also a clear link with the known magical and medicinal use of runes in ancient Scandinavian rituals and the common use of runes in Estonia, either in the form of runic or staff calendars, or as symbols of protection on homes and for divination.[9] Such connections are, of course, understandable due to the close proximity of the various cultures, and the extensive trade routes that crisscrossed the territories involved. Along with the movement of trade goods, ideas, religious concepts, and cultural and spiritual practices could have traveled the same pathways and thus had an indelible impact on the populations with which they came in contact. Indeed, shamanism in all of its various manifestations could have just as easily followed identical paths laid down by this same movement of peoples and goods, whether in lexical, ideological, or cultural form. Asbjørn sums this up in noteworthy fashion when he states that the

> observation, in conjunction with the pre-existent knowledge of early contact and lexical borrowings between the Finno-Baltic and Teutonic peoples, would suggest that deep analysis of the development of both Finno-Baltic shamanic deities and Óðinn may reveal instances in which tales that were traditionally associated with the exploits of one of these figures were transferred to the other. Such a discovery would certainly support the study of Estonian shamanism, as it would speed the process of recognizing purely Estonian elements of shamanic practice and belief. (1999: para 15)

The Role of History

History itself has played an important role in contributing to a heavy Scandinavian influence on Estonian culture, language, and traditions. During much of the Middle Ages, parts of Estonian territory were under Danish rule, and in the thirteenth century there were extensive settlements of Coastal Swedes on the islands and the western coast of the country, which they inhabited up to the beginning of the Second World War. The early modern history of Estonia was also characterized by both Swedish and Danish domination right up to the Great Northern War (1700–1721), leading to Sweden's defeat by the Russians (Estonia.eu 2014). One can expect that this constant influx of peoples, ideas, cultures, and customs had an impact on the native population, and ultimately helped mold the country as it is today. It is unclear whether this would have directly influenced shamanism in Estonia, but certainly the new invaders and settlers would have brought their own beliefs and customs, despite the fact that Christianity was the predominant religion of the time.

The interwar period of the twentieth century (between 1918 and 1940) can be characterized as one of intense cultural activity that served to establish the foundations for various movements and endeavors, as well as setting up a coping mechanism for what was to follow in what might be considered the darkest period in modern Estonian history. Here we can specifically look at the ways in which Estonians attempted to construct and define beliefs and practices linked to the ancient past, what internal and external influences affected them, and how the new esoteric movements, including neoshamanism, developed within a larger cultural context. The Estonian Institute (Eesti Instituut) posits a very interesting theory regarding the impact of World War II and the Soviet occupation on Estonian cultural life, going so far as to say that it split Estonian culture into two parts: cultural lives in exile and at home. The article goes on to state that "Estonian culture in Soviet Estonia had to resist forced Russification and restrictions to creative freedom; its ultimate success guaranteed the continuation of Estonian culture" (Eesti Instituut 2010). At the same time, religious life was equally under heavy pressure, with authorities insuring that the church and all other aspects of spiritual life were under control. Again, the Estonian Institute says, "The political and economic separation of Soviet Estonia from the rest of the world, accompanied by an extensive (but still incomplete) information blackout from Western spiritual developments and directions had negative results" (ibid.). What some of these "negative results" are will become clearer as we proceed through this chapter.

It is also vital to consider the types of information and materials produced, and the methods of dispersion to interested parties. Perhaps we can categorize the types of materials as follows: original archival materials (both local and international [Soviet]); original materials smuggled into the country through various channels, which are then translated, transcribed, and distributed; information and materials collected and compiled during expeditions—both internal and external; information and materials acquired through visiting lecturers, seminars, and conferences (mainly in the late Soviet and post-Soviet period); information (mostly oral) provided by returning Estonian populations and their families; and, finally, information and materials provided by other populations living within the territory of Estonia (for example, Russians and Roma people). Examining how and by whom these different source materials were used will provide a better picture of how belief systems survived and thrived in Soviet Estonia.

Some of the groups or circles from the Soviet Estonian intellectual sphere who found themselves under tremendous ideological pressure to prevent the spread of free thinking in society were able to find specific ways to circumvent it. As I see it, three main groups can be examined: artists, writers, and academics. It would seem that information on esoteric topics, or even those that mildly hinted at some form of spirituality, usually could only be accessed by certain people in particular circles. These circles were generally the ones made up of people who had access to materials, information, and contacts throughout the former Soviet

Union and its satellite countries, and perhaps even in the West. By far the largest of these groups were those that had an interest in certain signs and symbols, or the combination of patterns and colors, and that were at the same time interested in the deeper spiritual meaning behind these constructs—namely artists (including musicians, who were searching for the roots of the past within the context of contemporary Estonian music). Secondly, there were those who might be called writers and poets, and who wanted to consider the written word and how it was used in the past, and perhaps how it developed from its original meaning. And finally, the third kind of people were the academics, especially those working in the fields of anthropology, folklore, and linguistics. The last two categories overlap in many instances, as writers are in many cases also scholars.

Painting a Picture

Artists and musicians, many of whom had a strong interest in the eso-teric, were also able to discuss a wide range of related topics within several different contexts, and in many cases they were students of art history at the University of Art (*Kunstiülikool*), in Tallinn. In Soviet Estonia, the cultivation of a national handicraft movement developed as a reaction to the severe Stalinist repression of the late 1940s to the early 1950s.[10] This was to some degree a veiled protest against the communist ideology of the time that was advocating an interpretation of the arts and literature from the perspective of "social realism" in the social sci-ences. In 1966, the Association of Handicraft Masters, called UKU, was founded to produce affordable household items and souvenirs depicting a traditional Estonian national style. It employed over 1,500 artisans who "crafted artifacts either modeled on the originals deposited in various Estonian museums, or produced according to designs by modern artists in the style of folk art" (Reeman 2004). Looking at the first and largest category of people, the artists were mainly responsible for conducting extensive research into certain signs and symbols for inspiration. One well-known artist in Estonia was Kaljo Põllu (1934–2010), who exam-ined Sami symbols as well as the cultural and artistic background of the northern peoples. During the late Soviet period, one was permitted to investigate other peoples and cultures, and, through this research, a few felt that indeed there might have existed a native form of shamanism in Estonia. However, it was not possible to openly speak about it, but rather one had to transform the information somehow within the con-text of other cultures. Põllu created numerous pieces of graphic art based on Northern European shamanism and Northern Siberian shamanism, which was tied indirectly to Estonian shamanism. He was one of the few artists who developed this new theme of shamanism and the ideas and concepts behind it. During this era, the only way that one could learn about the symbols, customs, and traditions related to shamanism was through expeditions to Northern Siberia and other parts of the Soviet Union, and Põllu was responsible for organizing many of these excursions. Generally, those who participated in these expeditions were art history students who, during the course of their travels, were responsible for researching the meanings of various symbols and runes, and were required to meticulously draw them in great detail. These were later sent to the Art Museum archives. In addition to the symbols and runes, clothing and costumes, designs and colors, patterns, and other crafts, were also drawn and submitted to the collection. Because of the way this material was collected, recorded, and stored, it became a vivid portrait of the artistic and cultural traditions of the people it was meant to represent.

Another key figure in this method of collecting authentic data and finding ways to position it within an Estonian context from broader cultural and ethnological perspectives was Lennart Meri (1929–2006). He was the former president of Estonia for two terms between 1992–2000. However, before the start of his political career, Meri spent many years organizing expeditions to remote regions of the Soviet Union to study the cultures of small ethnic populations. He also had a strong interest in the discovery and colonization of Siberia, and through these travels generated extensive materials, both written and videographic, which even managed to penetrate the Iron Curtain at the time. In fact, one of his films, *The Winds of the Milky Way*, a coproduction with Finland and Hungary, was banned in the Soviet Union.[11] During the filming of this documentary, Meri produced another film that would have a profound influence on the understanding and study of shamanism in Estonia, entitled *The Shaman* (1977). It was filmed in the northernmost corner of Eurasia, on the Taymyr Peninsula. This material depicts a *Nganasan* shaman performing an incantation. On the heels of this film, Meri produced another documentary, *The Sons of Torum* (*Toorumi Pojad*, 1988–89), depicting an ancient Khanty bear feast ritual estimated to be about 3,000 years old. Together with these documentaries on other Finno-Ugric cultures, practices, and traditions, and the increasing number of expeditions by Estonian artists and scholars, the groundwork was laid for discovering how Estonia fit into the constellation of peoples making up its ancestral past. As the former cinematographer for Meri put it, "Lennart's passionate searches for roots, which had a more universally human and broader significance than the historical and cultural connections between Finno-Ugric peoples...formed...a mosaic-like magic mirror that was capable of showing what was transcendent of time and distance, and what was transient" (Maran 2009: 2).

Concurrently, there were also the musicians and composers, who were able to pursue ethnic contexts through the folk and runic songs, and music styles that were found in archives. Perhaps the most well-known Estonian composer is Veljo Tormis (1930–), who

> is famous for his imaginative use of authentic archaic folk material—first of all Estonian and Finnish runic songs (*regilaul*), but also old traditional songs of other peoples. He is not attracted by the exotic sound of a distant tradition, but interested in the meaning of singing, and often working together with ethnologists he always goes deeply into the background of the songs he is using. (Tormis 2013)

It was only in the 1960s, following the death of Joseph Stalin when there emerged a certain degree of intellectual liberation in the Soviet Union, that Tormis was able to develop an Estonian national style based on the use of folk music. His composing matured into creating music based on ancient folk tunes, branching out into compositions based on other cultures, such as, for example, the Livonians (*Liivlaste pärandus* [Livonian Heritage], 1970), and perhaps his most important work, Forgotten peoples (*Unustatud rahvad*, 1970–1989), a series of song cycles based on the ancient folk songs of Balto-Finnic peoples. In fact, Tormis worked with Lennart Meri on the film *The Sounds of Kaleva* (*Kaleva Hääled*), a three-act film-essay about memory and the historical-cultural ties of the Finno-Ugric peoples. In this film, an ancient smelting and blacksmith ritual is set to Tormis' cantata "Curse upon Iron."[12]

Examining the Written Word

When we speak about examining the information and materials found in archives and those acquired in expeditions, several key figures stand out. As a reaction to the Soviet attempt to eradicate cultural differences by creating a uniform society based on the principles of a socialist culture, there were some older professors who furthered this cause by providing mostly covert information on these forbidden topics through personal research and expeditions. Having to work within a restrictive system meant that research on topics that were not a part of the party line required finding a means to explore this information under the pretext of one's own field of study. One such man was Heino Liimets (1928–1989), a literary scholar who actually examined the etymology and movement of language through literature, and found a path to, and interest in, the esoteric world. Another was Lembit Andresen (1929–), a pedagogical scholar and writer, who used his research into the historical roots of Estonian folk schools to examine Livonian[13] history and culture. Certain rituals and customs that no longer exist today were preserved by the Livonians. In the fields of literature and linguistics, they were some of the most influential figures during this period.

Both Liimets and Andresen worked in the Tallinn Pedagogical Institute in the Department of Pedagogy and Psychology, which intermittently had close ties with Tartu University during the late Soviet period. Therefore, it was in these institutions that it was possible to learn something more about an otherwise hidden and quite forbidden world. However, it was still an extremely limited group of people who knew anything. To a lesser degree, handwritten and copiously copied materials on esoteric concepts and ideas also circulated in the world of psychology, as well as sporadically into the hands of certain other individuals.

Channels of information flowed from different directions into Estonia during the Soviet period. For example, Andresen had both German and Russian roots, and the majority of his source materials came from those two places—in addition to Livonia—since he researched that area extensively. In 2002, Andresen published an article comparing Estonian and Livonian folk schools. In contrast, Liimets was more interested in the linguistic side of Estonian culture and the old traditions and customs that might have survived. Most of his material came from a more local cultural context, in which it was common practice to do fieldwork in the countryside, collecting old songs and traditional sayings and interpreting them from a linguistics point of view.

Perhaps both scholars and others in the field received their inspiration from the work of renowned linguist and folklorist Oskar Loorits (1900–1961). In 1920, Loorits began making expeditions into Livonia, where he set about learning the language and writing a monograph on the belief system of the Livonian people (Krikmann 2000). He visited the area many times, actively promoting the rights of Livonians, until 1937 when the Latvian government revoked his right to enter the country any longer. Loorits immigrated to Sweden in 1944, where he continued his scholarly work at Uppsala University in the Dialect and Folklore Archives. His ethnographic work and methodology have been pivotal in all research related to Estonian folklore and linguistic studies.

Siberian Express

Another phenomenon may have occurred during the Soviet period that had a lasting influence on folk beliefs and the introduction of shamanism back into the Estonian mainstream. As Tuisk states, "Estonia is a nation with a sizable Diaspora. In the early twentieth century about a sixth of Estonians lived outside their ethnic homeland. In the context of

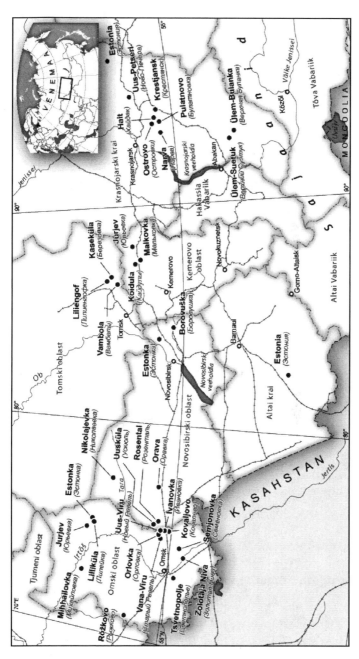

Figure 6.2   Map of Siberian Estonian Villages (*Siberi Eesti Külade Kaart*).[14]

expatriation, Siberia has been a significant destination at various periods in history" (2005). Throughout history, the reasons why Estonians moved to Siberia were varied: some were deportees, others went for religious reasons, such as to build Lutheran settlements, and many went to colonize new territories (see Figure 6.2).

By the postwar period, there was an exodus of Estonians from the settlements due to assimilation, urbanization, and dissatisfaction with the repressions carried out by the Soviet government. Many Estonians returned home, bringing with them a rich cultural admixture of folklore and beliefs from the local native population. Over time, many of these traditions merged with local ones, including Siberian shamanism. In Estonia, there is an old tradition of also calling village healers, or "doctors," *Maatark*, literally meaning a person who is wise about the land. Generally, this person had a good deal of herbal knowledge and was experienced with working with the natural world (in Estonian, *maarohtudega,* land medicine). One such *wise woman* whom I was able to interview, let us call her Linda, explained the above situation as follows:

> These beliefs are very important, especially as more Russians came in [to Estonia], bringing with them their own beliefs and legends, mixing them with both the Russian-speaking and Estonian peoples. They use a lot of black magic over there, and often we say that many of these magical practices and rituals have come from Russia. And some of them were brought over by the returning Estonians who were exiled, as they interacted with the people in the villages.[15]

Interestingly, she adds a third category of people to the list of Russians and returning Estonians who were considered as sources of information and carriers of cultural traditions and beliefs:

> Well, they [beliefs] also came with the Roma people. It is known, after all, that they have witches, and people believe in what they do. This probably already began before World War II, when they were even more feared and people believed in what they did. During the Soviet times, they put them to work and tried to make them melt into the local population.[16]

Those deportees who returned to Estonia were still fearful of reprisal, and did not develop or explore their understanding of these cultural traditions and practices further. However, the background and influence were there, and would later help establish foundations for the new movements that found momentum following independence. It is from the time period following Stalin's death that the term shaman was introduced into the Estonian vocabulary, where it had hitherto been coined as nõid, as was discussed earlier in this chapter.

As previously mentioned, the Soviet era was marked by the active implementation of Marxism-Leninism doctrine, which consistently advocated the control, suppression, and total elimination of religion from society. Under these circumstances, where people could not attend church without consequences or even celebrate Christmas, it would also have been unimaginable to walk into a forest and sing to a stone, or tie a ribbon on a tree and say a prayer, without fear of being sent to a mental institution. In fact, one of the greatest fears people struggled with was being perceived as different in some way, as that meant they might be diagnosed as mentally ill, placed in an insane asylum, and given powerful medications to counter their supposed delirium. In many cases, people who were completely normal were made mentally ill by undergoing such experiences. As a result, these institutions were full of people who had the abilities and calling to be healers and shamans, but through the abuse of medication were reduced to shells of their former selves.[17]

According to Shaman Mikk Sarv, materials could be found during the Soviet period if one knew where to look for them. He says,

> A very memorable experience happened in 1973 when I attended a lecture giving an in-depth overview of both Western and Russian literature. In fact, these materials are the same, after all, and the Russian archives, ethnographic collections, and proceedings were not secret at all. I myself have been to Siberia and researched the archives while doing fieldwork in 1977 and 1978. It was considered more as relating to the development of regional culture. (2011)

Wise Woman Linda corroborates this, although she indicated that many materials were passed around in secrecy:

> In Tallinn, toward the end of the 1960s and during the 1970s, there was a pastor in Holy Ghost Church (*Pühavaimu kirik*) who translated the works of Castaneda[18] and distributed hand-written copies around to certain people. I received a copy in the 1970s. They were sometimes typed, copied, and passed from hand to hand. Those who really wanted to get their hands on them did get them. (2011)

What Happens Next

The tradition of collecting data outside of Estonian borders in order to define the cultural inheritance of a nation continued into the post-Soviet period. One person to undertake this was the artist Kadri Viires, who is currently working at the University of Art. Viires herself states that

> knowledge of the existing wealth of folk traditions and the preserved heritage of folk art is very important. In my textiles I have not interpreted specific,

recognizable traditional symbols, but have been inspired by nature, colors, and the world view and folklore familiar to Estonians and our distant linguistic relatives—the people who speak Finno-Ugric languages. In my work this tends to be expressed in the form of an abstract connection with the heritage of the culture of the natural world, as well as with the spirituality of folk traditions. (2006–7)

It has been said that Viires follows a shamanic tradition herself, drawing upon those elements of design and tradition that make it uniquely Estonian.

Furthermore, following the Soviet period, many people felt a vacuum in their spiritual lives. As a result, many undertook a search for a specifically native Estonian belief system, and they began to experiment with new faiths and forms of spiritual practice. However, author and researcher Mare Kõiva believes that this phenomenon happened much earlier, as early as the 1980s. She says,

> I believe that our neo-shamanic movement had its roots in Scandinavia. Many teachers were invited here from Denmark and Sweden. This was a very important period. Already Leonid Brezhnev himself when he was ill used a lot of alternative healers, as well as the whole cabinet of older men surrounding him, also very happily used these healers and alternative methods to get a little boost. (2011)

Kõiva claims that the birth of neoshamanism in Scandinavia had a great influence on Estonia, and that the first teachers of shamanism who entered the country introduced the methods and works of Harner. Kõiva states, "He [Harner] himself came here a couple of times, I believe!" (2011). Furthermore, she feels that both the Sami and the Native American cultures were highly regarded in most circles. American Indians were invited over as soon as it was possible to do so, and contacts with Sami representatives were developed. But the activities that became very popular at the time were the influx of shamanic practitioners who came over from Finland, Sweden, and Norway, performing various songs and rituals. Harner had created an organization named the Soviet-American Shamanism (SAS) Program, which

> included sponsoring, and financially supporting, grassroots shamanic training workshops in Kiev and Moscow, as well as in such countries in Eastern Europe as Hungary, Latvia, Estonia, Poland and, even before the Berlin wall came down, East Germany. The Foundation also had a contract with the Soviet Ministry of Health to introduce shamanic healing methods (there known as "Psychorhythmo-therapy [Harner Method]") for the drug-free treatment of alcoholism and addiction problems. Michael Harner and the Foundation cooperated with anthropologists of the Soviet Academy of Sciences with regard to

the study of shamanism and introduced the experiential study of shamanism to the anthropological academic community there.[19]

Despite the fact that Kõiva feels there is evidence that the neoshamanic movement, which was sweeping Scandinavia at the time, had some influence in Estonia during the late Soviet era, evidence has shown that this was not the case. In a telephone interview with Jonathan Horowitz, a student of Harner and a teacher and field researcher from 1984–1993 in the Foundation for Shamanic Studies, he confirmed that Harner himself had never visited Estonia. However, Horowitz did visit Estonia twice to give workshops, which he described as being experiential journey-style events. He worked closely with Shaman Mikk Sarv, who organized the events in a nonacademic setting (Parks 2013). Sarv confirms that Horowitz visited Estonia two times between the years 1990 and 1991, and then came along on two joint expeditions to the Russian Sápmi territories, once in 1992 and again in 2002. Clearly, these visits occurred post factum, following the collapse of the Soviet empire. When asked whether he could recall if there ever were any workshops or lectures on shamanism given by foreign visitors during the Soviet period, Sarv said that there were none to his recollection, with perhaps the exception of researcher Mihály Hoppál, who visited during the very last years of the Soviet era in Estonia (Parks 2013). Furthermore, none of my interviews with current practitioners of shamanism and healers indicated any evidence that someone had attended a lecture or workshop given by a foreign practitioner of shamanism during this period.

This chapter hopefully provides a clearer picture of the methods Estonians have used in attempts to construct and define shamanic beliefs and practices in their country, by linking them to the internal aspects of homegrown shamanism and fusing them with other external factors that have influenced and affected its development. Fusional shamanism provides a methodological framework from which to build on other aspects of metroshamanism in contemporary Estonian society.

Conclusion

The path of shamanism in Estonia has been a complex one, fraught with controversy, insecurity and a myriad of obstacles. But it has, in a sense, made a full circle in its journey. We know from our ties with other Finno-Ugric tribes that shamanism must have been practiced by Estonians in one form or another at some point in history. There are tantalizing bits of that past in the ancient chronicles and buried in the archives. In this chapter, we discussed the connections that exist within the context of the local traditions of witches, healers, and shamans that fall under the

Estonian label of nõid. We have also analyzed the term shamanism itself and the dilemma its definition presents within contemporary ethnological and religious research by proposing an alternate term or methodological description that might more accurately portray the religioscape of modern shamanic practices—namely metroshamanism. We can find clues in music and art, and in the epic poems that emerged during the process of national awakening. We examined history and Estonia's close links with its Scandinavian and Eastern neighbors, and how they impacted religious and cultural life in this small nation. It was ultimately the ravages of war, occupation, and repression within the last hundred years or so that contributed to the Estonians' losing touch with their shamanic past. But when they had the freedom once again to search for the soul of their ancestors, they looked to their neighbors and kin, and in that moment were able to find a path for shamanism to return to Estonia, where it found its roots and began to flourish once again. The shamanisms of the north are intimately entwined with each other, held together by the binds of history, culture, traditions, language, and religion.

Notes

1. Znamenski explains in great detail how the word *shaman* came into use in other languages and cultures: "Since Russians were the first to use the word shaman to generalize about Siberian spiritual practitioners, some writers mistakenly assume that Russian authors introduced this expression into Western literature and scholarship. In reality, the people who brought the word shaman into Western usage and intellectual culture were the eighteenth-century Germanic explorers and scientists who visited Siberia. They used the word *schaman* to familiarize educated European and American audiences with ecstatic séances performed by native Siberian spiritual 'doctors.'" Andrei Znamenski, *The Beauty of the Primitive: Shamanism and Western Imagination* (Oxford and New York: Oxford University Press, 2007), p. 5.
2. Michael Harner, *The Way of the Shaman* (New York: HarperOne, 1990 [1980]).
3. Mircea Eliade, *Shamanism: Archaic Techniques of Ecstasy* (Princeton, NJ: Princeton University, 2004 [1951]).
4. From the film, *The Secret Helpers* (Original title: *De gode hjelperan*), directed by Harry Johansen and Torill Olsen, 2012, Norway, Aage Solbakk speaks about the Sami worldview of the time.
5. According to Sven-Erik Soosaar of the Institute of the Estonian Language, the roots of the word nõid are to be found in the etymology of the Finno-Baltic Sámi, as well as in the more distantly related Ugrian language of the Mansi, who live within the Tyumen Oblast of Russia. In that language, it means "shaman" or "witch." What is noteworthy is the fact that this root

word has only survived among the Mansi, whereas it does not exist in the Khanty language, a people who reside in the same region. Soosaar believes that the root word is derived from the original proto Finno-Ugric language, and that possibly with the demise of shamanic practices among those peoples, it can be postulated that the root word also similarly vanished from other Ugrian languages of the Uralic family (IF mgt 2011/124:1–2. Interview with Sven-Erik Soosaar in Tallinn, Estonia. May 9, 2011).

6. The concept of metrolingualism is discussed in detail by Emi Otsuji and Alastair Pennycook in their paper on "Metrolingualism: Fixity, Fluidity and Language in Flux." A methodological adaptation of this concept to shamanism creates a good framework from which to build an understanding of the practice, and is the basis for the term metroshamanism.

7. Jüri Kurman, translator. Afterword of *FR. R. Kreutzwald. Kalevipoeg: An Ancient Estonian Tale* (Moorestown, NJ: Symposia Press, 1982). Kurman adds that "As for the folkloristic authenticity of *Kalevipoeg*, it can be said that at least three fourths of the epic is directly based on Estonian oral tradition, with folk tales furnishing the bulk of the material, fairy tales contributing substantially (about one third), and folk songs accounting for approximately one eighth of the verses of the epic. The portion of the poem not based on Estonian folklore is either Kreutzwald's own creation, or, in the case of about five percent of the verses, is based on Finnish materials" (p. 287).

8. For a comprehensive history of the island of Saaremaa, see http://www.saaremaa.ee/index.php?option=com_content&view=article&id=277&Itemid=306.

9. An eminent Estonian shaman, Thule Lee, continues to practice the art of divination by throwing and reading runes. This is a common phenomenon among many of the Estonian practitioners. In his book, *Estide (tšuudide) hingestatud Ilm: Teadaandmise Raamat* (Männisalu 2001), Aleksander Heintalu, better known as Vigala Sass, describes in great detail runes that he feels are innately Estonian in nature, and provides an interpretation and use for them.

10. "A part of the Soviet cultural politics was the selective destruction of cultural heritage created by the preceding generations. During the post-war years, libraries were emptied of the 'heritage of bourgeois society'; in the course of this activity, a considerable number of periodicals and books of fiction, published during the period of independent Estonia, were destroyed and most of the remaining copies were kept under restricted access. In addition to all this, the whole society was drowned in propaganda that was meant to subject the spiritual sphere of life to the control of the ruling regime" (Eesti Instituut, 2012).

11. Lennart Meri's film The Winds of the Milky Way (original title: *Linnutee Tuuled*), produced: 1976–1977, was the winner of the Silver Medal at the 22nd New York International Film and TV Festival in 1979.

12. The Sounds of Kaleva (original title: *Kaleva Hääled*) is replete with shamanic symbols, including drums and other paraphanalia as a part of the ritual that is portrayed in the video.

13. Livonia (Est. *Liivimaa*) was the historic region of the Finnic Livonians, who lived along the eastern shores of the Baltic Sea, and encompassing parts of present-day Latvia and Estonia.
14. Astrid Tuisk. Estonian Folklore Archive, 2005, 2013. http://www.folklore .ee/estonka/files/index.php?id=157&keel=eng. Accessed: January 28, 2014.
15. The Wise Woman wished to remain completely anonymous and would only allow me to take notes on what she said; therefore, there is no official source. Interview: Kuressaare, Estonia. July 16, 2011.
16. Ibid.
17. A compilation of comments made by the Wise Woman, Linda. Interview: Kuressaare, Estonia. July 16, 2011.
18. Carlos Castaneda wrote several books during the stated period, among them: *The Teachings of Don Juan: A Yaqui Way of Knowledge*, 1968; *A Separate Reality: Further Conversations with Don Juan*, 1971; *Journey to Ixtlan: The Lessons of Don Juan*, 1972; *Tales of Power*, 1974; and *The Second Ring of Power*, 1977.
19. Michael Harner, "The History and Work of the Foundation for Shamanic Studies," *Shamanism*, 25th Anniversary Issue 2005, 18(1&2). Note: I have not been able to verify the exact dates of their visits to Estonia.

References

Andresen, Lembit. 2002. "Pestalozzi ja Eesti. J. H. Pestalozzi kaudmõjud Eesti- ja Liivimaa rahvakoolide arengule 19. sajandi kahel esimesel aastakümnel." (Pestalozi and Estonia. J. H. Pestalozzi's Indirect Effects on the Development of Estonian and Livonian Folk Schools). *Haridus. Eesti pedagoogilise üldsuse ajakiri*, 1: 59–61.

Asbjørn, Jøn. 1999. *Shamanism and the Image of the Teutonic Deity, Óðinn.* Folklore (Tartu) January 1999; Source: DOAJ. http://www.folklore.ee/folk-lore/vol10/teuton.htm. Accessed: January 21, 2014.

Curry, Andrew. 2013. "Two Remarkable Ships May Show that the Viking Storm Was Brewing Long before Their Assault on England and the Continent." *Archaeology*, June 10. http://www.archaeology.org/issues/95-1307/features /941-vikings-saaremaa-estonia-salme-vendel-oseberg. Accessed: January 21, 2014.

Eesti Instituut (Estonian Institute). 2010. "Control over Cultural Life. Estonica: Encyclopedia about Estonia. Created: February 25, Last Modified: October 10,2012.http://www.estonica.org/en/History/1945-1985_The_Soviet_Period /Control_over_cultural_life/. Accessed: April 9, 2013.

Eliade, Mircea. 2004 [1951]. *Shamanism: Archaic Techniques of Ecstasy.* Princeton, NJ: Princeton University Press.

Esslemont, Tom. 2011. "Spirituality in Estonia—The World's 'Least Religious' Country." BBC News: Europe. August 26. http://www.bbc.co.uk/news /world-europe-14635021. Accessed: September 21, 2011.

Estonia.eu. "Estonia's History: Chronology." http://estonia.eu/about-estonia /history/estonias-history.html. Accessed: January 23, 2014.

Harner, Michael. 2005. "The History and Work of the Foundation for Shamanic Studies," *Shamanism*, 25th Anniversary Issue, 18(1&2).

———.1990; 1980. *The Way of the Shaman*. New York: HarperOne.

Høst, Annette. 2001. "Thoughts on 'Neo shamanism,' 'Core Shamanism,' 'Urban Shamanism' and Other labels: Modern Shamanic Practice." First written for the shamanic newsletter *"Spirit Talk,"* issue 14, with the title "What's in a Name?" Scandinavian Center for Shamanic Studies. 21.01.2014. http://www.shamanism.dk/modernshamanism.htm. Accessed: January 20, 2014.

IF mgt 2011/120. Interview with Mare Kõiva in Tartu, Estonia. May 3, 2011.

IF mgt 2011/121. Interview with Mikk Sarv: Tartu, Estonia. August 4, 2011.

IF mgt 2011/124:1–2. Interview with Sven-Erik Soosaar in Tallinn, Estonia. May 9, 2011.

Johansen, Harry, and Torill Olsen, Directors. 2012. *The Secret Helpers* (Original title: *De gode hjelperan*), Norway. Film, 59 minutes.

Krikmann, Luule (ed.) 2000. Liivi rahva usund. I: *mit einem Referat: Der Volksglaube der Liven* (Livonian Beliefs. I: with a paper: The Folk Beliefs of the Livonians), Tartu Ülikool 1926, 270 lk; II 1927, 280 lk; III 1928, 284 lk; I-III köite kordustrükk: Eesti Keele Instituut, Tartu 1998, 870 lk; IV-V köide (käsikirja järgi avaldatud esmatrükk): jt; tõlked saksa keelest (translated from German): Reet Hiiemäe; tõlked liivi keelest ja eessõna (translated from Livonian and Forword): Kristi Salve, EKM, Tartu 2000, 394 + 180 pages.

Kurman, Jüri. (trans.). 1982. Afterword of FR. R. *Kreutzwald. Kalevipoeg: An Ancient Estonian Tale*. Moorestown, NJ: Symposia Press, p. 287.

Maran, Rein. 2009. "He Knew How to Be…" *Lennart Meri Soome-Ugri Rahvaste Filmientsüklopeedia* 1970–1997. Encyclopaedia Cinematographica Gentium Fenno-Ugricarum (Soome-Ugri Rahvaste Filmientsüklopeedia: Viis Dokumentaalfilmi 1970–1997) DVD booklet.

Meri, Lennart (dir.) 1977/1007. The Shaman (original title: *Šamaan*), digitally remastered: Tallinnfilm. Encyclopaedia Cinematographica Gentium Fenno-Ugricarum (Soome-Ugri Rahvaste Filmientsüklopeedia: Viis Dokumentaalfilmi 1970–1997) DVD.

———. 1988–1989. The Sons of Torum (original title: *Toorumi Pojad*), digitally remastered: Tallinnfilm. Encyclopaedia Cinematographica Gentium Fenno-Ugricarum (Soome-Ugri Rahvaste Filmientsüklopeedia: Viis Dokumentaalfilmi 1970–1997) DVD.

———. 1985. The Sounds of Kaleva (original title: *Kaleva Hääled),* digitally remastered: Tallinnfilm. 2009. Encyclopaedia Cinematographica Gentium Fenno-Ugricarum (Soome-Ugri Rahvaste Filmientsüklopeedia: Viis Dokumentaalfilmi 1970–1997) DVD.

———. 1976–1977. The Winds of the Milky Way (original title: *Linnutee Tuuled*), produced: 1976–1977, digitally remastered: Tallinnfilm. 2009. Encyclopaedia Cinematographica Gentium Fenno-Ugricarum (Soome-Ugri Rahvaste Filmientsüklopeedia: Viis Dokumentaalfilmi 1970–1997) DVD.

Otsuji, Emi, and Alastair Pennycook. 2010. "Metrolingualism: Fixity, Fluidity and Language in Flux," *International Journal of Multilingualism* 7(3): 240–254.

Pall, Valdek (ed.). Dialectological Dictionary of Estonia (*Väike murde sõnaraamat*). The Institute of the Estonian Language (*Eesti Keele Instituut*). Tallinn: Estonia. 1982–1989. Online word search for *nõid*. http://www.eki.ee/cgi-bin/murdekaart.cgi?num=34214&sona=n%F5id. Accessed: January 21, 2014.

Parks, Henno. 2013. Telephone Interview with Jonathan Horowitz. "Visits to Soviet Estonia." 18:50, April 10.

———. 2013. Telephone Interview with Mikk Sarv. "Visits to Soviet Estonia." 20:45, April 10.

Reeman, Vaike, and Piret Õunapuu. 2004. *Crafts and Arts in Estonia: Past and Present*. Eesti Instituut: Estonian Institute Publications.

Tormis, Veljo. 2007–2011. Veljo Tormis Databank. http://www.tormis.ee/VTindex.html. Accessed: April 9, 2013.

Tuisk, Astrid. 2005. "Estonians in Siberia." Estonian Folklore Archive. 2005. http://www.folklore.ee/estonka/files/index.php?id=32&keel=eng. Accessed: 09.04.2013.

Viires, Kadri. 2006–07. "My Textile—My Text Style," Cloth and Culture Now. University College for the Creative Arts. Lesley Millar. http://www.clothand-culturenow.com/Kadri_Viires.html Accessed: April 6, 2013.

Webb, H. S. 2013. "Expanding Western Definitions of Shamanism: A Conversation with Stephan Beyer, Stanley Krippner, and Hillary S. Webb," *Anthropology of Consciousness*, 24: 57–75. doi: 10.1111/anoc.12000.

Znamenski, Andrei. 2007. *The Beauty of the Primitive: Shamanism and Western Imagination*. Oxford and New York: Oxford University Press. (p. 5).

7

New Age Medicine Men versus New Age *Noaidi*: Same Neoshamanism, Different Sociopolitical Situation

James R. Lewis

As a movement, neoshamanism has propagated the idea of a universal shamanism as being the traditional religion of all indigenous people. And whether this portrayal is accurate or not, neoshamanism has become a global phenomenon. However, some academic observers have articulated certain themes about the politics of essentialized indigenous identity and spirituality that paint the production of neoshamanism as artificial and inauthentic. This has particularly been the case with certain forms of North American neoshamanism in which Euroamericans have adopted/adapted Native American spiritual traditions, a pattern that has been harshly criticized as cultural colonialism.

However, although core practices and ideas might be similar, one finds that neoshamanism has taken root in contrasting sociopolitical situations. In the Sami case, we know comparatively little about traditional Sami spirituality. "Sami shamanism," or whatever one wishes to call "traditional" Sami spirituality, has been largely created by contemporary Sami individuals who were, at least initially, informed by Michael Harner's core shamanism and a New Age view of universal indigenous spirituality. Subsequently, in sharp contrast to commercialized Native American spirituality, many Sami have adopted this contemporary spiritual form. And because so many of the "natives" have become participants, both academic and nonacademic observers have been reluctant to characterize "traditional Sami shamanism" as inauthentic. This chapter will analyze the contrast between the contexts of New Age Sami shamanism and New

Age Native American shamanism, and how they are differently regarded by the respective indigenous peoples.

Background

The phenomenon as well as the current popularity of neoshamanism arises from more than one source. To begin with the movement's intellectual background, it has regularly been noted that a lineage of three academicians—Mircea Eliade, Carlos Castaneda, and Harner—articulated and popularized the notion of shamanism. Additionally, Joseph Campbell's romantic neo-Jungian approach to mythology exerted a major influence on many neoshamans (Dubois 2009: 266–267). In Eliade's original conceptualization, shamanism was a complex of particular ideas and practices that were widespread but not universal. Thus, for example, in sections of the book in which he covers shamanism's presence in different world cultures, *Shamanism: Archaic Techniques of Ecstasy*, Eliade does not even attempt to discuss parallel phenomena in Semitic or in traditional African societies—which he viewed as cultures without shamanic traditions. However, by the time we get to Harner, shamanism has become a generic label for a certain kind of religious specialist found within small-scale traditional societies all over the world. Castaneda left academia to promulgate his fictionalized shamanism (Hardman 2007) in a way that "established key elements of later neoshamanistic explorations, as well as the broader New Age ideology" (Dubois 2009: 267). Harner went a step further by leaving the ivory tower to actively teach shamanic techniques in workshops on what he called core shamanism at his Foundation for Shamanic Studies (Jakobsen 1999: 159–165).

Another way of viewing contemporary neoshamanism is in terms of its appeal to romantic primitivism. The image of the Noble Savage dates back to the early modern period, when cultural critics used the putative nobility of people in a "state of nature" to criticize various aspects of contemporaneous "civilized" society. By the nineteenth century (von Stuckrad 2002), admiration for so-called "primitives" had filtered down to the level of romantic fiction. Such peoples were viewed as being free from the various constraints imposed by bourgeois culture, and this supposition made them attractive to Westerners oppressed by their socioeconomic environment and repressed by internalized cultural norms. The ambivalence toward the constraints of Western culture worked itself out in tragic narratives that portrayed the inevitable demise of savages (noble as well as ignoble) after being confronted with "civilization." Thus the reader of such tales could imaginatively participate in the imputed freedom and lifestyle of people in a state of nature and simultaneously feel that the culture to which he or she was otherwise committed was ultimately superior and would, in the long run, completely supplant "savagery" (Barnett 1975; Dippie 1982).

By the time the sixties counterculture arrived, this mixed attitude had given way to all-out admiration for peoples outside of Western culture and idealization of "tribal" lifestyles (e.g., "Why Tribe?", in Snyder 1969, 114–115). But some participants in the counterculture were eager to directly experience the spirituality and lifestyle of traditional peoples, which gave rise to such phenomena as the Bear Tribe (currently, the Panther Lodge Medicine Society), a "tribe" comprised of non-Indians, although founded by an individual of Ojibwa descent, Sun Bear (Vincent LaDuke). In the postcounterculture period, romantic primitivists were still attracted to selectively experiencing aspects of indigenous spirituality, but, unlike the Bear Tribe counterculturists, they wanted to do so without actually abandoning the comforts of their middle-class lifestyles.

The alternative spiritual subculture that became visible after the demise of the sixties counterculture—referred to variously as the cultic milieu, occulture or, most commonly, the New Age—is where neoshamanism has taken root. As discussed elsewhere (e.g., Lewis 1992: 10), one of the confusing aspects of this milieu is the extent to which it is characterized by fads. For example, if we understand the New Age as a movement that came into being in the 1970s, then the early New Age was dominated by an interest in imported Asian religions. Subsequently, by the time this alternative spiritual subculture became the focus of news media attention in the latter half of the eighties, items like crystals and activities like channeling were popular. When interest in these specific phenomena waned, observers began pronouncing the "death" of the New Age. But what was actually taking place was that people in alternative spirituality circles were simply changing the focus of their collective interest to other topics, such as angels, Native American spirituality and, eventually, neoshamanism. The difference, however, is that neoshamanism has had an influence beyond the alternative milieu, which has given it staying power.

In significant ways, the attractiveness of neoshamanism is based on the attractiveness of a highly romanticized image of traditional indigenous societies for whom shamanism is the natural religion. "Values relating to nature and to the landscape mark a distinction between a place-oriented, peaceful, holistic, traditional, and eco-friendly indigenous culture and a modern western capitalist society" (Fonneland 2012: 165). Furthermore, by virtue of the logic of this oppositional structure, the West is implicitly or explicitly portrayed as place-less, violent, disconnected, exploitative and so on (Kraft 2010: 57).

This idealized vision of indigenous cultures has become a global ideology (Kraft 2009). Certain themes in this discourse about indigenous peoples have particularly been articulated in United Nations documents and regulations—documents that go so far as to assert that indigenous peoples have a special spiritual relationship with—and therefore certain special rights over—landscapes regarded as part of their spiritual traditions (Fonneland and Kraft 2013: 139–140). Thus, for example, Article 25 of the 2007 United Nations Declaration on the Rights of Indigenous Peoples (UNDRIP) asserts that indigenous peoples have "the right to maintain and strengthen their distinctive spiritual relationship with their traditionally owned or otherwise occupied and used lands, territories, waters and coastal seas and other resources."

The notion that indigenous peoples universally regard themselves as having "a special spiritual relationship" with the natural landscape perfectly reflects the older romantic idea of the Noble Savage. This picture has been brought up to date and propagated primarily by participants in the New Age milieu. As discussed by Trude Fonneland and Siv Ellen Kraft, "Regular references to indigenous peoples as children of Mother Earth are similarly common in UN fora, along with references to a holistic worldview" (2013: 140).[1]

Beyond the articulation of a vague spiritual relationship between the natural world and indigenous people, in Article 34 the UNDRIP also explicitly asserts that aboriginal peoples have the "right to promote, develop and maintain" their distinctive customs, including their spiritual traditions. Additionally, Article 24 recognizes that indigenous peoples "have the right to their traditional medicines and to maintain their health practices," such as, presumably, the medical practices of such traditional healers as "shamans."

It took over a quarter of a century for UNDRIP to be formulated. When it was finally put up for a vote in the UN General Assembly, it passed overwhelmingly. Only Australia, Canada, New Zealand, and the United States voted against it—countries containing remnants of indigenous populations that had achieved a measure of legal recognition. These four nations eventually endorsed the declaration as well.

New Age Appropriations of Native American Spirituality

Although the ideology postulating a universal indigenous spirituality—a key component of contemporary neoshamanism—seems to have been generally accepted, neoshamanism has not. Native American spokespeople in particular have taken offense whenever nonnative peoples adopt and practice select parts of indigenous spiritual systems, and especially when Native entrepreneurs teach traditional practices to nonnatives. A key accusation found in Native discourses about opposition to

White adoptions of their traditions is cultural imperialism: for centuries, Euroamericans stole the lands of American Indians; now they want to steal Native religions.

This accusation is fundamental, and has been stated in multiple ways in numerous places. Thus, for example, Janet McCloud, Tulalip elder and fishing rights advocate, says that "First they came to take our land and water, then our fish and game....Now they want our religions as well. All of a sudden, we have a lot of unscrupulous idiots running around saying they're medicine people. And they'll sell you a sweat lodge ceremony for fifty bucks. It's not only wrong, it's obscene. Indians don't sell their spirituality to anybody, for any price. This is just another in a very long series of thefts from Indian people and, in some ways, this is the worst one yet" (qtd. in Churchill 2003).

McCloud's evaluation is not unique. Thus, for example, in an evocatively titled article published in the popular *Ms. Magazine*, "For All Those Who Were Indian in a Former Life," Andrea Smith asserts that "While New Agers may think they are escaping white racism by becoming 'Indian,' they are in fact continuing the same genocidal practices of their forebears" (1991a). Elsewhere, Smith observes that "The 'Indian ways' that these white, new-age 'feminists' are practicing have very little basis in reality....these New Agers do not understand Indian people or our struggles for survival and thus can have no genuine understanding of Indian spiritual practices" (1991b: 18).

Pam Colorado, an Oneida activist, goes further: "The process is ultimately intended to supplant Indians, even in areas of their own customs and spirituality. In the end, non-Indians will have complete power to define what is and is not Indian, even for Indians. We are talking here about an absolute ideological/conceptual subordination of Indian people in addition to the total physical subordination they already experience. When this happens, the last vestiges of real Indian society and Indian rights will disappear. Non-Indians will then 'own' our heritage and ideas as thoroughly as they now claim to own our land and resources" (qtd. in Rose 1992: 405).

Whatever one might think about these statements, it is not difficult to understand why—given the ugly history of Euroamerican dealings with Native peoples—the indigenous people of North America would hold such views. One might wonder, however, why non-Native scholars would similarly express harsh criticisms toward the New Age appropriation of American Indian spirituality. Excerpts from two different academic articles will suffice to exemplify the tone of this discourse.

In the first paragraph of her essay on Eliade and Åke Hultkrantz, Alice Kehoe describes these two scholars as marked by "an arrogant cultural imperialism that denies full humanity to the first nations of the Americas" (1996: 377). On the last page of her article, Kehoe adds that these men and others promoted the myth that "there is a dazzling present world transcending the dull empiricism of the bourgeois West...a myth that far away the long ago still exists. There in the wild places, noble savages preserve the true spirituality cast out of our cities" (388). She also flatly asserts that "Educated men cannot become shamans," a strange statement, which clearly (if unintentionally) implies that the only true shamans are people lacking such an education.

Slightly less acerbic but no less critical, Lisa Aldred, in her article on "Plastic Shamans and Astroturf Sun Dances," examines the New Age appropriation of Native American spirituality, especially the character of participation in the New Age subculture, through the lenses of a series of different critical commentators and social theorists. The resulting portrait is unflattering, to put it mildly, and Aldred can find nothing positive about the appropriators other than to say that, on the whole, New Age consumers appear to have good intentions. As for the people who create relevant products for such consumers, "plastic shamans, as well as other New Age entrepreneurs, could be viewed as "ransackers" of Native American spiritual traditions in search of ways to market them to consumers. They produce new interpretations by fusing bastardized versions of these traditions with self-help pop psychology, as well as exotic blends appropriated from other cultural traditions" (2000: 342–343).

While not all scholars of Native American traditions express this kind of disdain for New Age appropriations, the fact that these two pieces both appeared in the respected journal *American Indian Quarterly* indicates that such a perspective enjoys the support of mainstream scholarly specialists in this area of study. This way of framing the New Age interest in Native spirituality treats it as if it were some sort of a disease or at least an aberration, unworthy of serious study. Hence, by implication the only legitimate response to this phenomenon is critical and dismissive.

Traditional New Age *Noaidi*

At first glance, the situation of the Sami, an indigenous people located in northern Norway, Sweden, Finland, and northwest Russia, seems quite similar to that of Native American groups in North America. Some writers have even referred to the Sami as the "White Indians" of the Nordic region (Gaski 1993). The strongest parallel is that the Sami were oppressed by the dominant non-Sami peoples in all four countries. For example, land was confiscated, the Sami language(s) was(were) suppressed, their indigenous religion(s) was(were) destroyed, and Sami women were sterilized against their will, particularly in Sweden. As with the situation in North America, in more recent years steps have been taken in Nordic countries to partially undo centuries of cultural genocide.

There are, nevertheless, differences. In the first place, the non-Sami Nordic peoples are not colonizers in the sense of being foreign invaders who supplanted the Sami, although Nordic peoples did, in a sense, "invade" the northern regions and then ruled over the Sami. Also, despite claims to the contrary, most Sami do not stand out as racially different from their Nordic fellow countrymen.[2] Another major difference is that while Christian missionaries in North America tried but in most cases failed to destroy Native American religions, Nordic missionaries managed to completely disrupt traditional Sami religion as a comprehensive religious system. One obtains a clear sense of this destructive process from studies such as Håkan Rydving's *The End of Drum-Time* (2004 [1993]).

So where does the current phenomenon of "traditional Sami spirituality/Sami shamanism" come from? In a complete inversion of the North American situation, it has primarily been people who are ethnically Sami[3] who have adopted both the notion of a universal "indigenous spirituality" as well as a form of neoshamanism based on Harner's core shamanism—modified to conform to what little is known about the *noaidi*, the religious specialist of pre-Christian Sami culture.

The history of how this came about can be traced, on the one hand, to Ailo Gaup, a Sami who was raised by foster parents in Oslo. After he grew up, Gaup traveled to northern Norway in search of a noaidi who could teach him about his spiritual roots. However, as already indicated, the aboriginal spirituality of the Sami had, for the most part, died off long before. What he found instead was a Chilean refugee who had studied under Harner and who was able to introduce him to neoshamanic trance journeys via a Chilean version of core shamanism. Gaup then traveled to the United States to study directly under Harner, later returning to Oslo and establishing himself as a professional shaman (Gaup 2005). As neoshamanism grew, certain other Sami (as well as other indigenous groups) approached Harner, "requesting that he teach core-shamanism to restore their sacred knowledge formerly disrupted due to conquest and missionisation" (Wallis 2003: 221–222).

Another development that helped prepare the way for Sami neoshamanism was the growth of the New Age subcultural milieu in Nordic countries. As noted earlier, this milieu has been especially receptive to the notion of a universal indigenous spirituality that is portrayed as congruent with New Age thought. It has been participants in this subculture who have been particularly interested in neoshamanism. As discussed by Christensen, it was approximately five years into the new millennium when the northern Norwegian New Age milieu began to turn its collective attention to Sami shamanism (2007).

Yet another development that helped prepare the ground for the rebirth of Sami indigenous spirituality lies in the emergence of Sami national consciousness and Sami cultural revival, generally regarded as having its roots in the ongoing demonstrations against the damming of the Alta Kautokeino river in the Sami area in northern Norway—protests that began in the late seventies (Hætta 2002).

> Artists, musicians and young scholars who wanted to improve the political situation of the Sami began to explore the old Sámi culture, searching for building blocks for a new and proud Sámi identity. The traditional Sámi folk costumes were more commonly worn by young people, traditional crafts were revitalized, and folklore material was investigated in the search of a common background. (Mathisen 2010: 68–69)

This revival utilized nonreligious aspects of the Sami tradition to symbolize "Sami-ness," such as traditional clothing (the *kofte*) and the traditional Sami tent (the *lavvo*). Although many Sami belonged to Læstadian churches—a distinct pietistic tradition within the Lutheran state churches of the Nordic countries that tended to set the Sami apart from other Nordic peoples—the cultural revival movement did not initially draw from religion as an identity resource (Fonneland and Kraft 2013: 133).

As more and more people began to identify as shamans and as self-identified followers of traditional Sami spirituality grew into a popular movement, observers naturally questioned the movement's authenticity. This problem was solved, in part, by portraying Læstadianism as a preserver rather than as a destroyer of the traditional Sami way of life—a notion that Henry Minde claimed to find in the work of Johs Falkenberg (1941) and Robert Paine (1965), and that Minde subsequently designated as "the cultural preservation thesis" (2008: 8). However, although Læstadianism might traditionally have provided a refuge for Sami identity, the idea that the core of pre-Christian Sami spirituality was somehow secretly preserved within Læstadian churches is improbable.[4] This has not, however, prevented contemporary Sami neoshamans from adopting some version of the cultural continuity thesis as a way of imaginatively establishing an unbroken lineage back to an idealized Sami pagan past.

Given the contemporary nature of traditional Sami spirituality and some of its spokespeople's claims about representing a manifestation of a previously hidden religious lineage, one might expect that Sami shamans would become the targets of the same kind of scorn as that meted out to New Age shamans in North America. Self-proclaimed Sami neoshamans have certainly not been less commercially oriented than their North American parallels (Fonneland 2012; Fonneland 2013; Fonneland, forthcoming; Mathisen 2010). In general, however, Sami neoshamans *have* managed to avoid this sort of intense criticism. While the mainstream media in Nordic countries—especially in Norway—have been extremely critical of the New Age in general (Kraft forthcoming), anything with the aura of being "indigenous Sami" is given a free pass. A few examples will suffice to illustrate this point.

In her article on Polmakmoen Guesthouse, a retreat facility in Finnmark in northern Norway founded and run by Sami entrepreneur Esther Utsi, Trude Fonneland describes the staging of a product that, at its core, embodies the New Age stereotype of indigenous spirituality, clothed in traditional Sami trappings. Thus, for example, Fonneland remarks that on the Guesthouse website, "healing with crystals and pendulums are transferred from their New Age context and presented as a natural part of a Sami pre-Christian religion, here known as Sami shamanism" (Fonneland 2012: 170). Despite the marked tendency of the Norwegian media to harshly criticize "New Age entrepreneurs as concerned only with economic gain," in both local and national media, Utsi is consistently "portrayed and celebrated as a courageous entrepreneur full of ideas and energy, who has helped put Finnmark on the economic map" (169).

For another example, in an article on discourse about "tradition" in discussions of Norwegian neoshamanism, Torunn Selberg recounts a newspaper story in *Dagbladet* about Biret Maret Kallio, another Finnmark resident. Kallio aroused antagonism from local Christians because of her shamanic practices and her claim to be a noaidi. Accused of being a representative of the devil, Kallio is quoted as responding that "It was the Christian people who brought God and the Devil to the Sami people, not me." One particularly interesting aspect of the story is that the reporter gives Kallio the final word in the story, indicating that the reporter has implicitly taken her side. In her concluding statement, she claims that she is a representative of an unbroken tradition from pre-Christian times: "My work has nothing to do with New Age; this is *Old Age*. The drum is a vehicle for contact with one's inner self, with nature, with the forefathers, and the spirits" (Selberg 2001: 71–72). Kallio's references to "one's inner self" and to a romanticized "nature," of course, imply an entirely different story about her links with New Age ideas.

Earlier in the same article, Selberg briefly discusses a Norwegian book by Bjørg Vindsetmo, *Sjelen som turist: Om religion, terapi og magi* (Spiritual tourism: about religion, therapy and magic) that trashes alternative religiosity. The author is particularly harsh in her treatment of neoshamanism. The book's year of publication, 1995, indicates that *Sjelen som turist* appeared before Sami neoshamanism became prominent in Norway. One wonders how Vindsetmo would have approached her subject matter in the current atmosphere, in which criticism of anything attributable to the Sami tradition is either muted or left unstated.

Nordic academicians have, of course, noted the discrepancy between the claims of Sami neoshamans to represent ancient traditions and their romantic reconstructions. But even their most critical observations are mild when compared with the harsh critiques leveled by scholars of Native American traditions against White neoshamans. Thus, for example, in *I Modergudinnens fotspor* (In the Mother Goddess' footsteps), Marit Myrhaug asserts that in "its worst form of expression this romanticizing has resulted in something I would describe as "reverse cultural imperialism." Earlier one was concerned with destroying Sami religion based on an understanding that it was a bad thing. [Currently,] one is again in danger of abusing religion, but now based on a 'positive' understanding of it"[5] (Myrhaug 1997: 10).

To take another example, in 2007 there was a broad-ranging discussion regarding a neoshamanic performance at the Riddu Riddu music festival in the *Nordlys* newspaper. As part of that discussion, the Sami researcher Harald Gaski expressed criticism of "New Agey flirting with old Sami traditions," saying that "The [socio-cultural] context of the old belief is gone. Thus searching for it is a regressive nostalgia rather than a liberating experience. One easily ends up trivializing what one wants to praise, because the time is no longer appropriate for this once powerful faith" (*Nordlys* July 19, 2007).

At the most general level, the point of the present juxtaposition of American neoshamanism with Sami neoshamanism is clear enough: the same reconstructed neoshamanism that receives such extreme criticism in the North American context has been popularly accepted as an authentic expression of indigenous spirituality in northern Europe. The primary reason for this difference is also obvious: whereas the bulk of neoshamans in North America are White outsiders to Native American cultures, the majority of individuals self-identifying as Sami shamans have Sami heritage.[6] Additionally, academicians in North America feel free to rhetorically thrash neoshamanism, whereas Nordic researchers tend—even in nonacademic forums such as newspaper interviews—to express their criticisms with less rhetoric. The source of the difference in tone between these two sets of academicians is unclear, although one might speculate that some American researchers feel prompted to reproduce the outrage of their informants.

Another, less immediately obvious, component of the Nordic context is that, as mentioned earlier, many Samis are Læstadian or from Læstadian backgrounds. And while these people generally tend to support the Sami nation-building project and to be proud of many aspects of their Sami heritage, they are quite averse to the project of resuscitating pre-Christian Sami religion. However, the voices of these Christians tend to drop out in mainstream secular press accounts except when traditionalist Christianity is implicitly criticized, as in the story about Kallio mentioned earlier.

Thus, and in sharp contrast to the North American situation, indigenous critics of neoshamanism in Northern Europe do not generally receive media attention. To speak only about Norway and Sweden, it is clear that one factor at work in this area of the world is that liberal Scandinavians feel guilty about their nations' past mistreatment of the Sami. As a consequence of this postcolonial conscience (Kraft 2011), the media tends to treat any story about the Sami with extreme care to avoid accusations of racism. Academicians—the present writer included—are similarly cautious.

Conclusion

What can be learned from this analysis is a corollary to one of the basic lessons that were learned in the wake of the rejection of Eliade's system-building project. Like James Frazer before him, Eliade had built the case for certain universal religious patterns by juxtaposing apparently similar phenomena that he presented minus their original cultural contexts. The principal drawback of this approach is that—at the ground level in their original contexts—superficially similar patterns can, and often do, embody quite different meanings. This is, in part, the thrust of the accusation of "essentialism" that has been leveled against Eliade and others. "Shamanism" was one of Eliade's best-known essentialized products.

Harner took this artificial product one step further by creating the essentialized *working system* he referred to as core shamanism. Part of his vision was that people from different backgrounds could then build upon core shamanism by adding elements from their own religiocultural traditions (Harner et al. 1990). However, what most of us studying the contemporary impact of Harner's creation tend to remember the most clearly is that it is an essentialized artifice. What we tend to forget is that, as people adapt core shamanism to local situations—as the system indigenizes in different corners of the globe—new contexts supply new meanings.

In the present case, what this means is that, despite superficial resemblances, the neoshamanisms found in North America and the neoshamanism that has taken root in the Nordic region of Europe have come to embody different social significances—one of which has been discussed in this chapter. Undoubtedly the same is the case with many of the neoshamanisms that have been adopted in other areas of the world. Although observers have not been unmindful of local adaptations, in the future we need to grasp this point with greater clarity so that we do not fall back into essentializing modes of analysis all over again.

Notes

1. For a discussion of the UN context of "indigenism," refer to Niezen (2003). The idea that precontact Native Americans had a conception of "Mother Earth" has been systematically critiqued in such academic studies as Gill (1987) and Bierhorst (1994). As a counterpoint, this perspective has been disputed by Native scholars. See, for example, Churchill (1988) and Weaver (1996).
2. There are slight differences, but the strong racial "otherness" seemingly evident in older photographs of the Sami is the result of staging meant to emphasize differentness (Baglo 2001).
3. It should be noted, however, that Scandinavians have also been involved in Sami neo-shamanism. Thus, for example, a key person involved in the development of Sami neo-shamanism in Sweden has been Jørgen I Eriksson, who is not ethnically Sami.
4. Fragments of pre-Christian healing practices seem to have been preserved in Sami folk medicine. In this regard, refer, e.g., to Sande and Winterfeldt (1993) and Miller (2007). One striking element of these practices is so-called "blood stopping," the focus of a 2012 documentary by Torill Olsen and Harry Johansen, *De gode hjelperne* (The good helpers), http://tv.nrk.no/program /koid75001113/de-gode-hjelperne. The film is discussed in Caroline Rugeldal's short article, "Avslører gamle hemmeligheter" (*Revealing ancient secrets*) published by NRK (Norway's national news service) December 27, 2012, http://www.nrk.no/nordnytt/avslorer-gamle-hemmeligheter-1.10853683.
5. Translated by Trude Fonneland.
6. Non-Sami Norwegians who become shamans tend to assert that they are Nordic rather than Sami shamans (as discussed in Fonneland, forthcoming).

References

Aldred, Lisa. 2000. "Plastic Shamans and Astroturf Sun Dances: New Age Commercialization of Native American Spirituality." *American Indian Quarterly* 24(3): 329–352.

Baglo, Cathrine. 2001. "From Universal Homogeneity to Essential Heterogeneity: On the Visual Construction of 'the Lappish Race.'" *Acta Borealia* 18(2): 23–39.

Barnett, Louise K. 1975. *The Ignoble Savage: American Literary Racism*, 1790–1890. Westport, CT: Greenwood Press.

Bierhorst, John. 1994. *The Way of the Earth: Native America and the Environment*. New York: William Morrow.

Christensen, Cato. 2007. "Urfolksspiritualitet på det nyreligiøse markedet. En analyse av tidsskriftet Visjon/Alternativt Nettverk." *Din: Tidsskrift for religion og kultur* 1.

Churchill, Ward. 1988. "Sam Gill's *Mother Earth*: Colonialism, Genocide and the Expropriation of Indigenous Spiritual Tradition in Contemporary Academia." *American Indian Culture and Research Journal* 12(3): 49–67.

———. 2003. "Spiritual Hucksterism: The Rise of the Plastic Medicine Men." *Cultural Survival Quarterly* 27(2): 26–28.

Dippie, Brian W. 1982. *The Vanishing American: White Attitudes and U.S. Indian Policy*. Lawrence, KS: University of Kansas Press.

DuBois, Thomas A. 2009. *An Introduction to Shamanism*. Cambridge: Cambridge University Press.

Eliade, Mircea. 2004 [1951]. *Shamanism: Archaic Techniques of Ecstasy*. New York: Bollingen Series; Princeton, NJ: Princeton University Press.

Falkenberg, Johs. 1941. *Bosetningen ved indre Laksefjord i Finnmark: Optegnelser fra 1938*. Oslo : Etnografisk Museum.

Fonneland, Trude. 2012. "Spiritual Entrepreneurship in a Northern Landscape: Spirituality, Tourism and Politics." *Temenos* 48(2): 155–178.

———. 2013. "Sami Tourism and the Signposting of Spirituality. The Case of Sami Tour: a Spiritual Entrepreneur in the Contemporary Experience Economy." *Acta Borealia* 30(2): 190–208.

———. forthcoming. "Changing Religious Landscapes: The approval of a northern Norwegian shamanic association," in James R. Lewis and Inga Bårdsen Tøllefsen (eds.) *Nordic New Religions*. Leiden: Brill.

Fonneland, Trude, and Siv Ellen Kraft. 2013. "New Age, Sami Shamanism and Indigenous Spirituality," in Steven J. Sutcliffe and Ingvild Sælid Gilhus (eds.) *New Age Spirituality: Rethinking Religion*. Durham, UK: Acumen Publishing, 132–145.

Gaski, Harald. 1993. "The Sami People: The 'White Indians' of Scandinavia." *American Indian Culture and Research Journal* 17(1): 115–128.

Gaup, Ailo. 2005. *The Shamanic Zone*. Oslo, Norway: Three Bears Company.

Gill, Sam. 1987. *Mother Earth: An American Story*. Chicago: University of Chicago Press.

Hardman, Charlotte E. 2007. "'He May Be Lying But What He Says Is True': The Sacred Tradition of Don Juan as Reported by Carlos Castaneda, Anthropologist, Trickster, Guru, Allegorist," in James R. Lewis and Olav Hammer (eds.) *The Invention of Sacred Tradition*. Cambridge, UK: Cambridge University Press, 38–55.

Harner, Michael J., Jeffrey Mishlove, and Arthur Bloch. 1990 [1980]. *The Way of the Shaman*. San Francisco, CA: Harper & Row.

Hobson, Geary. 1981. "The Rise of the White Shaman as a New Version of Cultural Imperialism," in Geary Hobson (ed.) *The Remembered Earth: An Anthology of Contemporary Native American literature*. Albuquerque, NM: University of New Mexico Press, 100–108.

Hætta, Odd Mathis. 2002. *Samene: Nordkalottens urfolk*. Kritiansand: Høyskoleforl.

Jakobsen, Merete Demant. 1999. *Shamanism: Traditional and Contemporary Approaches to the Mastery of Spirits and Healing*. New York: Berghahn Books.

Kehoe, Alice B. 1996. "Eliade and Hultkrantz: the European Primitivism Tradition." *American Indian Quarterly* 20(3/4): 377–392.

Kraft, Siv Ellen. 2009. "Sami Indigenous Spirituality: Religion and Nation Building in Norwegian Sápmi." *Temenos: Nordic Journal of Comparative Religion* 45(2): 179–206.

————. 2010. "The Making of a Sacred Mountain: Meanings of Nature and Sacredness in Sápmi and Northern Norway." *Religion* 40(1): 53–61.

————. 2011. *Hva er nyreligiøsitet?* Oslo: Universitetsforlaget.

————. forthcoming. "New Age Spiritualities," in James R. Lewis and Jesper Aagaard Petersen (eds.) *Controversial New Religions*. New York: Oxford University Press, 2nd edition.

Lewis, James R. 1992. "Approaches to the Study of the New Age," in James R. Lewis and J. Gordon Melton (eds.) *Perspectives on the New Age*. Albany: State University of New York Press, 1–12.

Mathisen, Stein R. 2012. "Indigenous Spirituality in the Touristic Borderzone: Virtual Performances of Sámi Shamanism in Sápmi Park." *Temenos* 46(1): 53–72.

Miller, Barbara Helen. 2007. *Connecting and Correcting: A Case Study of Sami Healers in Porsanger* 151. Leiden: CNWS Publications.

Minde, Henry. 1998. "Constructing 'Laestadianism': A Case for Sami Survival?" *Acta Borealia: A Nordic Journal of Circumpolar Societies* 15(1): 5–25.

Myrhaug, May-Lisbeth. 1997. *I Modergudinnens Fotspor: Samisk Religion Med Vekt Pa Kvinnelige Kultutvere Og Gudinnekult*. Oslo: Pax Forlag.

Niezen, Ronald. 2003. *The Origins of Indigenism: Human Rights and the Politics of Identity*. Berkeley: University of California Press.

Paine, Robert. 1965. "Laestadianismen og samfunnet." *Tidskrift for samjunns-forskning* 1: 60–73.

Rydving, Håkan. 2004 (1993). *The End of Drum-Time: Religious Change Among the Lule Saami, 1670s–1740s*. Uppsala, Sweden: Uppsala University.

Sande, Hans, and Sigrun Winterfeldt. 1993. "Four Sami Healers: A Preliminary Interview Study." *Nordic Journal of Psychiatry* 47(1): 41–51.

Selberg, Torunn. 2001. "Ideas about the Past and Tradition in the Discourse about Neo-shamanism in a Norwegian Context." *Acta Ethnographica Hungarica* 46(1): 65–74.

Smith, Andrea. 1991a. "For All Those Who Were Indian in a Former Life." *Ms. Magazine*, November/December.

————. 1991b. "The New Age Movement and Native Spirituality." *Indigenous Woman*, Spring.

Snyder, Gary. 1969. *Earth House Hold*. New York: New Directions.

von Stuckrad, Kocku. 2002. "Reenchanting Nature: Modern Western Shamanism and Nineteenth-Century Thought." *Journal of the American Academy of Religion* 70(4): 771–799.

Wallis, Robert J. 1999. "Altered States, Conflicting Cultures: Shamans, Neo-shamans and Academics." *Anthropology of Consciousness* 10(2): 41–49.

————. 2003. *Shamans/neo-shamans: Ecstasies, Alternative Archaeologies and Contemporary Pagans*. London: Routledge.

Weaver, Jace, ed. 1996. *Defending Mother Earth: Native Perspectives on Environmental Justice*. Maryknoll, New York: Orbis Books.

8

More or Less Genuine Shamans!: The Believer in an Exchange between Antiquity and Modernity, between the Local and the Global[1]

Bente Gullveig Alver

This article deals with those who in daily life maintain a relationship with a transcendental universe and a thought-world in which "power," and the ability to use this power, are central, and hold the belief that magic is something that *acts*, that *influences*, that *causes something to happen*.

We shall follow a Sami woman, Ellen Marit Gaup Dunfjeld, on the basis of the narrative of her life story. Ellen Marit was born in 1944 in Masi in Finnmark and died in Bergen in 1991. She was the firstborn of nine children. She looked at herself as a mediator and a bridge between people and "powers." She practiced as a wise woman[2] and especially as a healer. It was through my work with alternative treatment in the Norwegian health system that I became interested in her.

Ellen Marit belonged to a generation of Sami who experienced major changes in lifestyle. Economic centralization, market-economic management, and an increasingly capital-intensive technology created an entirely different framework for settlement and industry. Ellen Marit spoke of the community's changing relationship to settlement, which she did not view as straightforwardly positive, even if it was more convenient, saying that it was a move "away from nature" for the Sami people:

> In the 1960s, it was like this, that everybody should settle in a house. And there was a deliberate plan by the authorities. I am in a way the last generation to have lived in tents. I thought it was wonderful to live in a tent. I really liked it. You lay there and were at one with the earth. It was just the canvas that

separated you from the wilderness and the stars and the moon. You were really *there*. People lived very close together....In the sleeping tent there were a lot of people lying in a row under their pelts. (EFA. Protocol GD, p. 94)

An awakening took place socially and mentally at this time among the Sami: they formed a new pride in being Sami, and this honed the notion of being an indigenous people and of indigenous peoples' rights to the countryside and food resources, and pointed them in the direction of requiring Sami self-government.

We need to look at how Ellen Marit moved between an older Sami conceptual world and a neo-religious universe, how she was torn between her loyalty to the small, tight community and the local, and the opportunities and challenges offered by the world at large and globalization. She and her development in belief, in thought, and in action are interesting as an example of the diversity and especially the complexity that operates in popular religiosity, and particularly within belief. Taking the complexity into account, my treatment may be too highly colored by attempts to create order and categories based on what Ellen Marit related. I can but state that I agree with the anthropologist Marit Myrvoll; after fieldwork in the Måsske community in Tysfjord on continuity and rupture in the Sami understanding of reality, she notes that "the attempt at professional categorizations has its shortcomings, and belief enters into a field which is larger and broader than oneself" (2010: 256).

My treatment here is a portrait of Ellen Marit in a few strokes. I will look at the various shifts in her conceptual world, try to understand the kaleidoscopic patterns that characterize and create a life, and highlight important events, which she believes were turning points and milestones. But it is also a treatment of popular religiosity and the contemporary relationship with traditionalization, continuity, and change, toward transformation and innovation.

An Authentic Shaman—What Actually Is It?

Ellen Marit's father, Mikkel Gaup, popularly called "Miracle Mikkel," was a well-known "wise man" in postwar Norway. He was also known outside Norway, and there he bore the nickname "Healing Fox" (Gaup 2005: 86, Strøm 2013: 102). Until the early 1990s he described himself, as did those around him, as a "reader"[3] or healer (Fonneland 2010: 156). This indicates that he used words and formulas in his practice. Later he was called a shaman. Inspired by the neoshamanic movement, the term "shaman" came to be used more commonly through the 1980s and beyond. When I interviewed Ellen Marit in the mid-1980s, she called herself and her father not just shamans but the last true shamans in Finnmark. When interviewed about the course of her life in 1990, she used the concept of the shaman rather than *noaidi* of both her father and herself. But what was it about her, and her father's conceptual world and practice as a "wise person" that in her opinion made them eligible not merely to hold the status of shamans but moreover to be regarded as authentic? The Sami shaman, the noaidi, in the form we know from ancient sources, is long gone.

Ellen Marit had a background in a tradition-rich reindeer-herding setting. She composed the book *Reindrift: Samisk næring—samisk fremtid* (*Reindeer-herding: Sámi sustenance—Sámi future*) on traditional reindeer herding (Gaup 1979). In the setting in which she grew up, the old Sami conceptual world was still alive, and this was maintained by the family's older generation, both through stories and through behavior. Right from childhood she had a keen interest in this universe, believed it and acted upon it. She was already as a child aware that she had special supernatural powers. As she entered her teens, her father supported her in this and began to carefully teach her more about how he saw the world. Through him she had a close relationship with nature to inspire her, with the dead and the world of the dead, with the spirit world, and with helping spirits in the form of various birds and animals.

It was her close relationship with this thought-world and with her own religious experience that resulted in her calling herself and her father genuine shamans. She seems to set authenticity in opposition to neoshamanism. This she encountered, for example, among Ailo Gaup's ideas about Sami shamanism, which he publicized in the book *Sjamansonen*, first published in 1987. It was a type of approach that had little to commend it to Ellen Marit. She says,

> I do not think shamanism can be learnt the way I understand shamanism. But you can learn to develop or use your own resources. It's a completely different thing. But it is not shamanism: shamanism belongs to religion in a culture. It must be interpreted in relation to nature and a particular way of life. You cannot just drag out bits and bobs and call it shamanism. I would not do it. But I think you can teach people to develop their spiritual sides more....I think myself I am a shaman. We call it *noaidi* in our culture. If I am not well integrated into shamanism, then I would like to see the person who is more integrated than me! Apart from my father. (EFA. Protocol GD, p. 61)

Neoshamanists' relationship with nature as divine, and magical practices as a central part of religious expression were matters that both Ellen Marit and her father could well recognize in themselves. Nonetheless, she claimed that her father called neoshamans fraudsters: man was born with supernatural powers; it was not something that could be learned or you could read up on. The shaman was chosen by the spirits. It was not something you could decide or control.

But it turned out as time went by that Ellen Marit herself was not immune to neo-religious ideas. In the late 1980s, she came into contact with the American neo-religious "goddess movement." Although she denied it when questioned directly, this relationship with and even burgeoning of neoshamanism was to color both her conceptual world and her terminology. I will return to this matter.

I Never Promised You a Rose Garden!

Ellen Marit told me her life story while she was seriously ill, six months before she died. When she realized how sick she was and had to admit that her life was ebbing away, she asked if she could tell her story to me. She believed she could better understand her life by putting it into words. I was not that close to her; I had learned of her through my university background. But we had respect for each other, and for her it was important that she should be able to relate things freely without regard to loyalties. Although she mainly wanted to understand who she was, she also wanted others after her death to understand who she had been. She was herself fluent in writing and would probably have preferred to write her own story. But she realized she was too ill to do so.

Telling one's life story shapes a life, teases out the tangled threads, explains and justifies, and fits things in so that there is coherence and harmony. The kind of emotion that a life story opens is both backward looking and future oriented. The past is used to construct the present and to direct the way to the future.

Long afternoons I sat by Ellen Marit's sickbed and heard her recount her tales. The world around left us alone in peace. I walked with her along wayward paths, and I did not stop her to ask her to explain the way, even though I was not always clear why we went the way we did. It was her life—her quest. She repeated things rarely and never interpreted. The short autumn days with the failing light blurred all the contours of the room. It almost hid the symbols of power of the "goddess friends"— mostly the bear in all its forms—which were fighting for space with the glass of water and the fresh flowers that stood on her desk every day. I did not always see her face clearly on the embroidered pillowcase on which she demanded to rest her head. But out of the soft light, out of the metallic smell, out of the pain and sadness of the past, out of the closeness between two women grew a story about the magician—about mankind in constant motion, searching for meaning.

Ellen Marit knew it was the last time she would put into words who she was or who she wanted to be. It made this version of her life story special. It is a narrative that shows the level of imagination and creativity someone can unfold in order to create a consistent whole and an understanding of her ways in and out of different worlds of the imagination and explanations of the many choices. Striking too is her affirmative and accepting attitude toward her religious experiences with the spirit world, with divine nature.[4]

Her Father's Daughter

Throughout her life Ellen Marit considered her father to be her spiritual guide. Mikkel Gaup was visited by very many people asking for help, and he was also known for his ability to treat the sick by "remote healing": he is said to have been so strong in his thought that he appeared to them physically, treating them over the phone, while he was many miles away (Ailo Gaup 2005: 86 ff., Eriksson 2003: 37, Strøm 2013: 102 f.). This he explained as a form of visualization and transfer of energy (Strøm 2013: 103). He had lost both his parents very early on and grew up with his father's parents, who were also known to have "had knowledge of more than the Lord's Prayer." It was his grandfather who had taught him.

People who have met Mikkel Gaup talk of a man with strong charisma. Another "wise person," Bergit Loen Hatlenes, who was a friend of his, says of him:

> Never, before or since, have I met a man with such power and charisma as Mikkel Gaup...Mikkel was actually a shy and reserved man. He was not that easy to fathom. But I felt that he opened up to me, and it was a delight to hear him recount. For example, he related that he was born on a rock on the plain, and he had been initiated into the shaman tradition by his grandfather. He was knowledgeable and insightful, and yet so different from any other man I had met before, let alone after. He was an exceptional man, he had nature within himself and spread goodness wherever he went. The times when he looked into the future something happened to his eyes and his whole figure. It was as if he disappeared into a separate world—only to return. (Strøm 2013: 101)

Ellen Marit admired her father's ability and willingness to help people, and especially his knowledge of nature and of the pre-Christian Sami religion and the conceptual world of an older day. He was her teacher, but she was his protector against the pressure from the world outside. Among the many who visited him were various neoshamans, who looked upon him as a guru or teacher. This was the case, for example, with Ailo Gaup, who was a relative. Ailo Gaup relates that in 1970 he quit his regular job as a journalist in Oslo and traveled to Lapland to find someone who could teach him the shamanic art. Here he ended up with Mikkel Gaup, and he says of him,

> Mikkel was for me a *noaidi* in the old tradition, a word-healer and distance healer, and he taught me much about the art. The holy sacred *sieidi* stones on the plain were well known to him. He could point in the direction of the rocks, such that the next moment it was as if we were surrounded by their energy. He nodded toward the sun and the sun's power opened up in me. He lived right next to the famous Kautokeino river and had the plain behind. All this and life in the mountains could be read in his face. He was the one who kept the fire alive for many through a dark time. (2005: 86)

Ailo Gaup has much respect for Mikkel Gaup and the knowledge he possessed. Long after Mikkel's death, claims Ailo, the hours he spent with him continue to influence his development and lead him onward (375).

Trude Fonneland, who interviewed Ailo Gaup for her doctoral work on neoshamanism, cites an enthusiastic Ailo recounting Mikkel Gaup's efforts in the Alta conflict, a conflict to which we shall return. Ailo highlights how for Mikkel there was a symbiosis between the political and the spiritual:

> Yes, crisis creates rituals, you know. It creates a mood of "it is now the case." It created an "us against them" feeling. I remember Miracle Mikkel was involved there and had almost sort of ritual moments where he spoke out that this is against the spirit of nature and that nature will fight back, and that it is nature that we should stick to. He had an amazing effect, maybe one that worked on me especially, more than anyone else. But he had an underlying ideology. Mikkel Gaup helped motivate me and others, in a language beyond politics, beyond the slogans. He had a perspective that was different. (cited in Fonneland 2010: 150–151)

The legacy Ellen Marit received from her father was a similar symbiosis, as we shall see.[5] Ailo Gaup also provided a good description of Mikkel Gaup's ritual way of dealing with things:

> Once I came to a healing at his place. Then he donned his healer robe and we went into the bathroom. Then he asked me to sit down on a chair. Then he began work. He drew his hands up and down my body, until they stopped at one spot. Then he yoiked and "growled" a bit. This was a kind of sound-healing, while his hands were like wolf snouts sniffing out filth inside me. When I went my way, I was much lighter in body and mind. This happened sometime in the early 1980s and was my first experience of healing. Did it help? Everything he did affected me, whether it was conversation or healing or just seeing how he acted towards others. (2005: 86–87)

Ellen Marit had seen her father treat the sick many times, and her method was basically very similar to her father's. She also wore his red "shaman robe" when she practiced, and both Mikkel Gaup's robe and her own were Ellen Marit's idea. Red is the traditional Sami color symbolizing strength and power. She used not just her hands on bare skin when she practiced, but she used her "whole self," she said. She concentrated hard to let the power flow through her to the patient. Often she strengthened her concentration by formulating inside herself what she was doing and what she wanted to happen. Thinking in this way was bound up with specific formulas that she had probably learned from her father and did not want to reveal to anyone. Like him she also used yoiking in her therapy. She claimed that she was not clairvoyant. But she formed an impression of the person she was treating, partly by reading their thoughts and partly through impulses from the body, which she felt as pain or vibrations in her hands. She said that the different diseases produced different vibrations. But she also received help from the spirit world through a "voice" that told her where she should lay her hands on the sick person's body (cf. Alver and Selberg 1992: 108–109).

Michael Harner, the father of "core shamanism," was also one of the neoshamans who visited the aged Gaup.[6] Ellen Marit was very much opposed to neoshamans coming to see her father, and she thought he was too gullible toward them:

> Father does not understand that he gives Ailo Gaup information that gets used, and then he gets drawn into this in a way. But he does not understand this. Michael Harner has been at father's. He has been there twice. There was a Finnish colleague of Michael Harner's who came with him the first time. I do not remember his name. Then he came, that Finnish colleague, by himself sometime later. He wanted to make a film with father where he wanted to get into shamanism through it. But he didn't get permission from me. I did not want father to be abused in that way, because I do not think he had a clear enough idea about why he was making the film and how it should be made. (EFA. Protocol GD, p. 66)

She tried to shield her father from what she saw as exploitation because she did not take neoshamanism seriously. She also tried to persuade him not to make statements to reporters, whom she always feared would ridicule him. But she also drew the spirit world into the argument over why there should be no filming and interviews. The spirit world should be shown respect and not abused, talked about, or disturbed unnecessarily. She showed me this clearly some years before the life-story interview with her. We were sitting in my house and talking about how she was consecrated as a shaman. My phone rang, but it was obviously a wrong number, and there was no one on the line when I answered. Immediately and obviously rattled, Ellen Marit got up and wanted to go. "Well, I said some spirits don't want me to continue talking," she said, and left me.

The Brave New World of Books

Only Sami was spoken in Ellen Marit's home in her early childhood. She was four years old when she first came across "the white man" and his language. She was so afraid that she and her brother climbed to the top of a tree, and they had to be lured down with both encouragements and threats when the danger was over. She encountered Norwegian in earnest at the age of seven when she started school. She knew no Norwegian, and the teacher no Sami:

> I could not manage Norwegian—could not say a word in Norwegian, so I didn't understand what was said....The teacher knew no Sámi and nor did any of the children. It was a purely Norwegian-speaking school. I sat there day after day, trying to copy the other kids and the teacher tried to read to me....In the breaks they tried to be friendly with me, the girls, and talked to me. I began to copy them, felt like a fool, and I learned a lot of words that I didn't understand the meaning of, and they really laughed when I said those words....But I gradually discovered that they were teaching me a lot of bad words, and they thought it was a real laugh. (EFA. Protocol GD: 14)

Gifted as she was, Ellen Marit soon learned Norwegian, and she came to like going to school very much. She wanted to learn, and she wanted to completely understand what she was reading. The books opened up a wider world for her. It was a joy to her, because she did not know that there was a world outside her Sami universe.

She was very excited when she discovered fairy tales in the books. She loved the fairy-tale world, and she seemed to possess the ability to glide smoothly between fact and fiction, in and out of different worlds: "At first it was a fairy tale that I was taking part in—it *did* come true, for me in any case" (EFA. Protocol GD, p. 7). Her parents did not like her enjoyment of reading, but she secretly borrowed books from the school library and read by torchlight under the blanket late into the night. She thought it was exciting to enter the fairy-tale world, which she felt she could recognize from her father's stories. He was a good storyteller, as when, in spare moments, the whole family, neighbors, and others gathered around him. But there were many other good storytellers in Ellen Marit's immediate surroundings:

> There was great-grandmother and her children. And father and his siblings. They grew up with their grandmother. And there were lots and lots of people

there. And they told stories, many kinds of stories. Fairy tales and legends and everyday stories. The stories were often sort of like there was some teaching in them. So through these little stories or fairy tales you got an introduction to the so-called supernatural part of our existence. (EFA, Protocol GD: 91)

Ellen Marit was fascinated by the fairy tale "The White Bear King Valemon." She lived completely in this tale, and she took turns to be each of the various characters in it. Sometimes she was the great enchanted bear, but mostly she was the princess, delicate and bright riding on the bear's back. She lived the role of princess so deeply that she felt the animal's rocking motions under her and could smell the strong, raw bear fur. But she was never the evil troll.[7] When Ellen Marit read, she became the people about whom she was reading, and she sensed the story's sounds and smells. She existed inside fairy tales, but could quickly jump over and change worlds when adults called her.

Ellen Marit is not the only one to have been hooked into getting into older Sami culture in this way. Brita Pollan, who has produced several studies of Sami shamanism, has claimed that she became aware of Sami culture through Sami fairy tales. She found them different from other tales and became curious about the reality behind them (1993: 17). She set out to investigate whether there was a possible connection between what she calls "shamanistic experiences" and the composition of Sami tales.

Courage to Stand Up to Parents

After elementary school Ellen Marit's parents said this was enough schooling. She was needed for work at home. They wanted her to marry a reindeer-herding Sami, and she did not need any more bookish knowledge. In our conversations Ellen Marit portrayed herself as strong by nature and very stubborn. She strove to the last to enter the so-called "continuation school." Her teachers thought she should continue to secondary school and had applied for a place for her there. But her parents said absolutely not. Especially her mother was strict when it came to her daughter's future and her Sami identity. She did not want, among other things, for Ellen Marit to wear anything but Sami clothes. When she was confirmed, she was not allowed to wear a white robe, like the others, but had to wear her Sami attire:

When I reached the teen years, there was a conflict. I wanted to wear more normal clothes, and there was a real fight over it, especially with my mother. She said that I should wear my Sámi clothing: I was a Sámi, and I would never be anything but a Sámi. But the whole time I was different from the others. But after a while I argued my case for wearing regular clothes and I walked around in them even if mother did not like them...I felt that it was important for me to be like the others and not stick out in everyone's eyes. I just did not want it. But everyone knew that I was a Sámi. And fortunately, I will say, my parents were so strict right at these times of upheaval, otherwise I could have veered over to becoming Norwegian. But they were very strict with me, so I grasped how it was so important for me to keep my Sámi identity, to be proud of it. And of course I was....It was much easier for my siblings. They did not have the same problems, because we had lived in Eiby a while and were more assimilated. (EFA. Protocol DG: 7–8)

Her mother placed great emphasis on educating her in everything that a reindeer-herding Sami woman should know, and not just know, but know well. For the young Ellen Marit, as for other Sami women, this meant heavy chores. Although she was closely bound to her father her whole life, and he was her guide in the spirit world, as an adult she saw clearly her mother's role in the family, as the one who holds it together in everyday life, amid the chaos of people visiting Mikkel Gaup:

Father always had a good time sitting and talking nonsense with all the people who came. So mother had to be responsible for keeping everything in order and looking after the work. So I felt really sorry for mother for that. She has had a lot of hardships. And had she not been the strong type that she was, it would not have been so good. It was she who kept everything in order and was at home the most. Father was with the reindeer and could be gone for days....It was usually like that with all the reindeer-herding men. They are not at home so much. So it is the woman who is in charge with everything to do with the home and children and everything going on. (EFA. Protocol GD: 24)

But despite what Ellen Marit portrays as a strict upbringing, with an emphasis on inculcating Sami norms and rules, she says that right from childhood on she was treated lovingly and much admired by the family. Hence she had the courage to stand up to her parents, even though she was raised to believe that this was not done: Sami youngsters should respect their elders and their opinions.

But in one area, she always listened to her mother. This was in her mother's warnings against evil forces. Her mother especially warned her against the evil that some women could invoke by means of church sand or soil from the cemetery. It was a notion in which Ellen Marit believed firmly. It was a destructive magic that her mother thought thrived during festive gatherings, because it could be difficult to control in situations in which many people were gathered. Ellen Marit told of the fear of this kind of magic once when there were baptisms in the family:

There were two women who were known to have devil's sand or church sand, which they used. Weddings and baptisms were suitable occasions to release

some devilry. Mother sat and watched them surreptitiously throughout the evening. And do you not think that they went up to the cooking pots more and
more often? And she was afraid they were going to put something in the pots,
so she just had to watch. Because there are some families that are known to
operate with evil forces. So you have to take care, otherwise you get demons
inside you. They can put them in through liquor or food or anything else. They
do it mainly out of worship of the evil power, and they have pledged themselves
to the evil one....If sometimes I was allowed to go alone up to Kautokeino,
I had to prepare myself. I could never accept anything from strangers, drink
anything or eat anything. If you had to have it, you always had to do a ritual
first....It was mother who taught me that. (EFA. Protocol GD: 30)

And so Ellen Marit went her own way as best she could. As she looked
back on her life, she was very aware that she belonged to a generation in upheaval; she went "from the pure Sámi culture directly to the
Norwegian," and that was tough. Her enjoyment of books, which gave
her a window onto another and bigger world than the Sami, also produced a split in her. She wanted to be Sami, but she also wanted to be
"Norwegian."

"I am the modern nomadic Sami"

Ellen Marit married young, maybe to get away from home or to get out
into the world. She did not choose a reindeer-herding Sami as her parents
wanted her to—they had looked into many marriage candidates for her
whom they thought suitable. She fell in love with a Sami from a southern
region in Norway. She married him when she was 20, and together they
went to the south of the country and settled in a major city, where he
began legal studies:

> Since it was determined by his family's closest members that he would become
> a lawyer, because the Sámi people needed it, that was the path he chose to fol-
> low. He was very involved and is very involved and is up among the experts in
> the field today. He has worked very hard for the Sámi cause.... We have worked
> actively together. I have often been an interpreter for him, especially during the
> Alta case. (EFA. Protocol GD: 98)

Many in Ellen Marit's own family were interested in politics, and she
asserted that she had always been engaged in politics and in what was
happening around her. But she thought that as far as getting a hear-
ing goes, it was a problem that when young she was very shy. It was a
shyness that she eventually overcame. Through her husband's work as
a lawyer for the Sami she realized that it was important to raise your
voice in political matters. Her political commitment was strengthened
through her collaboration with her husband. The couple moved several

times, following wherever his work led them, both within Norway and abroad. But amid all these moves Ellen Marit took on various jobs to assist. She worked in a grocery store and a kiosk, she sewed fur coats and hats at a furrier's, took a typing course, and had foster children, along with the two children she had in her marriage. But when her husband began practicing as a lawyer, she also wanted to have the education she had dreamed of. She applied to a school of journalism and was trained as a journalist.

In her narration, Ellen Marit gave an impression that the city and the people in the city, and the life they lived, was scary. Here she was possibly influenced by her father's ideas about the city and urban life, but perhaps more generally by neo-religious ideas. She claimed that her father pleaded with people from the town and said to them,

> You call my land a wilderness, but it's your town that's the wilderness. My land is not wild. It has been the way God created it here for hundreds of years....It is you who have made the wilderness. (EFA. Protocol GD: 46)

Wilderness or not, Ellen Marit was attracted to city life. But here too she flitted between different realities—between the hectic life of the city and the tranquility of open spaces in Finnmark. One of her close friends says that while Ellen Marit lived in Oslo, she liked to sit at a window table at the Grand Café, which has its windows facing the main street, Karl Johan. She wanted to see, but she also wanted to be seen. Additionally, she visited the city and mixed with the public as a journalist—for example, on the television screen on the popular entertainment program *Sommeråpent*. Above all, though, she was a public figure in the fight for Sami rights and in her efforts in the Alta conflict. But she always yearned for Finnmark and the great lonely plains:

> I usually say that I am a modern nomadic Sámi. It's a fact that I carry my home with me and in me. And when I'm here in the south, I have it all in myself. I can be there in thought. Through the mind, through the spirits, I am there whenever I want and I can. I can see it and I see my loved ones, my friends and relatives and parents and siblings. I see them. I can call them by yoiking. So I use yoiking a lot when I'm alone. Through yoiking you can call who you want. Then they are there, and you're not alone. So then you can be anywhere. So yoiking is one of the most amazing things about the spiritual part of people. Through it you can express yourself and communicate over a very wide range. You can contact the spirit world. You can get in touch with this world through the spiritual part of yourself. (EFA. Protocol GD: 71–72)

But she was not content with being at home in Finnmark on just a mental level. She felt a great responsibility for what happened at home and followed the yearly round and the pulse of her family's life as reindeer herders. In the fall she took herself home and took part in the women's work at the slaughter and the harvesting of berries. But when as an adult she really began work as a "shaman" with her father as a spiritual guide, she also went north to be with him and to recharge her batteries from nature at the family's sacred sites and centers of power.

The Alta Conflict

The Alta conflict was, for Ellen Marit as a politically conscious person, both a milestone and a turning point. It is instructive to see how her involvement in this conflict illustrates how her life as a magic practitioner melded with her role as a political activist. What was the Alta conflict about?[8]

In 1978 the Storting, Norway's national assembly, adopted a proposal for the production of hydroelectric power from the Alta-Kautokeino river system, which involved an area that was important for Sami reindeer-hearding. One of the Sami activists against the project, Eirik Myrhaug, says in the book *Sjaman for livet* (Shaman for life):

> The authorities claimed that the core of the Alta case was to carry out a resolution passed lawfully by parliament to dam large areas to build a power plant in what was then perhaps Europe's most magnificent and unspoiled wilderness. Many saw more sides to the case. The Sámi and many others viewed it as a crime against the indigenous populace perpetrated by society at large. The environmental movement saw in it a symbolic cause. But this was also true for the protection of cultural heritage, and many thought it was a matter of prestige at the center of the political establishment, and many people and many politicians were really opponents. It was grist to the mill for prestige theory when Gro Harlem Brundtland admitted that the development was probably not necessary. But even if the dam were built, the publicity would make out that the Sámi had won a victory in achieving a positive outlook for Sámi autonomy. It was also a victory for the environmental movement. (Brynn and Brunvoll 2011: 124–125)

In the years following the parliamentary decision, one demonstration after another took place against the project. The demonstrations attracted many people—a motley crew of environmentalists, nature lovers, and left-wing radicals. But very quickly Alta became a cause for Sami rights. The demonstrators on the Sami side took drastic measures. In late 1979 the Sami movement put up a *lavvo*, the traditional Sami tent, in front of the Storting, and seven young Sami went on hunger strike for many days to stop the project. Prime Minister Oddvar Nordli had to give in to pressure and promised to delay construction. But everyone knew that this only meant a reprieve, and in January 1981, work started anew. Ellen Marit says,

> Finally, the government sent a ship up to Alta with 600 police. That was in January 1981. It was worse than during the war. The state of things in Alta was absolutely horrific then. Hostility was rife even within families. And a lot of informing going on. It was totally unacceptable. You must understand that the Sámi people are not a homogenous group. There are as many opinions as in the Norwegian population. But we had experts on our side that proved the detrimental effects. We held meetings and conferences. But it only helped a little.... So the police ship came up. So the same seven guys started a new hunger strike in Oslo. And one of them was my brother Ante, who was now on hunger strike for the second time.... I started to get anxious. How would it turn out? And mother was anxious.... I don't know who left it up to me, but it just came over me that now I had to do something. So I went home by myself and did a ritual and prayed for guidance and strength to do what I had to do. For I would not want them to die, those young boys. (EFA. Protocol GD: 101)

The Sami movement had formed an action group, which sent the prime minister a letter in which they demanded a clarification of Sami rights and demanded an end to the construction work. Nordli promised an investigation of the issue, but rejected the request to cease construction. It was at this point that the young Sami went on hunger strike again.

As Ellen Marit emphasizes, the concern for her brother contributed to her, along with a few other women, starting a petition in Finnmark against the construction.[9] Later they decided to go to Oslo to see what they could accomplish there. When they set off, this group of women had no appointment with the authorities. But they were lucky enough to get to the city on February 3—the day Norway got a female prime minister, Gro Harlem Brundtland. According to Ellen Marit's narrative, they managed to get an appointment with her, and on February 6 the prime minister received the 13 Sami women in her office, and they told her that they were staying there until construction was halted. Brundtland left the office after a short time, but the Sami women stayed there for 18 hours until they were removed by police. The hunger strikers were also arrested but later released.

Both the hunger strike and the occupation of the prime minister's office received great attention. Afterward, Ellen Marit felt that the Sami had achieved a great deal, thanks to the Alta conflict and the focus on looking at the rights of the Sami as an indigenous people. But she was angry that the women's efforts were swallowed up among the men's:

> Of course I would have wanted the river to be saved. It was really the big wish. I also believe that the women's group which was involved, at least many of

them, look at it like this. Yes, now we can go and be happy that what happened did happen, even though they called us protesters and abused us. But had it not been for us, it would not have turned out as positively as it did within the Sámi culture. But it has always been like that, that when women do something, it sinks into oblivion. What has been written about the Alta case has been about what the men did. When history is written, it's the men's story, not the women's. (EFA. Protocol GD: 118)

Although she welcomed the way the Sami had been made visible as an indigenous people, and the fulfillment of rights and the new pride in being Sami, she was disheartened by the change she saw in reindeer-herding, and especially by her people's relationship with nature and their lack of respect for it. She cited a list of negative impacts on nature, which the Sami themselves supported. In particular, she was skeptical toward the motorization of movements on the plains, which she felt destroyed the grazing land: she felt it was not just the authorities who were responsible for the destruction of nature.

The Political and Religious Activist in Symbiosis

In both the Alta conflict and later, Ellen Marit spearheaded an inter-national campaign demanding recognition of Sami rights. Her political activity was always closely connected with her religious and magical conceptual world. As she mentions (see above), she spent precious time asking the spirits for advice and conducting rituals to bring success for the trip to Oslo before the group of Sami women went down there. The night the women stayed at the prime minister's office, several of them had dreams, and these were interpreted by the oldest woman in the group. The dreams and their interpretation were important for Ellen Marit as a political activist, and acted as a sign that the spirits had chosen her to accomplish something in the Vatican and elsewhere in the world. Together with two other Sami women she ended up seeing the pope in Rome and got to talk to him for a few minutes about the Sami people's situation. She also later went to the UN human rights' office in New York with an appeal.

The involvement of Ellen Marit and her whole family in the Alta con-flict was a major turning point in her view of herself as a Sami, and it deepened her pride in her Sami identity. As part of this, in 1984 she applied to the University of Bergen to take a major in folklore. She wished to compile and translate her father's stories from Sami to Norwegian and thereby elucidate his thought-world and what she saw as its roots in his practice as a shaman. She wanted to use the past to shape and legitimize her present.[10]

The World of the Spirits—The House of the Spirits

In Ellen Marit's worldview, "power" was a key concept, and she related to it both as a noun and as a verb. Based on his father's thought-world, she understood power as something that through particular rituals she invoked to herself from the outside—from the world of the spirits, from the dead and from nature. The noaidi of yore had an important role in sharing in the power of nature, including through being out in nature. For neoshamans who mostly live in cities and do not have daily contact with nature, "sitting out" is an important ritual for getting in touch with the spirit world and with their own inner self. Fonneland writes about this ritual:

> "Sitting out" is a ritual that provides the practitioner with experiences of nature and the forces that operate there, and thus also opens up the chance for the practitioner to acquire a certain status in the community. The idea is that nature through ritual can function as a mirror that reflects and gives answers to the individual player. In the same way as in the ritual of the sacred places, "sitting out" opens up contact with the spirit world. To "sit out" in nature, with all that implies, works here as a means to break down the boundaries between our world and that of the spirits. (2010: 124)

As Fonneland mentions, one can also make contact with the spirit world by being in certain places, the so-called "holy places," which might be special mountain areas or special rock formations that stand out from others. (On the holy places, see Fonneland 2010: 114–123.)

Ellen Marit and her father had a strong belief in the power of these holy places, and they went to see them together and individually. Different families could have their own holy places, and Ellen Marit might take close friends and peers along to the family's sacred place, but they had to perform the same cleansing rituals as she did. She speaks of the family's sacred place:

> Our family shrine is near where we live now. It's called "Kolmalaitri" and has been used for generations. You can go there when you like, but you do not need to go there more than once a year. It is not necessary. You can summon the spirit where you are. Whether you are alone or just two of you, which I and my father were. But mostly you should go alone. Whenever you go, you should ask permission. It is also very important that you ask for permission when you settle down and need to rest. You ask the spirits of the place if you are allowed to do it and say why you have to do it.... You mustn't just make yourself comfortable. You have to make an offering too. You can give whatever you want. You can give coins, money or whatever you may have—jewelry.... We were brought up to it, otherwise they might bring evil upon you. (EFA. Protocol GD: 69)

The spirit world, as Ellen Marit reiterated time and again in her narrative, was a dangerous world to visit. It was her father who taught her this. You had to approach it in a very specifically regulated way and perform certain rituals if it was to succeed. When rituals were performed, for example, against illness, the spirits needed to be asked for permission because rituals release power. You had to approach the holy sites with respect and caution. And you had to have a reason to visit these sites:

> The dead must not be disturbed unnecessarily. It was said that the reasons that many Sámi have graveyards on the islands is that they have a notion that there should be running water between the realms of the living and the dead. That is why there is always water near the offering place, the holy site... Then you must do a ritual where you wash yourself and send a prayer to the gods, the spirits, and then turn some of your clothes inside out before you pass over. The same when you go away from there. (EFA. Protocol GD: 71)

It was only during the last year of her life that the spirit world became a brighter and friendlier place for her, thanks to her finding out about the American "goddess world," but not least as a result of the death of her two sons, whom she saw as part of this spiritual world. She could not look upon her beloved boys as dangerous; she needed to relate to them as friendly helpers.

Ellen Marit had a dramatic story that illustrates well what Mikkel Gaup had taught her and her extended family on the dangerous world of the spirits and the measures that needed to be taken with it. She related that one of her brothers once camped in the mountains not far from a fishing lake, where he and some friends wanted to fish. But this brother had forgotten his father's admonitions to ask the spirits for permission to camp. Those sleeping in the tent had a very restless night, with voices chattering outside the tent and clattering and crashing. Eventually, the tent was struck so it fell on those who were trying to sleep. Enough was enough. They took to their heels and ran off. The next day her brother went back, and he discovered seven graves there with long stones that were stacked in a special way, as the Sami in earlier times used to do, all facing in an east-west direction. He then found out that he had raised the tent on a grave that was slightly higher than the others in the surroundings, and he thought it might be a shaman's grave. When he came home and related the incident, Mikkel Gaup blamed his son for forgetting what he had taught him: to ask the dead for permission before camping— and especially when it concerned a dead shaman's grave. He got what he deserved, thought Mikkel Gaup (EFA. Protocol GD: 70).

According to an old Sami concept, to become a great shaman demanded certain characteristics—often seen as male qualities—such as courage, endurance, physical strength, resourcefulness, and natural and local knowledge. But if we go to the older written sources we have about Sami shamanism, it is not just men who were shamans, even though they are the majority, but women too are spoken of (Tolley 2009: 143–149, Pollan 1998: 97–103). In Ellen Marit's family it seems to have been both men and women who believed they had inherited special abilities and practiced as "wise men" or "wise women."

Ellen Marit was particularly concerned in her practice with medical treatment, and perhaps had little to do with "big matters." But in her account of her life, she creates a story that has as its highlight the meeting with the spirits and the way they test her courage and strength. She related both to a more undifferentiated spiritual world, in which she claimed that the spirits could take on any form, including human form, and to spirits whom she called by name (cf. Tolley 2009: 203–205). The names she used were names from the pre-Christian Sami religion. She did not seem to distinguish clearly between what she called the spirits and the dead, or between the spirit world and the world of the dead. She was aware of this herself:

> There are other spirits in nature than just dead people. Like some who might have got a little further towards complete development. I have not entirely clearly sorted out the idea for myself, whether the pure nature spirits are a level higher than human spirits. I think I have understood from the stories that it's the dead person who is at the lowest level. And so one can develop until one reaches the divine. I imagine that nature spirits have progressed further than the deceased. That's the way I imagine it. It is a kind of hierarchy. (EFA. Protocol GD: 70–71)

Although it was not quite clear to me which spirits she was talking about at any particular time, the belief in them and communication with them was an underlying note in her narration all the time, like the subtle chiming of a wind harp at the weakest breeze. The note is just there, but it breaks through more clearly when she talks about her personal crises, about how she visits holy sites, or performs certain rituals, or receives a message.

When she got a message from the spirits, as she often did, it was mostly about what she should do, or what she should leave be. Spirits expressed themselves through a voice that commanded, that gave orders that could not be contravened. The spirits were generals, while she was just a soldier.

Dream and Vision as a Divinatory Arena

The will of the spirits can be read from events or from certain signs and omens, and can be expressed in dreams and visions. For Ellen Marit, dreaming was important in her communication with the spirits. Some dreams and their interpretation create a structure in her narration and stand, if not as turning points, at least as milestones in her life. When young and inexperienced in interpreting dreams, she often turned to her father. Later she did not ask him for advice on interpreting the dreams, except in the most critical situations. But he was of great importance as an interpreter of the young Ellen Marit's dream of her dead grandmother calling her to her grave. This dream he interpreted as the spirits' choosing Ellen Marit, and the event signified a turning point in her life.

Three nights in a row Ellen Marit dreamed her dead grandmother was calling her. The grandmother saw her come to her grave and put flowers on it. The grave was a long and arduous day's journey away, where part of the journey had to be by rowing a boat and on foot. Ellen Marit wanted at first not to understand the dream's message. According to the older shamanic tradition, the election to be a shaman roused resistance from the one chosen. It was a responsibility that was not undertaken willingly. But after consulting with her father, she realized that it was not something she could refuse: then the dead would punish her. When the dead woman called a third time, there was no way around it if she wanted to hold on to life and health:

> So she came again the third night and said the same thing, and then I got a move on. Then I went to my father and told him that grandmother had visited me three nights in a row and asked me to come with flowers to her grave, "Well, you must understand what you have to do. You *have to* understand what you must do!" "Well, what shall I do then?" "Well, you must do what she tells you to." And so I did. (EFA. Protocol GD: 52)

No spirit comes a fourth time for a good purpose. If you did not understand the seriousness after the third time, it was all the worse for you. Ellen Marit's father understood the seriousness. He told her to do what the dead demanded, but first he taught her the rituals she needed to approach the realm of the dead and be protected against them. Ellen Marit also belonged to a tradition in which she did not have much choice when it came to the fate she was assigned in terms of the Sami community's views on naming. As the firstborn, she was given the name Marit after the long-dead grandmother who was now calling her. The name Ellen she received from her great-grandmother, who had raised Mikkel Gaup. Both of these women had special abilities and were able to treat disease. According to Sami and Norwegian folk belief, someone takes on the personality and skills of the person after whom they are named. The story of Ellen Marit's calling reflects a traditional society's focus on the group's influence on the individual's choice and the course of life marked out for him or her. It is not the individual who has free choice. The choice is bound up with the traditional regulatory framework and the group's preferences.

Ellen Marit's father and her husband followed her for the first part of the way to the grave, but then she had to go on alone. She got lost and walked and walked for many hours, but did not find it. Eventually, she got help from another member of the spirit world—a helping spirit in bird form:

> Suddenly there is a small sparrow which stops in front of me by the road-side—up in the air—and it flaps its wings, and stays perfectly still. I am as it were caught by this sparrow. So it flies to the left. Then I follow it with my gaze and see that only fifty meters from the trail lies the cemetery! I just had not seen it, although I had walked past it many times. So I did some rituals before I went through the church gate, and rituals when I came to the grave. It has a picket fence around the grave. So I put the flowers there, finished and left. Afterwards I realized that this was a test of my endurance, my patience. Thirdly, it was a test of obedience, that I could learn how to take a message and obey. My father taught me the rituals I should use. And he also made me aware that I would make that kind of contact and come up against tests like this. (cited in Alver 1999: 155–156)

Ellen Marit saw this religious experience as a final confirmation of election by the spirits, represented by her grandmother, and that her father would guide her all the way to becoming a "fully worthy shaman." She knew from him that to get the knowledge and insight that was needed, she had to expect that life would become tough for her. She had to build up her strength through mastering the challenges the spirits proffered. They wanted to test her to see if she was strong enough, good enough.

Later in the course of her life Ellen Marit's dreams continued to provide dream symbols that fit into an older Sami conceptual world. But as time passed and she gained more insight into a neo-religious thought-world, she adapted the interpretations of her dreams toward a brighter universe.

Chosen by Fate

A person's fate can be revealed through signs or a message from another world. Ellen Marit knew that her two sons would not survive her, and she told me this early on, before the elder one died. She had been given a message through a dream that still came back to her. It was a dream in which she and her sons were run down by black runaway horses, and she found herself on the roadside with the bleeding, dying boys pressed close to her.

But she did not just know *that* they were going to die but also *how* they would die. Her youngest son had a birthmark on his neck, as Ellen Marit's mother immediately saw when he was a newborn. To the close family her mother had said she was uneasy about that birthmark. She saw it as a sign that the child would not grow old, and that he would die a violent death. Marks on the body have been interpreted from of old in both Sami and Norwegian tradition as a sign or message from "another world."

In 1981 Ellen Marit lost her youngest son in a tragic accident when he was 18. It caused her to have still more anxiety over her eldest son's fate. For he too had a birthmark that foretold his fate. It was shaped like a fish. It was interpreted by the family elder as a sign that he would die in the water. In addition he slept with half-open eyes, which was also a traditional sign of drowning.

The youngest son's death confirmed Ellen Marit's belief that it was fated, and she was reluctant to leave the place in which her elder son was living. She reorganized her studies and her life to be in the city where he was. She could not free herself from the dream of the black horse as a symbol of death and her lifeless boys. One day in 1984 her son disappeared quite suddenly. The family took it fairly calmly—youngsters often follow their own mysterious ways. But after some days Ellen Marit dreamed that she saw him lying floating in water with his face turned over. The dream made her certain that he was dead. No one completely believed her desperate tale, however, except her father. He confided to Ellen Marit that he had had a vision in which he saw the boy coming toward him, his clothes drenched. A few weeks later the boy was found drowned.

The Danish scholar Per Stounbjerg writes in his discussion of the autobiographical text that the text creates hierarchies:

> Some events are highlighted as the core events, others are just garnish. The story provides a sequence of pointers in the form of reversals and turning points, and thus transforms life into an intelligible whole. We recognize it as narrative: we are recounting not just our lives. The story itself is one of the most important metaphors we use to understand it at all. (1994: 45–46)

In Ellen Marit's life story the tales about the doomed and death are absolutely central. The loss of those dearest to her is associated with the thought of what she must endure in order to tread the "shaman path" and have a part in secret knowledge. She was to feel the force of her father's words: "I cannot give you my strength. It is you who must build up your strength." After her youngest son's death she was so grief-stricken that she did not have the energy to get up from her bed and go to the friends and family who gathered in the house when the accident was discovered. She was completely paralyzed, wanting only to sleep, to be gone, to avoid taking part. Her father went to plead with her. He asked her to get up, to join the other mourners. He thought she was not behaving appropriately as a shaman or Sami by her self-imposed isolation. He told her that such intense grief was not something the spirits favored. They decide, and humans obey. He reminded her that death is not an absolute, and that it is just the side of life seen in the mirror. Dying is a transition to another life, another dimension. One must get used to living with death on the left side. Her father spoke to her not only as her spiritual guide but from an old Sami conceptual world and from the traditions of its society. Grief must be lived out in the community and through certain rituals. Her father's admonitions about who she was and what was expected of her forced her to her feet. But he said that did not give her life meaning; her loss had made her life into something else. Her father spoke to the shaman in her, and perhaps to the Sami, but not to the mother, the person. It was her elder son who did this. The fact that he was still there got her to start eating again.

For the first time in the narrative process Ellen Marit questioned the conceptual world her father stood for. She needed something other than the spirits' dominance over her life and ideas of the realm of the dead as a dark and dangerous house of spirits of which her son was now a part. A few weeks after her father touched upon her sense of duty and talked the "shaman" onto her feet, she had an experience in a new community. It was a women's community, which triggered a sense of closeness and security that she needed and gave her loss and her life new meaning:

> I was invited to a conference in Gothenburg a few weeks after my younger boy died. I was going to cancel the trip, but luckily my family was so sensible that they insisted that I should go—and it was good that I went. I had a powerful experience on 6 August—Hiroshima day. It was celebrated by the women at this conference by launching light boats (pieces of cardboard with lights on) into the canal. It was a stream of light flowing down as far as you could see—a wonderfully powerful vision. It was so very powerful to me, that I was not the only one who mourned, that I was not the only mother in the world who had lost a child. There are women who lose children every single day, every second, all year round. Think of all those women who lost their children in Hiroshima. Then a great calm came over me. After that, it was not so tough. (cited in Alver 1999: 159)

Away from the Sami community and from family, from expectations and obligations, she gave up her feelings of violence. In a world of light moving in flowing water, in solidarity with women who light candles and commemorate their dead, grief grew lighter. From looking at her son's death as a grim reflection of fate, she allowed herself a few moments, a few hours, a few days to concentrate on being a mother: to see the unfairness of the boy's death, the unfairness in other children dying, and the incomprehensible in Hiroshima—but an injustice and incomprehensibility that she shared with many.

After both sons were dead, the world of the dead and the spirit world were very different for her, because her boys were now situated there. She poeticized a brighter world for them. She met her boys in her dreams and experienced them as loving helpers. On the level of feeling and experience she had close contact with them and it filled her with warmth. The spirit world lost some of its fear and terror, but perhaps something of its power too. It became more human and less dangerous.

> I saw the lads like stars twinkling at me as I lay in bed, half-unconscious. Two stars coming toward me and twinkling and flashing and shining. Then they changed—and they stretched their hands toward me. I saw them walk no further. Well, I saw the elder—he came to me. I do not remember how long afterwards it was. Then he says: "Mum, you must not cry for me. I am in the light." And it was so beautiful. (cited in Alver 1999: 157)

In many ways her depiction of life in the realm of the dead resembles the many contemporary tales of near-death experiences, permeated by a tone of beauty, light and joy (Alver 1999: 57–74).

Meeting the Goddesses

After the reverberations from the Alta conflict leveled off, Ellen Marit continued to fight for minority rights. Inspired by her friendship with the social psychologist and politician Berit Ås, she was also concerned with women's equality and peace processes more generally. Berit Ås had heard about Ellen Marit and invited her to speak at a Nordic conference on women in Denmark in 1979, which discussed politics and work in light of women's emancipation (Haslund 2008: 204–205). Ellen Marit agreed to attend. Here she appeared not only as a lecturer on male and female gods in the pre-Christian Sami religion but also as a "healer" for the various conference participants. And not just that: Berit Ås relates that Ellen Marit taught the conference women the ritual moon dance: "We danced in the middle of the night to various words that I do not remember: a large ring of over a hundred women charmed by Ellen Marit's beauty and individuality." Later Berit Ås and Ellen Marit met each other over a common cause in the Alta conflict both in Finnmark and in Oslo, and at the peace conference in Gothenburg in 1981. In 1987, Berit Ås wanted to examine how peace and women's studies were pursued at American universities and to try to create interest in raising money for a women's university in Løten, which was inaugurated 1985. Close political friends insisted that she had to have a secretary with her who would help her maintain a record of what she experienced and got out of the trip. Berit Ås asked Ellen Marit, who said yes. This six-week trip, in which she interacted closely with Berit Ås while visiting various American universities and other institutions, had a great influence on her, in both the political field and the religious (Haslund 2008: 202–215). Berit Ås's political enthusiasm for equality and peace affected Ellen Marit. In her life story it emerges in her reflections on the importance of forgiveness to achieve peace in the world, and how pure ritual can empty the mind of hateful thoughts. When it comes to the religious and the magical, it was also on this trip that she made contact within the academic world with a group of women who belonged to a neo-religious movement. Ellen Marit called them "goddesses" (see Orenstein 1990). Berit Ås had good opportunities to see Ellen Marit as both a political and a religious player on this trip. When I asked what she thought of her, she replied,

> I admired her for her strength and determination, her courage and strong integrity. That she behaved as if she had those powers and insights that she had, and did not give up or stop through other people's condescension, I see as something almost worthy of wonder. (Letter from Berit Ås, November 30, 2013)

The American goddesses looked upon Ellen Marit as an interesting acquaintance, because for them she was a "primeval woman," a shaman and an icon of their quest for the power of nature, for the protection of the environment and Mother Earth, and for the true and original. Central in this neo-religious contact network was the literary scholar and ecofeminist Gloria Orenstein. She and Ellen Marit made such a good contact that she visited Ellen Marit in Norway, as she wanted to learn about "real shamanism" from her. Orenstein found herself a private trainer so that she could physically cope with the hardships of the north Norwegian mountain landscape. Ellen Marit took her to the plains, and together they visited the ancient holy places and the centers of power. Ellen Marit related that Orenstein had come to the conclusion that the two were "soul mates" or twin souls, and that they had had contact with each other on the mental level before they met on Ellen Marit's American trip. For example, this soul friendship also manifested itself for Orenstein in that she felt the same pain in the body as Ellen Marit when Ellen Marit had cancer. Ellen Marit did not know what to think about this "soul mates" business, which did not entirely fit into her conceptual world, but the two had close contact with each other right up to Ellen Marit's death.

Both Orenstein and Ellen Marit spoke of their relationship as one between teacher and student. Ellen Marit influenced Orenstein through her teaching on the Sami conceptual world, but Orenstein's thought-world also colored Ellen Marit's way of thinking. As an effect of the influence of this world of ideas of the "goddesses," Ellen Marit's guide suddenly began to address her in English.

Orenstein discusses Ellen Marit as her teacher in the article "Toward an Ecofeminist Ethic of Shamanism and the Sacred" (1993). She puts her forward as a person who uses her dreams and visions as a baseline for her political work, and she says of her, "Being a political leader was being a spiritual leader, and vice versa." Orenstein recounts her visit to Ellen Marit in Finnmark, in which she felt that she was learning about "genuine shamanism" as opposed to what she had learned previously in neoshamanistic workshops. Orenstein describes very clearly some interesting differences between the two women's ways of thinking:

> From my own experience in Samiland, I know that I was always waiting to meet my "power animal" and my shaman teacher was always taking me to the real reindeer, the real birds, the real mosquitoes. It wasn't until she communicated with birds, brought them to us, talked with them, and sent them away, or until she "psyched out" the problem of a lost reindeer, that I began to understand how the neo-shamanic narrative from contemporary workshops had actually blinded me to the fact that real animals are also spirit and power, and, at least to my shaman teacher, they were every bit as important, or even more so, than her owl spirit guide who had appeared to her in childhood.
>
> Sometimes I used to feel that I had a more "shamanic" perspective than she did, because I was always coming up with sophisticated symbolic interpretations of dreams and I was always looking for "power animals," while she seemed to be more interested in the real animals and she understood the figures in dreams to represent the spirits of real people. The truth is that she made less of a distinction than we do between real and spirit people or animals. To her, all was real, all was spirit, all was sacred, simultaneously. There was no contradiction in that. (1993)

New Horizons

Encountering a new horizon of opportunity, and inspired by her feminist and neo-religious networks, Ellen Marit developed a rebellious attitude toward the control that she experienced on many levels from both forces and people. This rebelliousness is seen in her treatment in the last phase of her life of the stringent regulatory framework for rituals and ritual usage in the old Sami conceptual world, when she inaugurated a different approach to the rituals. The rituals became more individual, more personal, more creative. For example, one of her very last rites exemplifies a different view from what her father had taught her. She described how she helped a group of people rid themselves of hatred, for example against former spouses. Ellen Marit was at that time too ill to participate as a leader of the ritual, but it was conducted according to her instructions:

> They should get themselves two big cloths, one red and one yellow, big enough to put them around themselves. Then they should put on some old clothes, some clothes that they could discard. Then they should find a place to burn them or a river they could throw the things into.... First, they should put on the old clothes, then wrap them in a bundle and throw them into the water while wearing the red fabric around them. It symbolizes power. Then they should offer various prayers. These they could make up themselves, ritual prayers based on the idea that the spirits should help them get rid of hatred. When they have done this ritual, they should dress in different clothes and don the yellow fabric. The yellow symbolizes spirituality. They should pray the spirit to fill them, so that they would be filled with more love and that power of love should take the place where hatred had been.... You have to prepare yourself mentally for the rituals. You must build this up and plan it and enter it on the mental level too. You must conduct these rituals in this way. And the words you say, you must adapt to your situation and what affects you. There is no uniform recipe for this; it can suit all cultures and all people throughout the world. (cited in Alver 1999: 163).

The ritual has a traditional Sami feel, including the color symbolism and the way the evil is destroyed. But the reflexivity associated with what is said and done and the show of love power, replacing hatred and filling the mind space, seems to have originated in the neo-religious conceptual world.

Ellen Marit's rebelliousness is also seen in her struggle against the idea that her bitter fate was directed by the spirits, and that she had nothing with which to resist these trials. She was looking for a different understanding and found assistance in neo-religious notions. These neo-religious ideas had shown her a way through the grief over the loss of her sons and had opened up the notions of death and a friendly kingdom of death, which she did not find in older Sami ideology. She was confident that her sons were with her on a mental level, that she communicated with them daily in a different way from how she otherwise communicated with the spirit world. The grief opened up a religious experience in which she felt she was one with the universe, an experience of limits being effaced between humans and the powers, between life and death, between vision and dream, dream and reality. Before her elder son died, he painted a wall where he lived with a huge, brilliant sun. For Ellen

Marit, this was a sign that the sons were in a realm of light, in a kingdom of love—a land she too would come to. She found peace in the belief that they would come back in new shapes for a better life than the life they had been wrenched from so abruptly. "I have lost both my children. But I think that they were not supposed to have a longer time in this life. They had to move on. They were developed enough to proceed to the next phase" (EFA. Protocol GD: 125).

Love Power

In her final years, Ellen Marit expanded her views on the power that was central to her thought-world and to her actions, and its limits. She gave the power she related to a new name. She called it love power.

> It just gets clearer and clearer, the deeper one penetrates into this stuff. That what is important is love and the power of love. And love is what permeates all creation.... If you first discover the amazing power it is and what it can do, against all evil and enmity, so you are never in doubt any more. (cited in Alver 1999: 162)

This power, which she had attached to the spirit world and the dead ancestors and sacred places, we meet now in humanity itself. Ellen Marit flitted in and out of different thought-worlds and belief systems. She still talked about the spirits out there and their permission to develop and strengthen the power, but she also moved the center of power from something outside the person to something that exists in herself. She saw humanity as divine in a different way from before. But the belief that power can be used for specific purposes, that the magic works, is there all the time.

> Spirituality is there. And that's the biggest part of every human being. Some people have these abilities to a greater degree and can develop them more strongly than others. But everyone can develop them more than they actually do. You have to find your own answers through listening to your guide or guides, then you will arrive at the answer—the answer that is for you.... Your road or path does not need to look like my path, but the goal is the same. The goal is to become divine. What my guides have told me is that everyone can create their own rituals based on the position they are in, based on their own background.... When you do these rituals, it is the core of your being. What you do and what you say—the meaning of it is that you fix your whole attention on the core of spirituality, on the divine. It is the goal of every soul to be divine. (cited in Alver 1999: 162)

The goddess ideology gave her concepts and categories to fill in the words. She used the term "spirituality" and talked about development and the way into the core of the individual. It is as if the ego or the "I-person" gets bigger. She talked about the individual ways to go about finding my answers and yours. After she focused her thoughts on love power in her life story, she said that she did not think she could have explained so clearly what power was ten years earlier, because she did not have or did not want to use the words she now used. But for me the power at which she marveled and questioned a decade before was the same power to which she related as she lay on her sickbed.

Journeys Back and Forth

Ellen Marit essentially had little freedom within the older Sami conceptual world and the traditional reindeer-herding community, which was her background. Her role as the family's elect with powers of mediation was governed by the expectations of the family and community. But she made her choices. If one is to believe what she says, she followed her will from childhood on. That she managed to do so, she explained, was because she was a child who received much love and attention. Without doubt, her life story shows a child who was allowed to fend for herself early on, who had a great responsibility for siblings and daily home routines laid upon her, but who also, filled with fantasy as she was, found room for herself, a space to learn and play. She was not to be the wife material they tried to make her; she took her stand on getting more schooling and chose an academic career and to some extent a life in the city, instead of marrying into reindeer-herding.

She had a rebellious streak in herself, a desire to break free, but as is often the case, she paid for it with a longing to return. All her life she flitted between different belief systems and different contexts. Her practice as a shaman or "wise woman" was bound up with an older Sami conceptual world with her father as a spiritual guide. Although she was against all forms of neoshamanism, and she and her father looked at that kind of shamanism as deception, her own world of ideas, advice and treatment practices were gradually colored by neo-religious ideas, although she vehemently denied it. It may, of course, be because neo-religious ideas gradually became mainstream in Norwegian society. But her contact with Berit Ås, especially their week-long travels in the United States in 1987, the context of peace and women's conferences, and her relationship with the ecofeminist Gloria Orenstein were important for her development as both a political and religious player. The ideas of the "goddesses" about the protection of Mother Earth and nature, and humanity as divine, were reflected in Ellen Marit's imagination and helped open up a brighter spirit world than the older Sami one. Among the "goddesses" she also encountered a longed-for sounding board for the individual, for the proximate, for intimate relationships, feelings, and experiences, and not least an arena in which political and religious commitment fused. What separates Ellen Marit from many other Norwegian "wise women" is that she used her special abilities not only to benefit the individual but also for the group, for society. This creates a firm connection back to the ideas of the old noaidi.

One of late modernity's core concepts is creativity. "To be oneself and exist as a creative human, what higher happiness can be achieved? This is the highest value" (Hauge 1990: 58). Ellen Marit as a creative person regarded magic and the magical as the key to creativity, to shaping and changing. The belief in power, and that this power could accomplish and be used, was the essence, the very core, of her life's work toward forming an identity. Ellen Marit's life story is about how people use this magic to understand and recount who they are and what they want.

When in her narrative she lends shape and color to the power, she ends up beside her father, with what he said, what he did, what he was. There, on her bed, bound up in her body and her pain, loaded down with love energies from a network of friends who were more or less linked with neo-religious contexts, she waited for her father to come and make her healthy or—in the last stage—*whole*. She was convinced that she was in the last stage of her development to becoming a fully worthy shaman. But in her thoughts and her story her father underwent a transformation. He was like a savior and like the top of the hierarchy. His magical world and that of the "goddesses" merged into one universe in which the common denominator was nature as sacred, and in which he was the overseer of nature, of creativity, of love.

Ellen Marit asked to tell her story, to be allowed to remember, to understand why things had to be as they were, or turned out. Through narration her various identities and her various roles knitted together into a whole, something meaningful to leave behind. 'Life's pattern one recognizes only when one wanders life's paths anew" (Stounbjerg 1994: 45). What she told me relates to the events of her life. But through the journey back she gave form to what she thought lay ahead for her. There up ahead were her boys. When she had finished her long story, she was silent and became completely still. Her gaze slid past me and fixed on something far, far away: "Look," she said, "look at the boys! They're standing there at the gate like two twinkling stars, waiting for me."

Notes

1. The text is translated by Dr. Clive Tolley, Docent, Department of Folkloristics, University of Turku, Finland.

2. "A "wise" person perceives him or herself as someone with special abilities and as a channel for supernatural powers. As a wise woman she exists in a state of power deriving from the fact that her surroundings accept who she is, and treats her on the basis of the values and norms traditionally associated with this institution" (Alver and Selberg 1992: 61).
3. On the "reader" and the reader's characteristics, see Myrvoll 2010: 148–153.
4. My knowledge of her is not limited to this one text. I spoke with her many times about her attitudes toward and use of her special abilities, about folk medicine and about her way of understanding illness and treatment.
5. See also Fonneland on the wise woman Esther Utsi's vision of Polmakmoen Guest House. This vision goes beyond the idea of the guest house as just a place for holiday guests and conference participants. "Her hope is that the personal, spiritual and cultural experience she offers her guests will impact at a higher, political level, and contribute to the development of a new economic era" (2012).
6. On Harner's development of core shamanism, see Harner 1980. On Harner, see Svanberg 2003: 97–103. Svanberg says, "If it was Carlos Castaneda and books about meetings with Don Juan that established the interest in neo-shamanism in the West, it was Michael Harner who made sure that there was a practical approach to the practice of a view of life which previously it had long been possible to encounter only in literary depictions, expressing a shamanic interpretation of reality and ways of living. Literary shamanism is supplemented for Harner with practical application." (2003: 97)
7. Paradoxically the role of princess haunted her. In some ways she was different in the Sami communities in Finnmark. This otherness was in some groups considered arrogance, and she was called "princess." She was beautiful then too, as fairy-tale princesses always are.
8. See the description of the Alta conflict in Kraft and Fonneland's introduction, here.
9. In this campaign, this women's group met opposition from their own people. Especially the Laestadian Sami were against rising up against the authorities, something they looked upon as a sin against God. See the similar presentation of the issue in Myrvoll 2010: 230–252.
10. Before she got as far as the main subject, she became seriously ill and had to interrupt her studies.

References

Alver, Bente Gullveig. 1999. "At dø—og at vende tilbage! En moderne vision om det genvundne paradis" and "Det magiske menneske: Magi som perspektiv for identitetsarbejde og selvforståelse," in Bente Gullveig Alver, Ingvild Sælid Gilhus, Lisbeth Mikaelsson, and Torunn Selberg (eds.), *Myte, magi og mirakel i møte med det moderne*. Oslo: Pax, 57–74 and 147–164.
Alver, Bente Gullveig, and Torunn Selberg. 1992. *"Det er mer mellom himmel og jord": Folks forståelse av virkeligheten ut fra forstillinger om sykdom og behandling*. Sandvika: Vett & Viten.

Brynn, Grace, and Bente Brunvoll. 2011. *Erik Myrhaug: sjaman for livet*. Oslo: Nova.

Dunfjeld, Ellen Marit Gaup. 1979. *Reindrift: Samisk næring, samisk fremtid*. Tromsø: Norsk Reindriftsamers Landsforbund.

Eriksson, Jørgen I. 1988. *Samisk shamanism*. Umeå: h:ström.

Fonneland, Trude A. 2010. "Samisk nysjamanisme: i dialog med (for)tid og stad: En kulturanalytisk studie av nysjamanar sine erfaringsforteljingar—identitetsforhandlinger og verdiskaping." Doctoral dissertation, University of Bergen.

———. 2012. "Spiritual Entrepreneurship in Northen Landscape. Spirituality, Tourism and Politics," *Temenos* 48(2): 11–27.

Gaup, Ailo. 2005. *Sjamansonen*. Oslo: Tre bjørner forlag.

Harner, Michael. 1980. *The Way of the Shaman: A Guide to Power and Healing*. San Francisco: Harper & Row.

Haslund, Ebba. 2008. *Ild fra asker: Et portrett av Berit Ås*. Oslo: Pax.

Hauge, Hans. 1990. "Før, under og efter subjektet," in Hans Hauge (ed.), *Subjektets status. Om subjektfilosofi, metafysik og modernitet*. Aarhus: Aarhus universitetsforlag, 52–72.

Myrvoll, Marit. 2010. ""Bare gudsordet duger": Om kontinuitet og brudd i samisk virkelighetsforståelse." Doctoral dissertation. University of Tromsø.

Orenstein, Gloria Feman. 1990. *The Reflowering of the Goddess*. Oxford: Pergamon Press.

———. 1993. "Towards an Ecofeminist Ethic of Shamanism and the Sacred," in Carol J. Adams (ed.) *Ecofemnism and the Sacred*. New York: Continuum. Read on Web: http://www.babaylan.net/wordpress/toward-an-ecofeminist-ethic-of-shamanism-and-the-sacred/

Pollan, Brita. 1993. *Samiske sjamaner: Religion og helbredelse*. Oslo: Gyldendal.

Skånby, Sten. 2005. "Den mystiske indianen: Schamanism i skäringspunkten mellan populärkultur, forsking och nyandlighet." Doctoral dissertation. Stockholm University.

Stounbjerg, Per. 1994. "Livet som forbillede: Om den selvbiografiske fortælling." *K & K*, 21(76): 43–54.

Ström, Anne-Karine. 2013. Bergit: *Helbredende hender*. Oslo: Orfeus.

Svanberg, Jan. 2003. *Schamantropologi i gränslandet mellan forsking och praktik: En studie av förhållandet mellan schamanismforskning och neoschamanism*. Åbo: Åbo Akademi University Press.

Tolley, Clive. 2009. *Shamanism in Norse Myth and Magic*. FF Communications, 144, no. 296. Helsinki: Academia Scientiarum Fennica.

References

The interview material is stored in the Ethno-folkloristic Archive (EFA), University of Bergen. According to Ellen Marit Gaup Dunnfjeld's wish, it is closed and not publicly available before 2021.

Earlier short versions in Norwegian and Danish of Ellen Marit's life are found in Alver and Selberg 1992, Alver, Gilhus, Mikaelsson and Selberg 1999.

III

Neoshamanism in Secular
Contexts

9

Sami Shamanism and Indigenous Film: The Case of *Pathfinder*

Cato Christensen

Nils Gaup's 1987 *Pathfinder*[1] is usually referred to as the first ever Sami feature film. It was a genre-specific action-adventure film, set in an ancient past, in a harsh, snow-covered landscape. It told the story of Aigin, a young Sami boy, whose resourcefulness and etic values save his people from a band of murderous bandits.

The film was an immediate success, both commercially and critically. It was even nominated for an Academy Award. It was hailed for its grandeur, its visual beauty, its suspense, but perhaps most importantly, its ethnopolitical importance. The film was seen as a statement of the worth of Sami culture—to the world, but particularly to Sami communities. By the mid-1980s, many Sami had been assimilated into Norwegian-ness, and found themselves out of touch with their Sami ethnicity and even ashamed of links to anything "Sami." To them, *Pathfinder* was described as a boost for "pride and identity" (*Norwegian News Agency* 1987).

This chapter focuses on a somewhat neglected aspect of *Pathfinder* as an ethnopolitical phenomenon, namely its emphasis on religion. Drawing heavily on ethnographic accounts of Sami pre-Christian shamanism, so-called *noaidevuohta*, *Pathfinder* offers an elaborate portrayal of religious aspects of ancient Sami society. But the film's religiosity, I argue, was much more than a merely "apolitical" cinematographic adaptation; it was embedded in broader discourses of establishing markers of a new postcolonial Sami identity.[2]

I discuss *Pathfinder* from a cultural-analytical perspective (cf. Ginsburg 1991). Emphasis will be put on the film's mediation of meaning and its connection to broader discourses of Sami ethnopolitics. Besides the film itself, I will examine media coverage in connection with its 1987 release and interviews with filmmaker Nils Gaup. I also reference other films that shed light on the subject matter. The discussion is structured into five sections, but principally moves back and forth as it aims to conceptualize *Pathfinder*'s emphasis on religion, both in terms of broader discourses of reclaiming the Sami past, and processes of "indigenization" of Sami ethnopolitics.

An Ethnopolitical Movie

Coming home from a hunting trip, the young Sami boy Aigin (Mikkel Gaup) witnesses the murder of his parents and younger sister by a band of black-clothed marauders, the *Tchudes*. Aigin watches the Tchudes from a hilltop when he is noticed. He is shot and wounded by an arrow, but eventually manages to escape to a neighboring *siida* (reindeer community). In fear of an imminent Tchude attack, most of the nomadic Sami group leaves for safer territory by the coast. Aigin and a few other men stay behind to fight the Tchudes. The men are slaughtered. Only Aigin survives. He is captured and forced to act as a pathfinder for the Tchudes, to lead them to the Sami's coastal settlement...

Pathfinder was action oriented, fast moving, high on suspense, and brutal. The media emphasized its international and "Hollywood-like" profile. It was especially noted that the film bore a close resemblance to the Western genre (Iversen 2005, Solum 1997). It was referred to as a "Sami Western" or a "Northern" (Dahl 1987). Several newspapers also highlighted the fact that it was the first Nordic film shot in the grand format of 70 millimeter and equipped with Dolby stereo sound in six channels. Presumably, in 1987, this was an audiovisual power pack reserved only for the biggest blockbusters (Haave 1987a).

The film was a significant breach with the norms of filmmaking in Norway at the time, because of its grandeur and genre specificity, but most importantly because of its ethnic dimension (Iversen 2005). Although Norwegian cinema had occasionally featured Sami characters and, to various degrees, centered on Sami-related themes in the past, this was the first feature film ever to depict Sami culture from "the inside" (Christensen 2012a, Skarðhamar 2008). The director, Nils Gaup, was himself a Sami. The film used Northern Sami (*Davvisámegiella*) as the main language of dialogue. It was shot on location in the midst of the Sami core areas in Finnmark, the northernmost county of Norway, and most of the cast were local Sami amateur actors. Aigin was the first-ever true Sami hero on film (Mecsei, in Kulås 2008). The story of the film, although presented in the familiar cinematographic idiom of American adventure movies, was also deeply embedded in Sami culture and tradition. It was adapted from Sami folktales, framed in the title sequence as a "story that has been passed down from generation to generation for nearly 1000 years." The media reported that Nils Gaup, the director, had "first heard the story from his father, who in turn had heard it from his father" (Haave 1987b, my translation).

Pathfinder was born out of an ongoing process of Sami political and cultural revitalization. It was launched in a crucial period in terms of raising Sami ethnic awareness both inside and outside Sami communities (Eidheim 1998). The decade of the film's release, the 1980s, was initiated with the so-called Alta conflict (1979–1981). This event marked a watershed in terms of placing Sami rights issues on the Norwegian national political agenda, and finally putting an end to the politics of assimilation that had dominated the Norwegian-Sami relationship for over a century (ibid., Minde 2003). In the wake of the Alta conflict, the ongoing Sami social movement came to attract more and more people and to express itself in new ways and in new arenas, beyond strictly political channels. Art and popular culture now became tools for forging a new postcolonial Sami identity (Eidheim 1998).

Entwined in the cultural and political situation of the mid-1980s, *Pathfinder* took part in a broader discourse concerning "what it meant to be a Sami," what the characteristics of Sami culture were, and how Sami tradition and history should be viewed. In his extensive analyses, folklorist Thomas DuBois argues that the film, as such, should be seen an expression of the Sami "community's conscious choice to maintain and reassert cultural difference despite (or even because of) long-term processes of acculturation, language attrition, and political disenfranchisement" (2000: 256). *Pathfinder*, he argues, was "a proposition to Sami and non-Sami alike regarding the identity and future of Sami people" (ibid.). DuBois especially brings to the fore the film's promotion of cultural traits, as signifiers of ethnic distinction and communality. While not a prime concern in DuBois' analysis, religion—I argue—is perhaps most prominent as such.

Religion as a Cinematographic Theme

Religion plays a significant role in *Pathfinder*. Supplementing the action-oriented core plot, the film gives rich descriptions of the ancient Sami society's religious dimensions. With a seemingly impressive degree of historical meticulousness and heavily drawing on ethnographic material, the film depicts several known aspects of pre-Christian Sami noaide-vuohta. It features, for instance, a noaidi (shaman) as a leading character.

It depicts shamanic drum rituals, performed with a richly and beautifully decorated drum, and it depicts animal visions and bird omens. In general, the film presents a cinematographic universe wherein people's lives are highly determined by spiritual beliefs and notions, such as beliefs in predestination and the guidance of visions, and where undertaking religious rituals is an integral aspect of everyday life. For instance, an extensive sequence of the film is devoted to the traditional bear hunt ritual of the Sami (cf. Hultkrantz 2000). As the protagonist, Aigin, finds his way to a larger group of Sami while fleeing from the evil Tchudes, the whole group is involved in performing rituals following the killing of the bear: dancing around a fire, spitting chewed birch bark on the hunters to reduce "the power of killing."

Religion also forms the basis for a prominent subplot in the film, focusing on the growing bond between the young protagonist, Aigin, and the noaidi, Raste (Nils Utsi). The subplot is set even in the first sequence, before the opening credits. By voice-over, we hear a man telling about visions of seeing a reindeer bull for the third time. The man is later revealed to be the noaidi, and the vision is a foresight of his own death. This adds an extra dimension to the immanent Tchude threat, beyond the mere matter of survival. Knowing he will die, the noaidi Raste has to find his successor, to ensure the continuance of the religious tradition of the Sami. As the plot progresses and the significance of this religious tradition to the Sami is elaborated, we come to understand the severity of the situation. Religion is essential to the Sami society, its foremost characteristic and inducement. It is what constitutes them as a people and is inherently tied to their existence.

Religion is the primary cultural trait that differentiates the Sami from the Tchudes. A prominent leitmotif in the film is the contrast in worldview between the two ethnic groups. This is made particularly explicit in a core scene midway into the film, as the old noaidi conveys insight into his (the Sami's) worldview to the young, inexperienced Aigin. In this scene, Raste warns the young hero of losing site of the "interconnectedness" that binds him to his Sami community and his environment, or else he himself becomes a Tchude, "a man who has lost the path, stumbling blindly towards self-destruction." The religious theme culminates in the film's final scene. As the old noaidi has been killed in the fight against the Tchude villains, Aigin now becomes the Sami community's spiritual "pathfinder." With the aid of his resourcefulness, Aigin has managed to stop the Tchudes' attack, and now he also ensures that the spiritual foundation of the Sami people is upheld. "We always have a pathfinder," a woman states, as she hands Aigin the ritual drum. These are the final words spoken in the film.

From a purely technical perspective, these religious motifs, symbols, and props serve important aesthetic functions in the film. They add a touch of mystery to the story, making it more than a mere action film. They form a narrative strand to supplement the rather formulaic, hero-villain core story, providing an "extra layer" to characterization, imagery, plot development, and suspense. Lengthy sequences focusing on religious ritual, for instance, help give complexity to the Sami characters, hence promoting emotional investment among audiences in their well-being in the face of war and genocide. But in so doing, the weight given to religion in the film also goes beyond the merely aesthetic. The story of Aigin, his *rite de passage* and initiation as a shaman forms the basis of *Pathfinder* as a moral tale, about the essence and foundation of Sami culture, and its resilience toward outside threats. As such, religion sits at the core of the film's affiliation with a broader process of Sami identity construction, an articulation of the essence of Sami culture, its uniqueness and seminal foundation.

Recuperating the Religious Past

Pathfinder could be seen as an example of what anthropologist Faye Ginsburg (1991, 2002) referred to as "screen memories," that is, a cinematographic recreation of the past directed at rectifying alleged misrepresentations or neglect of the given community's past in the discourse of dominant society. While not portraying an actual historic event, *Pathfinder*'s folktale-based story expressed a retelling of history from a pronounced Sami perspective. The film resonated with broader discourses circulating at the time about reclaiming and recuperating the Sami history and past. As discussed by, for instance, anthropologist Harald Eidheim (1998), the conceptualization of an ethnically distinct history has been vital to the process of Sami cultural revitalization. A prime orientation of the Sami movement has been to collectivize a notion of the Sami as "a people who had established their homeland on the tundra, the coasts and the woodlands in the north long before the Nordic people arrived at the scene" (ibid.: 42). *Pathfinder*, envisioning a mythical past in which Sami natives faced the threat of invading outsiders, was arguably an enactment of such ideas.

In media coverage in connection with the 1987 premiere, such intentions with the film were prominent. The focus was, on the one hand, on the extensive course of research into Sami history and tradition that had gone into making the narrative, settings, props, and costumes of the film as authentic as possible. Allegedly, the film team had consulted both scholars and different museums, including the Tromsø University Museum—a world-leading center for research on Sami history and pre-Christian religion. In one interview, Gaup put it like this: "I have read heaps of books about Sami culture; even the ancient Romans have written down something about it. And we have consulted several scholars" (Bakkemoen 1987, my translation).

On the other hand, emphasis was on intentions within the film to recodify Sami history and tradition, to make it adaptable to the current ethnopolitical situation. For instance, the focus was on director Nils Gaup's "belief in the powerful potential of Sami culture" and his intention for the film to "give the Sami increased confidence their own identity and culture" (Berntzen 1988, my translation). As *The Norwegian News Agency* put it, "Unquestionably, his [Gaup's] driving force is to show the strength and diversity of Sami culture, and to accentuate the historical lines of this minority that have opposed Norwegian assimilation politics for centuries" (Tonstad 1987, my translation).

Infusing the film with religious motifs and symbols seems to have been at the core of the intentional "traditionalization" of Sami culture and identity. In interviews, the opportunity to convey Sami traditional religiosity to a contemporary audience was even stated to be the prime motivation for making the film in the first place. As Gaup himself put it,

> Originally, the plan was to make a film about a spiritual leader, like the film's Raste character. At one time I consulted a scholar of shamanism, but I abandoned the project because I could not find a good story there. I got the feeling that the story of the shaman lacked tension.... The story of the young boy and the Tchudes, however, that's pure suspense. In a way, it was my way of tricking people into getting something from both kinds of story (Gaup, in Løchen 2003: 102, my translation)

In terms of accentuating the historical lines of Sami culture, emphasis on pre-Christian shamanism was, arguably, all but natural. Probably no aspect of Sami culture and tradition was more in need of recuperation than the religious tradition.

Throughout history, religion has been a prime ethnic marker of the Sami people. Even the oldest known sources on Sami society emphasize their religiosity as a constituting cultural feature, what distinguishes them as a group, different from other "peoples" (cf. *Historia Norwegiæ*, tenth century). However, the descriptions of Sami religion have for the most part been derogatory, contrasting Sami heathenism, sorcery, and devilry to true Christianity and civilization (Kristiansen 2001). Such descriptions were at the core of the intense Christian mission directed toward the Sami from the seventeenth century onward, and also a foundation for the more extensive politics of assimilation that was undertaken from the middle of the nineteenth century, officially lasting up until World War II, and for all practical concerns even longer (ibid.). The result of the Christian missionizing and assimilation politics was that the old religion—the Sami noaidevuohta—gradually disappeared (Rydving 1993). As most Sami were christened and many came to affiliate with the Lutheran revival movement of Læstadianism, the pre-Christian religious past came to be commonly viewed as illicit (DuBois 2000). Oppressed and devalued for centuries, Sami shamanism and pre-Christian traditions came to carry little allure for most Sami. This was the situation even in the mid-1980s, during the time period when *Pathfinder* premiered. The process of raising Sami ethnic, cultural, and political awareness was well on its way, not least following the aforementioned Alta conflict. But the religious past, Sami pre-Christian traditions, remained a delicate matter.

While arguably in need of recuperation, Gaup's emphasis on religion was also probably, for the very same reason, somewhat risky. Indeed, as folklorist Thomas DuBois (2000) notes, the religious aspects of the film, the references to Sami pre-Christian religion, held a tremendously divisive potential in the Sami society of the 1980s. *Pathfinder*'s depiction of Sami pre-Christian religion could even have been, he argues, "a threat to the feelings of unity and consensus, which the revitalist work should evoke" (ibid.:268).

There might be several reasons why negative responses from Sami communities never came. Most notably in that regard, *Pathfinder*'s account of Sami shamanism was characterized by avoidance of the sorest elements of the Sami community's religious conflicts. For one thing, the narrative of the movie was placed in the era prior to the arrival of Christianity in Sami society. The film thus avoided making a dichotomization between Christianity and Sami noaidevuohta part of the plot, and also avoided taking sides as such. In other words, the film's account of shamanism just "blended in" as part of the narrative's time period, and with no other option, the film's Sami could hardly be blamed for their religious affiliation.

The film also excluded the potentially most problematic aspects of Sami pre-Christian religiosity from being represented. This included, for instance, the aspect of trance, perhaps the most disdained aspect of historical noaidevuohta. Reading from ethnographic sources, the noaidi falling into trance was a salient aspect of the Sami pre-Christian ritual (Bäckmann and Hultkrantz 1978). But over the course of Christian mission and assimilation politics, this element became a primary subject of suppression and disgrace in Sami societies—a symbol of heathenism, idolatry, sorcery, and sacrilege (Mebius 2000). Trance has also been associated with so-called "arctic hysteria" and has therefore laid the foundation for highly derogatory characterizations of Sami people as inherently mentally unstable by nature and especially predisposed to hysteria and obsession (ibid., Pollan 1993). Even today trance is still a somewhat shameful aspect of Sami pre-Christian religion, often associated with negative stereotypes about the Sami as drunken and staggering (Mebius 2000). So, even though trance, and shamanic trance journeys, is given a central place in ethnographic descriptions of traditional noaidevuohta, it was totally excluded from *Pathfinder.*

A similar point can be made about the film's treatment of the musical expression of *joik.* Joik is included in the film, both as part of the film score (by Sami artist Nils-Aslak Valkeapää) and the plot, but without the religious associations documented in much ethnographic material. Joik in pre-Christian Sami society was primarily linked to the noaidi, as a means of evoking trance (Olsen 2004). As such, just like trance, joik also has a history of being a somewhat delicate matter in Sami society. Several examples can be given illustrating that joik has been problematic and divisive for the Sami population, even quite recently (Kraft 2009a). For example, both Nils-Aslak Valkeapää's joiking during the opening ceremony of the Lillehammer Winter Olympic Games in 1994 and Sami artist Mari Boine's "hymn joik" during the Norwegian Crown Prince couple's wedding in 2001 met with strong objections, particularly in Laestadian milieus (ibid., see also Kraft in this volume). *Pathfinder's* emphasis on joik as a purely musical, rather than religious, phenomenon was inherently sensitive to such tendencies.

Other aspects of *Pathfinder's* version of Sami pre-Christian religion might be interpreted in the same way. Corresponding to the exclusion of trance and the secularization of joik, the film included neither elaborative accounts of shamanic initiation nor gods. In this way, the film further avoided provocative aspects of "the old Sami heathen religion." Additionally, the noaidi, Raste, is depicted as a highly sympathetic character. Raste is an active, responsible, and indisputably good community member. He represents common sound values such as harmony, compassion, selfless devotion, and ecological sustainability. Generally, the religiosity of the film was given only positive connotations. It was not only sensitive to potentially negative prejudices from the film's contemporary Sami communities, but arguably also sufficiently ambiguous as to conflict neither with Christian nor secular worldviews, for that matter. The depiction of religion in the film was, one might argue, accommodated so as to be acceptable and unifying even across disparities in a diverse Sami population. And Sami shamanism was promoted as the common ground upon which to assert this unified Sami identity.

Indigenous Spirituality

The weight given to religion in *Pathfinder* might also be understood beyond the national context of the Sami-Norwegian relationship and the stigmas associated with Sami pre-Christian religiosity. This brings to the fore that the Sami awakening out of which the film obviously grew was not restricted to its being a Norwegian or even a Nordic phenomenon. It also involved a larger world of international politics and rights, and intercultural contact between native groups from all around the world. The Norwegian Sami "became" an indigenous people officially in 1990, when the Norwegian state ratified ILO 169, but this was preceded by more than a decade of intense "indigenization," comprising changes of both political and cultural nature (Eidheim 1998; Minde 2003). In this process, an entirely new context for the formulation of self-image and the identification of a Sami cultural domain was created. New and alien symbols of indigeneity were adopted, in public discourse and at local levels, in towns, villages, and rural areas, and individually, in Sami individuals' concept of self. As anthropologist Harald Eidheim put it, "it became increasingly common for ordinary Sami people to view their existence and cultural survival in terms of an indigenous peoples' perspective" (1998: 37).

Over the last decade, a corpus of research has been devoted to religious aspects of such processes of "indigenization," not merely related to the Sami experience but also to the forging of "indigenous peoples" as a global category in itself.[3] Terms such as "indigenous spirituality" (Kraft 2004), "indigenous religion" (Niezen 2012), or "aboriginal spirituality" (Beyer 2007) have been coined to express the phenomenon. In different ways, these concepts all refer to processes in which the intercultural commonality between indigenous groups has become infused with notions of them as *one* spiritual community. Such notions, it is argued, have increasingly become part of "the common terminology of indigeneity," for instance, in UN fora and international law—a discourse into which indigenous delegates from around the world are "socialized" (Karlsson 2003: 406).

There is nothing new to "Western" spiritual fascination for the groups now labeled "indigenous." According to historian of religion Armin W. Geertz (2004), such fascination might even be seen as an expression of a primitivist ideology that ever since antiquity has influenced Western societies, and continues to do so. Among other things, it is commercialized on the global New Age/neoshamanism market, promoted by the likes of Michael Harner and Carlos Castaneda (cf. Wallis 2003). What is new, however, is what anthropologist Harald Prins (2002) calls "the paradox of primitivism," that is, the adoption of primitivist myths by "the primitives" themselves, as a counterhegemonic strategy. Increasingly, ideas of indigenous peoples as carriers of a common religious heritage that has been lost in Western dominant society are turned into an asset for and by indigenous peoples themselves (Beyer 2007). For ethnic groups in the process of gaining recognition for cultural particularity, the instrumentality of such ideas is marked. Assertions of a worldview fundamentally different from, and even opposed to, the "Western" world's religions and worldviews are a way of stating both cultural difference and inherent cultural worth (ibid.). It is a way of marking cultural boundaries in a process of group formation. The asserted unique religiosity of indigenous peoples is the "difference which makes a difference," to paraphrase anthropologist Gregory Bateson (1972: 276).

In terms of the Sami, research on the religious aspects of indigenization is growing.[4] Most prominently as such, historian of religion Siv Ellen Kraft has in a number of articles over the last few years placed emphasis on the utilization of religious heritage as a cultural asset and resource for the Sami (e.g. 2004, 2006, 2009ab, 2010). Indeed, there has been a marked change in the attitude toward Sami pre-Christian religion over the last decades. Although stigmas still exist, especially in pietistic Christian milieus, the general public discourse is characterized by positive references to the Sami religious past. There is also a broad tendency for the Sami religious past to be evoked more implicitly, encompassed in vague terms such as "Sami spirituality" and "Sami nature spirituality," and commonly ascribed to the Sami people as something like an inherent cultural essence (Kraft 2009a). In general, such concepts are part of an increasingly collectivized mythic discourse of the Sami, as indigenous peoples, with strong ties to a pre-Christian origin and a spiritual relationship to nature, the earth, and the landscapes that they traditionally have inhabited.

In many ways, it is this very same utilization of religion as a symbolic resource that was promoted with *Pathfinder*'s portrayal of Sami shamanism. The film's ideal of a religious past as a unifying force, of religion as a marker of cultural boundaries and difference from "others," and connotations of cosmological holism and ecological sustainability, all seem to reflect the repertoire of "indigenous spirituality." This also brings to the fore questions of the formative role of a film that is now almost 30 years old, as a catalyst, not just for legitimating Sami pre-Christian religion as a *positive* aspect of Sami culture but also for a discursive reorientation of "local" Sami religious history in global milieus.

A Cinematographic Formula—
Concluding Remarks

While leaving the question of *Pathfinder*'s role in legitimating Sami pre-Christian religion ultimately unanswered, it is at least worth noting that *Pathfinder*'s depiction of religion as a core to cultural particularity and continuity seems to be a formula that works in terms of filmmaking. Not least is this indicated in later productions by its director, Nils Gaup, who, in the increasingly vital, flourishing, and versatile field of Sami film, remains the best-known Sami filmmaker. For instance, in his latest production, *Hjerterått* (2013),[5] a teen drama television series, Gaup has the same actor as Raste in *Pathfinder*, Nils Utsi, reprise the role of a noaidi. The noaidi character is now even moved to a modern Sami environment. Besides hinting at the continuity of Sami noaidevoutha in the present day, the noaidi is, just like in *Pathfinder*, one of the good guys, devoid of the negative characteristics that have often, particularly in Christian circles, been connected to historic noaidevuohta.

A similar nod to notions of Sami culture as inherently tied to its pre-Christian religious roots can be found in Gaup's historical drama *The Kautokeino Rebellion*, one of the most viewed Norwegian feature films in 2008. Marking Gaup's return to his Sami roots after a series of productions without Sami content, the film featured a "Sami version" of the historic so-called Kautokeino rebellion, a violent rebellion among a group of Sami reindeer herders in 1852 that resulted in the killing of a police officer and a local merchant. Just like *Pathfinder*, *The Kautokeino Rebellion* is interesting in terms of both recuperation of the past in general, and particularly in terms of religion (Christensen 2012b). The historic rebellion is perhaps the most stigmatized incident in the history of the Sami in Norway, due to its having been explained as an outcome of Sami religious fanaticism (Graff 2009). Allegedly, the rebellious Sami had maintained a rather radical and fundamentalist approach to the Lutheran revival movement of Læstadianism, which spread in the Sami core areas of northern Scandinavia from the 1840s onward (ibid.).

Gaup's adaptation redressed such perspectives. Placing responsibility for the tragic events instead on Norwegian authorities and discriminatory policies toward the Sami, the film consequently gave a highly positive account of the religiosity of the rebellious Sami. Gaup's version of Læstadianism was entirely sympathetic and low key. It even took on many of the same characteristics as his recuperated version of Sami noaidevuohta in *Pathfinder*, being mostly a sort of nature-oriented cosmological holism. Gaup's rebellious Sami were children of the earth, characterized by communitas with each other, their reindeer, and their natural environment, and with a spiritual foundation in the past. Although pre-Christian religious practices are never depicted explicitly in *The Kautokeino Rebellion*—which focuses on a period after the Christianization of the Sami (cf. Rydving 1993)—it is still implicitly present in the film. It forms a basis for the film's entire discursive landscape, so to speak: the pre-Christian religious heritage of Sami culture remains, hidden and unconscious, but available as a resource in the darkest of hours. As Gaup himself put it in an interview, commenting on a scene in which a wrongfully imprisoned Sami turns to joik for comfort and strength, "Shamanism is the power that people can mobilize in painful situations in order to remain resilient, survive and move on" (qtd. in Morset 2009: 119).

While not conclusive for the scope of Sami filmmaking today, these examples, nevertheless, also point to a more general trend in filmmaking among many indigenous groups around the world (cf. Ginsburg 2002, 1991, Hood 2008, Dowell 2006, Cummings 2011, Columpar 2010, Singer 2001, Kilpatrick 1999, Fielding 2003). From the aboriginal Australian *Rabbit-Proof Fence* (2002, Philip Noyce), via Maori *Whale Rider* (2002, Niko Caro), to the acclaimed first Inuit feature film ever, *Atanarjuat: The Fast Runner* (2001, Zacharias Kunuk), there is a marked tendency to promote spirituality as a core characteristic of indigenous communities. It is perhaps no wonder. In fact, as filmmaking has been utilized by indigenous groups as a vehicle for internal and external mediation of culture, identity construction, and redressing of outside cultural domination, it is in many cases done so with *Pathfinder* as a shining "landmark" (Dowell 2006: 376). Being "the first and, so far, the only Indigenous film to be nominated for an Academy Award" (Wood 2008: 136), *Pathfinder* continues to screen at various indigenous and independent festivals and showcases around the world. *Pathfinder* has arguably been exemplary, demonstrating that indigenous people can make good feature films, even commercially successful ones, and with a thematic backdrop of religion as a crux to cinematographic constructions of identity. *Pathfinder* has itself become the pathfinder.

Notes

1. Original title in Sami was *Ofelaš*. In Norwegian, the film was entitled *Veiviseren*.
2. This chapter is based partially on a previous article, published in Norwegian (Christensen 2010), but it also adds new aspects to the analysis of religion in *Pathfinder*.
3. See e.g. Niezen 2012, Kraft 2004, 2006, 2009a, 2010, Tafjord 2012, Brosius 1997, Karlsson 2003, Cox 2007, Beyer 2007.
4. See e.g. Kraft 2004, 2006, 2009ab, 2010, Fonneland and Kraft 2013, Fonneland 2010, 2013, Christensen 2010, 2012ab, Christensen and Kraft 2011, Mathisen 2010.
5. In English, the title means something like "cruel."

References

Bateson, Gregory. 1972. *Steps to an Ecology of Mind: Collected Essays in Anthropology, Psychiatry, Evolution, and Epistemology*. Northvale, NJ; London: Jason Aronson.

Beyer, Peter. 2007. "Globalization and Glocalization," in James A. Beckford and N. J. Demerath III (eds.) *The Sage Handbook of the Sociology of Religion.* Los Angeles: Sage, 98–117.

Brosius, J. P. 1997. "Endangered Forest, Endangered People: Environmentalist Representations of Indigenous Knowledge." *Human Ecology* 25(1): 47–69.

Bäckman, Louise and Åke Hultkrantz. 1978. *Studies in Lapp Shamanism.* Stockholm: Almqvist & Wiksell International.

Christensen, Cato and Siv Ellen Kraft. 2011. "Religion i *Kautokeino-opprøret*: en analyse av samisk urfolksspiritualitet." *Nytt Norsk Tidsskrift* 1: 18–27.

Christensen, Cato. 2010. "Religion i *Veiviseren*: en analyse av samisk religiøs revitalisering." *Din: Tidsskrift for religion og kultur* 1–2: 6–33.

———. 2012a. "'Overtroen er stor blant Viddenes folk': om religion og koloniale relasjoner i samisk filmhistorie." *Tidsskrift for kulturforskning* 11(2): 5–25.

———. 2012b. "Reclaiming the Past: On the History-making Significance of the Sámi Film *The Kautokeino Rebellion*." *Acta Borealia* 29(1): 56–76.

———. 2013. *Religion som samisk identitetsmarkør: Fire studier av film.* Phd dissertation, Department of History and Religious Studies, University of Tromsø.

Columpar, Corinn. 2010. *Unsettling Sights: The Fourth World on Film.* Carbondale: Southern Illinois University Press.

Cox, James L. 2007. *From Primitive to Indigenous: The Academic Study of Indigenous Religions.* Hampshire: Ashgate Publishing Company.

Cummings, Dennise K. (ed.). 2011. *Visualities: Perspectives on Contemporary American Indian Film and Art.* East Lansing: Michigan State University Press.

Dowell, Kirstin. 2006. "Indigenous Media Gone Global: Strengthening Indigenous Identity On- and Offscreen at the First Nations/First Features Film Showcase." *American Anthropologist* 108(2): 376–384.

DuBois Thomas A. 2000. "Folklore, Boundaries and Audience in The Pathfinder," in Juha Pentikäinen (ed.) *Sami Folkloristics.* Åbo: Nordic Network of Folklore, 255–274.

Eidheim, Harald. 1998. "Ethno-Political Development among the Sami after World War II: The Invention of Selfhood," in: Harald Gaski (ed.) *Sami Culture in a New Era: The Norwegian Sami Experience.* Karasjok: Davvi Girji, 29–61.

Fielding, Julien R. 2003. "Native American Religion and Film: Interviews with Chris Eyre and Sherman Alexie." *Journal of Religion and Film* 7(1), www.unomaha.edu/jrf/Vol7No1/nativefilm.htm, accessed May 2014.

Fonneland, Trude A. 2010. *Samisk nysjamanisme: i dialog med (for)tid og stad. Ein kulturanalytisk studie av nysjamanar sine erfaringsforteljingar—identitetsforhandlingar og verdiskaping.* PhD dissertation, University of Bergen.

———. 2013. "Sami Tourism and the Signposting of Spirituality: The Case of Sami Tour: a Spiritual Entrepreneur in the Contemporary Experience Economy." *Acta Borealia* 30(2): 190–208.

Fonneland, Trude A., and Siv Ellen Kraft. 2013. "New Age, Sami Shamanism and Indigenous Spirituality," in Steven J. Sutcliffe and Ingvild Sælid Gilhus (eds.) *New Age Spirituality: Rethinking Religion.* Durham: Acumen Publishing, 132–145.

Geertz, Armin. W. 2004. "Can We Move Beyond Primitivism? On Recovering the Indigenes of Indigenous Religions in the Academic Study of Religion," in Jacob Olupona (ed.) *Beyond Primitivism: Indigenous Religious Traditions and Modernity*. New York: Routledge, 37–70.

Ginsburg, Faye D. 1991. "Indigenous Media: Faustian Contract or Global Village?". *Cultural Anthropology* 6(1): 92– 112.

———. 2002. "Screen Memories: Resignifying the Traditional in Indigenous Media," in Faye D. Ginsburg, Lila Abu-Lughod, and Brian Larkin (eds.) *Media Worlds: Anthropology on New Terrain*. Ewing: University of California Press, 39–57.

Graff, Ola 2009. "Fra skurker til helter." *Ottar—Populærvitenskapelig tidsskrift fra Tromsø Museum* 1: 46–55

Historia Norwegiæ (unknown author). 1999. Published in Roald E. Kristiansen, *"Finnene" fra Historia Norwegiæ [slutten av 1100-tallet]*. http://www.love. is/roald/, accessed May 2014.

Hultkrantz, Åke 2000. "Fifty Years of Research on Sami Folklore and Mythology," in Juha Pentikäinen (ed.). *Sami Folkloristics*. Åbo: Nordic Network of Folklore, 75–101.

Iversen, Gunnar. 2005. "Learning from Genre: Genre Cycles in Modern Norwegian Cinema," in Andrew Nestingen and Trevor G. Elkington (eds.) *Transnational Cinema in a Global North: Nordic Cinema in Transition*. Detroit: Wayne State University Press, 261–278.

Karlsson, Bengt G. 2003. "Anthropology and the 'Indigenous Slot': Claims to and Debates about Indigenous Peoples' Status in India." *Critique of Anthropology* 23(4): 403–423.

Kilpatrick, Jacquelyn. 1999. *Celluloid Indians: Native Americans and Film*. Lincoln: University of Nebraska Press.

Kraft, Siv Ellen. 2004. "Et hellig fjell blir til—Om samer, OL og arktisk magi." *Nytt Norsk Tidsskrift* 3–4: 237–249.

———. 2006. "Samisk folkemedisin og nyreligiøse plastikk-sjamaner: Et kritisk blikk på nyromantiske forskningsperspektiver." *Din: Tidsskrift for religion og kultur* 2–3: 43–52.

———. 2009a. "Sami Indigenous Spirituality: Religion and Nation-building in Norwegian Sàpmi." *Temenos* 45(2): 179–206.

———. 2009b. "Kristendom, sjamanisme og urfolksspiritualitet i norsk Sápmi." *Chaos: Dansk-norsk tidsskrift for religionshistoriske studier* 51: 29–52.

———. 2010. "The Making of a Sacred Mountain: Meanings of Nature and Sacredness in Sápmi and Northern Norway." *Religion* 40(1): 53–61.

Kristiansen, Roald. 2001. *Samisk religion. En kortfattet oversikt*. http://www. love.is/roald/samiskreligion.htm, accessed May 2014.

Løchen, Kalle. 2003. "Intervju: Om *Veiviseren*," in Margaret Ljunggren (ed.) *Fra idé til film: Veiviseren*. Nesbru: Vett og Viten AS, 99–107

Mathisen, Stein R. 2010. "Indigenous Spirituality in the Touristic Borderzone: Virtual Performances of Sámi Shamanism in Sápmi Park." *Temenos* 46(1): 53–72.

Mebius, Hans. 2000. "Historien om den samiske nåjden," in: Thomas P. Larsson (ed.) *Schamaner: Essäer om religiösa mästare*. Falun: Nya Doxa, 41–75.

Minde, Henry. 2003. "The Challenge of Indigenism: The Struggle for Sami Land Rights and Self-government in Norway 1960–1990," in Svein Jentoft, Henry Minde, and Ragnar Nilsen (eds.) *Indigenous Peoples: Resource Management and Global Rights*. Delft: Eburon Academic Publishers, 75–106.

Morset, Kari S. 2009. *Stemmene fra nord. Samisk revitalisering: Den kunstneriske kampen som levendegjorde en truet samisk kultur* [*Voices of the North. Sami revitalization: The artistic struggle that revived a threatened Sami culture*]. PhD dissertation, Scandinavian Studies, University of Wisconsin, Madison.

Niezen, Ronald. 2012. "Indigenous Religion and Human Rights," in John Witte and M. Christian Green (eds.) *Religion and Human Rights: An Introduction*. Oxford: Oxford University Press, 119–134.

Olsen, Kjell. 2004. "Heritage, Religion and the Deficit of Meaning in Institutionalized Discourse," in Anna-Leena Siikala, Barbro Klein, and Stein R. Mathisen (eds.) *Creating Diversities: Folklore, Religion and the Politics of Heritage*. Helsinki: Finnish Literature Society, 31–42.

Pollan, Brita. 1993. *Samiske sjamaner: Religion og Helbredelse*. Oslo: Gyldendal.

Prins, Harald. 2002. "Visual Media and the Primitivist Perplex: Colonial Fantasies, Indigenous Imagination, and Advocacy in North America," in Faye D. Ginsburg, Lila Abu-Lughod, and Brian Larkin (eds.) *Media Worlds: Anthropology on New Terrain*. Ewing: University of California Press, 58–74.

Rydving, Hakan. 1993. *The End of Drum-Time: Religious Change Among the Lule Saami 1670s–1740s*. Uppsala: Almqvist & Wiksell International.

Singer, Beverly R. 2001. *Wiping the War Paint Off the Lens: Native American Film and Video*. Minneapolis: University of Minnesota Press.

Skarðhamar, Anne-Kari. 2008. "Changes in Film Representations of Sami Culture and Identity." *Nordlit* 12(1): 293–304.

Solum, Ove. 1997. "Veiviserne," in Gunnar Iversen and Ove Solum (eds.) *Nærbilder: Artikler om norsk filmhistorie*. Oslo: Universitetsforlaget, 187–202.

Tafjord, Bjørn O. 2012. "Indigenous Religion(s) as an Analytical Category." *Method & Theory in the Study of Religion* 25(3): 221–243.

Wallis Robert J. 2003. *Shamans/Neo-Shamans. Ecstasy, Alternative Archaeologies and Contemporary Pagans*. London, New York: Routledge.

Wood, Houston. 2008. *Native Features: Indigenous Films from Around the World*. New York, London: Continuum.

Media

Bakkemoen, Edel. 1987. "På flukt i samenens land," *Aftenposten Amag* September 26, 1987.

Berntsen, Kristin V. 1988. "Navn i nyhetene: Nils Gaup," *NTBtekst* April 11, 1988.

Dahl, Henning Kramer. 1987, "En film som viser vei," *Morgenbladet* October 2, 1987.

Haave, Harald. 1987a. "'Veiviseren'—første spillefilm på samisk noensinne," *NTBtekst* June 4, 1987.

———. 1987b. "'Veiviseren'—Samisk film-thriller ut i den store verden," *NTBtekst* September 24, 1987.

Kulås, Guri. 2008. "Den første helten," *Klassekampen* January 11, 2008.

Norwegian News Agency 1987; "'Veiviseren' styrker samisk stolthet and identitet", *NTBtekst* October 2, 1987.

Tonstad, Per Lars. 1987, "Navn i nyhetene," *NTBtekst* October 1, 1987.

Films

Atanarjuat: The Fast Runner 2001. Zacharias Kunuk. Isuma Igloolik Productions.

Hjerterått 2013. Nils Gaup and Grethe Bøe-Waal. Original Film AS

Pathfinder [Ofelaš/Veiviseren] 1987. Nils Gaup. Filmkameratene AS.

Rabbitt-Proof Fence 2002. Philip Noyce. Rumbalara Films.

The Kautokeino Rebellion [Kautokeino-opprøret] 2008. Nils Gaup. Borealis Production.

Whale Rider 2002. Niko Caro. South Pacific Pictures.

10

Contextualizing Exhibited Versions of Sami *Noaidevuohta*

Stein R. Mathisen

Introduction: Circular Itineraries

An attempt to visit (and revisit) at least some of the exhibitions and museums in Arctic Scandinavia that present versions of Sami *noaidevuohta* had taken our group on a rather long detour during the summer of 2013—driving in a wide circle through the northern parts of Norway, Finland, and Sweden. One day we visited the Steilneset Memorial in Vardø, a spectacular monument to the memory of the victims of the Finnmark Witchcraft Trials 1600–1692. Opened in 2011, it had been created by the French/American artist Louise Bourgeois (1911–2010) and the Swiss architect Peter Zumthor (b. 1943). The site commemorates the 91 victims who were accused of practicing witchcraft and sentenced to death by burning, often after severe torture. One of the main components of the monument is a chair with an eternal flame burning at the seat, symbolizing the ordeals the victims suffered, while a 125-meter-long Memorial Hall exhibits the names of every one of the victims in small niches, together with a summary of the accusations made against them, and what little is known from the legal records about the everyday lives of these people (Willumsen s.a.). Some of the victims were, as might be expected, Sami healers who had practiced traditional noaidevuohta, but were sentenced to death after the violent encounter with the Church and legal representatives of the Danish/Norwegian government. The last victim recorded in this long list of "witches" was the Sami Anders Pouelsen, who in 1692 was "accused of having used a rune drum and of practicing godless witchcraft" (Willumsen s.a.: 97). I will return to this Sami who confessed to the use of a rune drum. In this connection I will just draw the attention to the fact that this monument communicates the very darkest side of the prosecution of people who were believed to be in contact with supernatural powers, which the intruding outsiders had associated with the devil and the dark forces. The memorial very strongly communicates the personal sufferings this led to, and stresses the illegitimate use of power and brutal force against people who confessed to other belief systems, or simply were accused of activities constructed by the visiting colonizers.

On the evening that very same day, our company arrived in the village of Anár/Inari in northern Finland, where we had planned to visit the Siida Sami Museum. We took quarters at the Hotel Inari. What immediately caught my attention in the hotel room was the large picture above the bed. It was a drawing of a little boy dressed in Sami costume, leaning over a rune drum about half of his own size, with a rune hammer in his folded hands. It was a child *noaidi*, very innocent looking, but still with something more determined in his eyes as he looked directly at the picture's audience. The colors, position, and facial expression seemed to be filled with harmony and peace. But the magical drawings on the drum had come to life, as if already setting out to act. I learned that the drawing was made in 2006 by the Sami artist Merja Aletta Rauttila, born in Kargasniemi, Utsjoki in 1960, and that it was also featured as a very popular postcard for tourist and visitors, for sale along with other similar motifs by the same artist in the hotel lobby.

The contrast between the sinister Witchcraft Trials' Memorial and the romantic drawing in the hotel room of the Sami child noaidi was striking: on the one side death, suffering, suppression, and violence; on the other side childish innocence and harmony. But the historical background for the two representations was still the same. Historical sources, literature, and other information about the Sami noaidi are to be found in abundance. But these knowledges have over the years been documented and represented in very different ways. In the end it has become a complex task to distinguish between myth and fact, because these two sides of the phenomenon have become (and were?) so closely interwoven.

The purpose of this study is, however, neither to find the one correct way of representing Sami noaidevuohta nor to provide any sort of authorized and "true" version of what these beliefs actually consisted of, or should be interpreted as. Rather, the intention is to understand some of the different interests that have been invested, by different actors, in the representations of this phenomenon in a historical perspective. In this case, the angle has to include important questions related to the colonializing of the area. Colonialism is here not just a matter of the initial conquest and the subsequent exploitation of natural resources. It also concerns how the subjugated people and their culture have been imagined and represented in later phases by the colonizers and by themselves. The whole range from denigration to romanticizing of indigenous cultures has produced representations that even today continue to leave their mark on relations between people living in the area. In putting a material object like the Sami *govadas*, the noaidi's rune drum, in the center of the analysis, I aim to better understand the substantial and concrete qualities of some of the immaterial communicative contexts generated around these objects. The focus of the analysis is therefore not on the drum in itself as an object, but on the various performances and narratives that have been attached to it and inscribed in it under different circumstances.

Noaidevuohta: Performed, Exhibited, and Commoditized

Given that there is no single narrative to investigate, this analysis has to consider a rather long history of narratives and performances relating to Sami noaidevuohta and the noaidi's govadas. At the outset, the task is to seek possible connections between different performances, exhibitions, commodifications, and connected communications related to the rune drum. There could be a kind of common meta-narrative behind all the different presentations, but these connections could just as well be connected by narratives that only at first glance seem to be about the drum. To find an answer to this, it is necessary to start the analysis not with the drum itself, but rather with an investigation of various actualizations where the rune drum holds a prominent position. These examples of communication taking place in recurring historical contexts will be the primary material of this analysis. This will take us through a long row of changing contexts, ranging from legal, religious, archival, and museal arenas, to contemporary tourism, souvenir shops, and digital shows in theme parks.

As has already been noted, some of the first documented narratives about the Sami noaidi's drum were the result of violent meetings between an indigenous population and the legal representatives of an expanding national state. It is not surprising that in a historical perspective the narratives are conflicting, and interpretations of the drum are seen from opposing points of view. This is of course interesting for several reasons when the narratives are analyzed from a postcolonial perspective. The noaidi and his drum have been at the center of the formation of narratives relating to views of the world that were in deep conflict. On the one hand authoritative versions represent the political, economic, and religious power of the state formation, and are usually univocal. On the other hand, more unofficial counternarratives have come out of contexts experienced as difficult and dissenting, and therefore the narratives often contain elements that are polyphonic, ambiguous, and opposing. This communication can be understood as a form of dialogic narration, building on the ideas of the dialogic of language as developed by Mikhail Bakhtin (1981). The rune drum can also be observed in exhibitions of various kinds, where the museum display, usually the trusted keepers of those few most "original" rune drums still kept today, would be the most obvious, but certainly not the only one to be considered.

This study will have its focus on contexts in which the Sami drum is being used when particular kinds of intercultural meetings are taking place, namely, in which a dominant majority has taken on the task of controlling, representing, or commercializing a cultural activity originally strongly tied to a minority group. Mary Louise Pratt uses the concept of "contact zone" to describe situations in which colonial meetings are taking place "to refer to the space of colonial encounters, the space in which peoples geographically and historically separated come into contact with each other and establish ongoing relations, usually involving conditions of coercion, radical inequality, and intractable conflict" (1992, 6). Following this way of looking at the colonial encounter, it should however *not only* be understood as a history of total domination from colonializing interests but also as a situation in which the colonized and subjugated people, often in spite of dominance and violence, tried to position themselves in various ways to make their situation more endurable. This most often takes on forms of communicative strategies, for example, in what Pratt calls "autoethnography," or "autoethnographic expressions," referring "to instances in which colonized subjects undertake to represent themselves in ways that *engage with* the colonizer's own terms" (7). This involves a perspective of looking for forms of resistance and agency among the colonized peoples, also in communicative acts that at first glance would seem to conform to the intruders' way of seeing the world, or even express subordination to a hegemonic culture. Closer analysis and contextualized readings of older texts and historical sources can reveal at least some of these strategies.

The exhibition of rune drums in museums and art collections in similar ways initially showed the drums in contexts in which the culture of the others (the colonized) became colonial trophies (Dicks 2003: 146), typically on exhibit in ethnographic museums of the imperial centers in Europe. Like other resources, they were first "discovered" on the colonialized peripheries, and then brought into the centers, where they could be gathered and become part of established collections (Clifford 1997: 193). This new contextualization also produced new orders and new meanings, with consequences both in the center and on the peripheries. But such processes of transculturation (Pratt 1992: 6) do not only work in unilinear ways. Postcolonial demands for the repatriation of the ethnographic materials once collected in the Sami areas raised similar questions of redefinitions of the collections, once they were brought back to their places of origin. Repatriation can, however, never reinstate some original condition, but only reestablish objects in their old surroundings as heritage. There are two major alternatives for this recontextualization: either connected to museum exhibits, or to tourism and similar commodifying projects.

So an important part of the question explored here is in the end what happens when symbols and images of cultural and ethnic identity enter the commercial area? Since cultural difference also exists as commercial products, especially in tourism and experience industries, there is always a risk that the ethnopolitical insistence on the relevance of cultural differences for rights and policies could be damaged by examples of commodification of the same ethnic expressions. As John L. Comaroff and Jean Comaroff put it in their book on the dilemmas of commercializing ethnicity,

> Those who seek to brand their otherness, to profit from what makes them different, find themselves having to do so in the universally recognizable terms in which difference is represented, merchandised, rendered negotiable by means of the abstract instruments of the market: money, the commodity, commensuration, the calculus of supply and demand, price, branding. And advertising. (2009: 24)

The demands of the market, as well as the specific characteristics of the new contexts in which Sami noaidevuohta is now appearing again might change the meanings being communicated, even when the objects and the symbols have been left relatively unaltered.

This means, for example, that representations, especially in the media (and in tourism) easily get caught up in primitivist discourses when they want to show and commodify cultural differences. Harald Prins calls this "the primitivist perplex" (2002: 58) with reference to media productions. What characterizes this field of exhibition and discourse today is therefore a prevailing multivocality and ambiguity, sometimes leading to unexpected reactions to actions and products intended to work in quite opposite ways. This is why historical contextualizations of the complicated translocations, transformations, and transculturations of the rune drum can clarify processes leading up to contemporary representations.

Performed: Noaidevuohta and the "Rune Drum" before the Court

It is important to understand how those historic representations of noaidevuohta that are available to us today have been formed by very concrete encounters between the indigenous population and representatives from the outside world, as well as interpretations of these meetings. To find the roots of some of the visual and textual representations of Sami noaidevuohta in museums and exhibitions, I will return once again to the Sami noaidi representing the last individual destiny in the long row of victims in the Bourgeois/Zumthor Memorial Hall in Vardø. On December 7, 1691, the old Sami Anders Pouelsen was arrested in Unjárga/Nesseby, where he lived, and an instrument called a *Runnebomen* (Willumsen 2010: 377, *n*4, 411: the rune drum; i.e., the noaidi's drum) was confiscated. Both he and the drum were then brought to the village of Vadsø, the administrative center of the area, located further out and north in the Varanger fjord. Then in the beginning of the next year, he appeared before the court in Vadsø, accused "on the grounds that he has owned and used an instrument they call a rune drum with which he has practised that wicked and ungodly art of witchcraft" (Willumsen 2010: 377). This witch trial resulted in very thorough written descriptions of the drum and its use (see the full court proceedings in Willumsen 2010: 377ff; see also Lilienskiold 1998, 257–273; Knag 1693, referred to in Hagen 2002), and these descriptions have in turn become important sources for later studies of the Sami rune drum and the Sami religion (among many, see Leem 1767: 467ff.; Friis 1871: 36ff.; Manker 1950: 433ff.; Rydving 1991: 38ff.). The written records are of course in the pen of the servants of the court and the magistrate, but if we choose to see this as a written report from an actual encounter between the Danish/Norwegian authorities representing their set of values, and an indigenous Sami representing a conflicting set of values and beliefs, it is still possible to understand how the relatively weaker Sami part in this confrontation is trying to negotiate himself into a more favorable position.

At the court's request, Pouelsen was asked to name every figure on the drum and explain its meaning. He explained the figures with names and references, sometimes to Sami belief and gods, and sometimes to Christian belief, gods, and institutions. It is not so easy to decide from the text whether this means that the cognitive world depicted on the drum was already in a process of change, or whether this was a conscious strategy from the noaidi to try to escape negative accusations of demonology. But the next phase of the court's investigations is more informative in this sense. What is really interesting, according to the court proceedings, is that the old noaidi Pouelsen was allowed to perform with his rune drum before the court, and to demonstrate how he used this instrument in his work as a noaidi. The description of this is therefore a unique account of an intercultural meeting.

> Now he picked up the rune drum and tried it, instructing the court how he plays, having first crossed himself and then made the sign of the cross over the drum. He recited the Lord's Prayer in the Karelian [Finnish] language, before he continued with his own prayer, Ætziem, achie, ja barne, ja Engilen, væche don, and other utterances that were supposed to mean God our Father, your Mother, and your Son, and the Holy Spirit, send us your help. All the while, he kept looking at his figures, and the top danced up and down and he beat with his hammer and uttered these words to the gods, And you God who hath created Heaven and Earth, the sun and the moon, and the stars, all humans, and birds, and all the fishes and the sea. And he confessed his sins saying, I am a sinful human, old and unworthy, I will be better off dead if you will not help the one we are pleading for, and he promises he will never again sin, and such-like utterances of worship. (Willumsen 2010: 385)

Besides the court book, there is another source, written by the deputy Court Judge Niels Knag, describing certain aspects of the demonstration of the rune drum in more detail (Hagen 2002: 329). This manuscript, now in the Royal Library in Copenhagen, describes how the accused after some time stopped drumming, and told the court that the gods could not come to an agreement, as to whether they would answer him or not. The gods were skeptical, because the call came from a "Norwegian house." The accused then called out loud to the gods that they should not be afraid of the Norwegians. Even if he was playing the drum in a Norwegian house, the Norwegians did not want to harm them in any way, he assured them, before he continued his drumming. At last he received answers (Hagen 2002: 328f., referring to Knag 1693). This passage shows Pouelsen's awareness of being an actor in a performance that could turn out quite differently from the healing sessions to which he had contributed in Sami local societies. Anders Pouelsen must have known that he was in a very difficult position when he was accused of witchcraft by the Danish authorities, and he was clearly attentive to the existence of differences in belief and worldview (see also Willumsen 2013: 318). Hence he tried to imitate sentences and formulations that he must have picked up in church sermons and at other Christian scenes, to create a sort of meeting ground or contact zone where the relations between the two groups could be negotiated.

But Pouelsen's strategies in this respect did not prove successful. On the contrary, the court was eager to show its authority and will to dominate the false beliefs of the indigenous population. They therefore declared that

> his practice is found to be extremely punishable, particularly the fact that he paints the Holy Trinity, God the Father, the Son and the Holy Ghost, whom he with his incantations and abuse, which God will judge, so grievously profanes, scorns, desecrates and outrages, and the fact that he recites the Lord's Prayer and makes the sign of the holy cross over himself and over the rune drum when preparing to play on it, and the reference he makes of his pictures as representations of God, God's created elements, telling them, You God, who hath created Heaven and Earth, the sun and the moon etc. and, finally, the fact that he paints Hell and the devils, and he is particularly reluctant to explain his dealings with them. (Willumsen 2010: 390)

The court found it "highly necessary to make a hideous example of such godlessness" (391). But since there were no witnesses declaring that he actually had harmed anyone with his evil deeds, they were not quite sure whether he qualified for a death sentence. In the demise of the witchcraft craze in Europe, the court found his case "indeed a most unusual one, requiring due consideration from superior authorities" (391). He was seen as guilty of committing witchcraft, but the court decided to imprison him, and to send his case to the Danish king in Copenhagen for further consideration regarding the possibility of a death sentence. While imprisoned, he was, however, killed only two days later with three blows of an axe to his head while he was asleep by Willum Gundersen, a servant working for the *amtmann* (regional governor), Hans Hansen Lilienskiold (1650–1703). In a trial that followed, the servant was declared insane: "he committed this killing in a condition of rage and confusion, when he was bereft of his senses, of which he has but little, for which reason he cannot be sentenced to loss of life in accordance with the claim from Anders Pouelsen's heirs" (402).

The scene in Vadsø's courtroom had already set strict limits for what an interethnic meeting, as well as intercultural communication, could be like in February 1693, and there was little possibility for Pouelsen or his relatives to gain any understanding for their version of how their beliefs and their healing practices should be understood in relation to the far more powerful regime of the Danish/Norwegian state. The court records can be understood as a filtered version of Sami beliefs and practices in the area as seen through the Danish/Norwegian judicial system at that time. But Pouelsen's performance before the court can perhaps be understood as an example of attempted auto-ethnography, an effort to communicate to the court the Sami values and their position, by using concepts and formulations that he himself thought or hoped would be acceptable to the court representatives. But to no avail. There was at this point no opportunity for a real dialogue between the two different ways of understanding the visible and the invisible world.

Described: The Collected and Decontextualized Religious Item

This could very well have been the end of Pouelsen's story. But together with the material sent to Copenhagen for further consideration was also the rune drum. When the drum arrived in Copenhagen in 1694, it had already started on a long journey through which it eventually would become an important part of future collections connected to Sami religion. What were the implications of these changes in contexts? One might say that the rune drum already was operated outside its original and "authentic" context when it was being played in the courtroom in Vadsø in 1692, even if it was being played by its proper owner. But this point of departure might prove futile, in the sense that it stresses and looks for some kind of integral essence in the drum and its use, some kind of original meaning that should be preserved. Alternatively the drum could be understood as a specific kind of instrument, which had been placed in various surroundings and situations. It is exactly the study of this specific drum's mobility that can reveal some of the instrumentalities and agendas that have been linked to it. According to Pouelsen's narrative when he was standing before the court, the drum had followed him on his travels to various places in the northern areas where he had been living for "a narrow century" (Willumsen 2010: 378). Now his playing on the drum before the court set the drum, already decontextualized, on a new journey, even after its owner's death. The rune drum, along with manuscripts describing its use and interpretations of the signs, eventually became part of the Royal Collection in Copenhagen.

When the description of Pouelsen's rune drum first appeared in print 75 years after the trial, it did so in Knud Leem's description of the Sami in Finnmark (1767). Only now there was no reference to the owner and user of the drum, in the sense that his name was not mentioned. He was just referred to as "a Laplander of Finmark" (467, here cited from the first American edition, in Pinkerton 1812: 475). Neither was there any reference to the witch trials nor to the contexts surrounding the confiscation of the drum. But the descriptions in Leem's book of the signs on the drum and explanations of its use (op.cit., 467–474) were clearly taken from a written copy of the court proceedings. It is likely that Leem had access to these written records while he worked in Copenhagen (Hagen 2003: 88). But the written reports were no longer used as evidence in a criminal court. Leem wanted to describe a religious practice that was understood as wrong, and consequently had to be corrected.

Leem's interpretations in the book must be understood as the result of the movement of the descriptions from one context to another. The descriptions had now left the system of law and entered a system of religious interpretation and missionary activity. In Denmark, the Missionskollegiet (Missionary Collegium) had been founded in 1714 to promote missionary activities in the Danish colonies. In addition to Danish colonies in the East and the West Indies (and later Greenland), this also included Finnmark, where Leem himself was commissioned and sent as a missionary to Porsanger in 1725. Leem later became a leading authority on matters of Sami language and culture within the Danish mission among the Sami, and was a professor of Sami language at the Seminarium Lapponicum in Trondheim from 1752 up to his death in 1774. He served in this capacity because the college educated teachers and missionaries to do missionary work among the Sami and teach them in their own language. In that vein the last part of Leem's book aims to represent the rune drum as material evidence for the existence of a heretical Sami religion, which could be understood as the antithesis of Christianity. This description in turn identified a concrete working field for the missionaries operating among the Sami. The description of the rune drum and the old Sami religion would make it easier to identify beliefs and practices that had their roots in heresy. The early missionaries used these writings as a starting point, added their own observations and other missionaries' reports to their own, and produced versions of a Sami religion that had been freed from any actual context, but that could operate as a proper antithesis to Christianity, and as a concrete object against which the missionaries could aim their work.

Within the history of religions, this has sparked an interesting discussion on how ideas about Sami religion had been constituted more as an antithesis to Christianity than as contextualized descriptions of religious practices in certain areas (Rydving 1991; 1993). Håkan Rydving understood this as a dynamic confrontation between two conflicting cognitive and religious views, in which changing drawings, and interpretations of the images on the drum, could be understood as forms of resistance:

> The role of the drums as symbols of Saami resistance is well attested in the sources from the 17th and 18th centuries. For the Saamis, the drums represented their threatened culture, the resistance against the Christian claim to exclusiveness, and a striving to preserve traditional values—i.e. "the good" that had to be saved. For the Church authorities, on the other hand, the drums symbolized the explicit nucleus of the elusive Saami "paganism"—i.e. "the evil" that had to be annihilated. (Rydving 1991: 29)

Rydving points to the court records as the only sources we have concerning Sami understandings of these violent religious encounters. In this perspective the different versions and interpretations of the drums can only be understood in light of the colonializing processes taking place in these specific historic contexts. This also points to the possibility that the drums themselves and their painted images could have been in a process of change, as a result of the violent encounter with the representatives of the new religion. What is important here is also that the documents and interpretations that came out of these violent and colonializing religious encounters in their turn became the raw material for the production of new interpretations and innovative cultural forms.

Exhibited: Indigenous Artwork and Creative Reinterpretations of the Drum

In Copenhagen, Poulsen's rune drum as an object had to follow the development and the reorganization of museum collections. From being a part of the Royal Collections, it ended up as a part of the Nationalmuseet (National Museum) in Copenhagen. But much later the rune drum was again returned to Finnmark where it had come from. Although the drum still formally belongs to the National Museum, it has since 1979 been deposited at the Sámiid Vuorká-Dávvirat (Sami Collections) in Kárášjohka/Karasjok. This is an early example of the repatriation of Sami objects kept in central European museums, a development and negotiation that still is going on today, and that concerns other rune drums as well (Ucko 2002; Silvén 2012). The idea has been that important items of Sami cultural heritage should be brought back to the areas where they had once been confiscated or collected. The process of repatriation should be understood as a typical postcolonial process taking place globally, and in certain ways challenging the old colonial structures of power. The process itself holds great symbolic value for the once (or still) colonized peoples. But it can also be understood as a productive development that in turn has produced new cultural manifestations of indigenous culture and identity.

The original rune drum once belonging to Pouelsen is of course safeguarded in secure surroundings in the Sami museum's magazine. But a copy received a very prominent and central place in the exhibition that was being established in the Sámiid Vuorká-Dávvirat (Sami Collections) in Kárášjohka/Karasjok. This exhibition was designed in cooperation with the Sami artist Iver Jåks (1932–2007), and marks a significant change in ideas of exhibiting Sami noaidevuohta. Earlier exhibitions, for example, at the Nordiska Museet (Nordic Museum) in Stockholm, had focused on the noaidi and his activity, most significantly by presenting mannequin models of the noaidi with the govadas in what was designed to give an impression of a historically authentic environment, or by arranging realistic dioramas that were meant to be "peep shows" depicting a true historical scene as naturalistically as possible (Mathisen 2004b: 11ff.). The diorama was a three-walled extension of the room where the visitors and the spectators found themselves, and the arranged nature of the spectacle could only be perceived if one paid attention to a dividing half-wall of glass. The frozen immobility of the scene also revealed the ethnographic gaze that had produced it, and made it a frozen element of culture, denoting a cultural reality that continued to exist only in the ethnographic present and as something that did not have to be seen as objects to be understood as parts of historical processes.

Iver Jåks' exhibition broke this ethnographic narrative, and focused more on the aesthetic aspects of the drum, thereby reinventing it as an object of art. This possibility had already been pointed to in books by Ernst Manker (1965; 1971), where the imagery of the rune drums was interpreted as a work of "art," in the Western sense of the word. The imagery on the rune drums could be compared to paintings, and sacrificial stones could be compared to sculptures (Manker 1965, 11). The noaidis' art of navigating in Sami cosmology was paralleled to representational work by professional artists in the Western world of galleries art exhibitions. In the same vein, Iver Jåks' interpretations paved the way for a situation in which the drum could be exhibited in museums as an isolated object, very much in the same way any object of art would have been presented to the public in an art museum. In the same manner, the ethnographic objects were not enclosed as exemplars in a glass showcase, or contextualized as belonging to social processes in dioramas, but rather displayed as unique sculptures, where form, materiality, and shape were important. In his own work, Jåks was also inspired by the world of images depicted on the skin of the rune drum, and this was (and became) the case for many other young Sami artists as well.

As a source of inspiration, other copies of Pouelsen's rune drum found their way into a wide range of museums and exhibitions. One copy is exhibited in Várjjat Sami Musea (Varanger Sami Museum) in Unjárgga/Nesseby (close to the area where Pouelsen lived when he was arrested in 1691), one at the Kulturhistorisk Museum (Museum of Cultural History) in Oslo, one at the museum in Alta, and at exhibitions at several other museums. These exhibited drums have in turn inspired Sami artisans (*duodjárat*) to make copies or versions of the Pouelsen rune drum, and some of these have also eventually been exhibited in art collections and art museums, or ended up in private collections. To sum up, the specific rune drum of Pouelsen has been copied and recontextualized in such a wide variety of new surroundings that it probably is no longer possible to give an overview of all of the examples of exhibitions that show it.

In addition to these copies are more creative (and interpretative) uses of the rune drum and its imagery by artists and authors. Most interesting in this connection is the path-breaking work of Sami artist Nils-Aslak Valkeapää (1943–2001), mainly because his work was so central in the ethnic revival of Sami identity, and because his artwork, poetry, and music had important ethnopolitical implications. In his book of poems, *Beaivi, áhčážan* (*The Sun, My Father*) (Valkeapää 1988, 1997), Valkeapää presents a wide collection of photos of Sami people that he gathered from ethnographic collections in major European cities like Oslo, Stockholm, Copenhagen, Helsinki, Hamburg, Paris, and London. He had the idea to, together with the poems, connect these images to the Sami areas where they originated, and also bring the persons pictured back to their relatives and families. This is a postcolonial reclamation of a lost cultural heritage, and an attempt to use this heritage to establish a new basis for an innovative Sami identity. This process is also directly associated with the rune drum. The image of the drum is featured in more ways than just on the front of the book. In Sami, the word govadas can mean both something containing a lot of pictures (like this book) and the rune drum, with its images and symbols (Hirvonen 2008: 195; see also Dana 2003).

But recontextualizations of the Sami drum and its images as works of art can also be problematic and contested. In the late 1990s, the Sami artist Lars Pirak (1932–2008), together with Swedish artist Bengt Lindström (1925–2008), was commissioned by the Luleå Arts Council, the municipality of Jokkmokk, and the Vattenfall hydroelectric company to decorate the Akkats Dam, part of a hydroelectric power station on the Lule River. The dam was decorated with large colorful murals, with motifs taken from Sami mythology. The north side of the intake building has a large version of a rune drum. It is claimed that this artwork reappropriates the surrounding nature and the man-made installations as genuinely Sami, as well as establishes the Jokkmokk area as an important center for Sami heritage and innovative creative artwork (Scheffy 2004: 226). This view was, however, not shared by some members of the Sirkkas Sameby, whose traditional herding routes were interrupted because of the dams along the Lule River, and several of the old sacrificial stones became submerged under water (Scheffy op. cit.). They felt that the artwork was a misrepresentation of traditional Sami interests in the area, and that the artwork in fact functioned as a cover-up to hide the theft of indigenous Sami resources and rights.

Commodification: Serialized Drums and Commercial Signposts

If the art world ran the risk of producing contested images and versions of Sami noaidevuohta, this is certainly also the case when images connected to Sami spirituality appear in various commercial enterprises. Many of these products are in some way or other connected to tourism. Both heritage tourism and cultural tourism are important areas for the development of a flourishing contemporary experience industry in Northern Scandinavia. The tourist boards of the area promote travel to the north to experience the Midnight Sun in the summer and the Aurora Borealis in the winter. But one recurring and important element in this tourism package is the opportunity to experience what is labeled "genuine Sami culture." While the vast northern landscapes are being experienced as mostly uninhabited wilderness areas by these urban tourist visitors, these sights combine well with the European narratives of an indigenous "nature people" living in close and perfect contact with their natural surroundings (Mathisen 2010). The Sami, and especially those among them who are occupied in semi-nomadic reindeer-herding activities, and who on some occasions also wear their colourful traditional dress, have become the picturesque materialization of this harmonic relationship between a barren Arctic landscape and its inhabitants. Therefore, this part of Sami culture is most often presented to outsiders, and in the tourism industry the reindeer herder is the "emblematic" Sami (Olsen 2004). In tourism the Sami are given roles as the ultimate and colorful others, although still indigenous to a part of the European area. But they are usually associated with the past, and stand in contrast to modern, contemporary life. With its closeness to nature, reindeer herding stands for a life based on traditionalism, harmony, spirituality, and ecological attitudes toward nature (Mathisen 2004a). Versions of Sami reindeer-herding culture have become central symbols for a way of life that represents harmony with nature and the environment and that offers a special kind of indigenous, spiritual conscience. This development in tourism has led to new uses of the image of the Sami noaidi's drum, this time within the field of commerce. One can therefore speak of a special form of modification of the rune drum called commodification.

Would the rune drum and its imagery retain this kind of critical function for the indigenous population, as proposed by the artistic use of Nils-Aslak Valkeapää as a shaman-poet (Dana 2003), even if it were transformed into more commercial contexts? Some cases from the world of tourism would suggest that there are good reasons to be skeptical about this possibility. The Suoma Sami Nuorat (Finnish Sami

Youth Organization) protested against fake "shamanistic" ceremonies in Rovaniemi, Finland, in which "Finnish persons impersonate a Sami shaman wearing dirty clothes and having a dirty face as well" (SSN Protest; see also Comaroff and Comaroff 2009: 159). This protest concerns a tourist ritual in the 1980s in which the performing "Sámi" "shaman" was dressed in a filthy Sami costume, had a sooty face, acted primitively, and marked the tourists' faces with soot as a kind of initiation ritual. This ritual clearly recirculated old images of an "ignoble savage." Another, more recent, example is a fake "Sámi" baptism that takes place in Santa Claus Land in Rovaniemi, where people dressed in "Sámi" clothing perform a ritual, marking the tourists' crossing of the Arctic Circle by touching them with a big Sami knife (NRK Sápmi November 4, 2008). A further blatant example of negative presentations of Sami spirituality is a deck of cards sold in some souvenir shops in Finland, in which the Joker card features the noaidi "as a deranged drug abuser getting his visions by eating fly agaric (mushrooms)" (SSN Protest).

Thus there is a discussion going on, in protest demonstrations in the streets and in the media, as to where the line should be drawn when it comes to tourism's use of images and rituals connected with Sami noaidevuohta. Some think that the Santa Claus Hotel's use of symbols from the noaidi's govadas as decorations on curtains and on bedclothes is disrespectful toward Sami values, while others think this might be acceptable (NRK Sápmi). Much of the indignation concerning tourism's use of Sami spiritual symbols questions whether the recontextualizations of these symbols can be understood as respectful or not. What kind of environment does a tourist site offer for the presentation of an indigenous spiritual heritage?

Sápmi Park in Kárášjohka/Karasjok is a modern tourist theme park established in conjunction with the hotels in the Norwegian Rica Hotel franchise in 2000. The whole idea behind this theme park was to present a genuine and traditional version of Sami culture. The village of Kárášjohka/Karasjok was, however, not seen as being able to meet the demands of a growing tourism in the area. The main problem was paradoxical: that this area in the middle of what is considered to be the heartland of Sami culture did not really look Sami enough to be appreciated by visiting tourists. A theme park could be tailored to meet the growing needs of the tourism industry.

This new tourist site was established only a couple of hundred meters away from the already mentioned Sámiid Vuorká-Dávvirat (Sami Collections) in Kárášjohka/Karasjok, where Pouelsen's original drum is kept in the magazine, and where a copy of the drum has been exhibited. The majority of the tourists who earlier visited the museum to get a taste of traditional Sami culture, now visited the theme park instead. Beyond what a museum is capable of, the Sápmi theme park aimed to give tourists the feeling of crossing the border between an everyday, ordinary Western and urban way of life, and becoming immersed in a way of life and thinking that belonged to premodern living conditions. This was signaled as soon as the tourists passed through the gate into the park, after they had paid the entrance fee, and were free to experience the newly constructed open-air museum. The Sápmi Park features the *lavvu* (tent) typical for this nomadic culture in different shapes, as well as old buildings in traditional design, in which the Sami lived when the reindeer were in their winter pastures. Tourists can experience live reindeer, or they can visit a Sami-inspired restaurant in a giant *darfegoahti* (turf hut) and consume dishes with reindeer meat.

But even in Sápmi Park the tourists soon meet the iconic image of the rune drum, govadas, only this time first as signposts, giving directions to the various attractions inside the park. If the govadas indeed played an important role for the Sami as an instrument for orientation in relation to a spiritual world, and as a supernatural helper to find the right path to follow whenever problems had to be solved, it had now been reduced to a simple signpost, advertising the direction to experiences, attractions, and consumption possibilities of various kinds. This means that the rune drum has been transformed from an image of an intricate symbolic world, into a denotative sign telling tourists where to consume. The "drums as signposts" in the theme park lead the tourists to, for example, the souvenir shop, where among other goods they also can buy copies of mass-produced rune drums (not the *duodji*-type of copies) at relatively affordable prices, available in a variety of sizes. The imagery of the rune drum is also for sale as decorations in a rich assortment of design products, ranging from drinking mugs to silverware, and from clothing to jewelry. These transformations of the Sami govadas in many ways have only very loose connections with the original content, but still function as markers of Sáminess, nurtured from multiple sources like history, spirituality, aesthetics, and commercialization.

Ecology and Equivocality: The Complexities of a Virtual Sami Shaman

One of the "drum signposts" inside Sápmi Park welcomes visitors to the main attraction at this tourist site: the Stálobákti Magic Theatre (and the Tourist Information, Coffee Shop, Shop, and Silversmith). This dramatized production takes place in a separate scene within the larger area of the theme park, and is designed to present the traditional worldview of the Sami people, and more specifically to give an impression of what noaidevuohta is, and what the symbols on the govadas really stand for. Realizing that a people's beliefs or worldviews are not easily represented in a traditional museum exhibition, the theme park's organizers decided to put considerable money and resources into the construction of a dramatic scene in which the ideas hidden inside people's heads could be presented visually. For that reason, this presentation was developed in cooperation with the international company BRC Imagination Arts (http://brcweb.com), and with the involvement and assistance of several contemporary Sami artists and culture workers (according to a credit poster at the entrance to the show). BRC Imagination Arts had already done work with digitalized storytelling in several different arenas, like movies, special effect theaters, modern exhibitions, experience museums, and theme parks. On their website, the company presents the Magic Theatre project in the following way,

> Located literally near the end of the Earth, at the Sápmi Cultural Park in Karasjok, Norway, the Sápmi Magic Theatre opened a unique window into the ancient mythologies of the reindeer herding people known as the Sami. (http://brcweb.com/Projects/sapmi-magic-theater/)

When the Sápmi Magic Theatre first opened in 2001, this kind of representation of Sami spiritual culture was both new and technologically innovative. Combining digital technology, pictures, and film to tell a narrative based on traditional knowledge and belief made it possible to develop a commercial product appealing to the experience industry in general and to the tourism business in particular. The combination of "ancient mythologies" and ultramodern visual technologies creates a sense of excitement, offering visitors the chance to enter a kind of time machine:

> Innovative combination of cutting-edge media technologies share the Sami myths and wisdom with new generations of locals and international tourists. The host for this enlightening adventure is an old Sami shaman whose face appears, via the magic of layered digital imagery, in the flames of a campfire. In-theater effects such as smoke, fiber optics and fog give shape to the tale he tells, opening hearts and minds to the unique Sami worldview. (http://brcweb.com/Projects/sapmi-magic-theater/)

One of BRC's mottos is "creating experiences that matter," and the digitalized, multimediated theatrical performance offers an ethnographic and historical account of Sami spiritual life. And as with all of their shows, the intention is that they also carry a moral obligation and imperative, in BRC's own words: "With every visitor experience we create, and in every heart that we touch, we strive to leave the world a better place by awaking the best in people" (http://brcweb.com/). The show's narrative certainly carries a distinct moral message, although it is less clear what the imperative of this should be for the visitors. So what is this narrative? The basic plot of the story is tied to the oppositional conflict between modernity and tradition, in which the intrusion of modern life and technology into Sami life is a real threat to the traditional values that once existed in Sami culture.

The narrative is enacted in two different sections. The first performance takes place in a square room, in which a film screen through the use of film clips from Sami everyday life relates a narrative of a transition from a traditional, harmonious, nature-based living, to a contemporary way of life based on technology, snow scooters, and helicopters. At the end of the film, the audience can watch an old Sami entering a helicopter, now used in reindeer herding in some districts. While they lift into the sky in turbulence and heavy noise, a voice-over rhetorically asks what the Sami forefathers would have thought of this kind of use of the tundra environments. The film ends, and the visitors are asked to continue to the next room, to learn more about the spiritual life of the Sami. Walking through a maze-like passage, one enters the next room, which is circular and has a high ceiling, imitating the interior of a large Sami tent. One half-circle of the room has seats for the spectators, and the other half is a screen.

While the spectators find their seats, the sound of a drum, imitating the human heartbeat, fills the room. In the middle of the room there is a fireplace, and in the artificial smoke from this fire the face of the old man who previously entered the helicopter reappears. Only now he presents himself as the timeless shaman of the Sami people, and his mission is to relate the true narrative of the Samis' relation to nature and the spiritual powers that can be found there. This narrative is accompanied by an impressive composition of digitally transmitted images, light effects, sounds, and musical scores. The screen shows an arrangement of pictures from rock carvings, images from the rune drums, and pictures from beautiful northern landscapes, while artificial stars and Northern Lights flash over the ceiling. The narrative about Sami spirituality itself is based on several of the sometimes contradictory historical sources discussed earlier in this article. But the specific narrative about the worldview of the Sami is linked with prevailing contemporary ideas of indigenous wisdom about nature, about inherently ecologically friendly ways of life, and about a kind of environmental concern that is lacking in the Western, modern, urban lifestyle. This way of thinking is recognizable to visitors. This linking of indigeneity, spirituality, and environmental concern is already known to national and international audiences from New Age literature, Hollywood movies, and a wide variety of media presentations.

The aspiration to provide a respectful version of the old Sami noaid-evuohta and indigenous spirituality, however, also evokes older images of indigenous peoples as either "ignoble savages" and primitives with heathen religions, or as "noble savages" who live in a prelapsarian harmonious contact with nature, freed from the corrupting forces of civilization and modernity. The problem is that when the tourists again enter the streets of Kárášjohka, this contemporary Sami village turns non-Sami in the eyes of the tourists, and true Saminess (and spirituality) is something that only belongs in a very distant past, or in the Magic Theatre's purely virtual reality.

The Multivocality of Circulating Narratives and Contextualized Exhibits

The Steilneset Memorial Hall that is dedicated to the victims of the Finnmark witchcraft trials does not flag any strong references to ethnicity. And the victims of the prosecutions indeed had varied ethnic backgrounds, although about 20 percent of the accused were referred to as Sami in the court proceedings (Hagen 2002: 322). The short text in Pouelsen's niche in the Memorial Hall reads abruptly that he was: "Brought before the court in Vadsø on 9 February 1692" and "accused of having used a rune drum and of practicing godless witchcraft" (Willumsen s.a.: 97). His confessions before the court cover a longer list, although none of them would really stand out as criminal acts for the contemporary reader. But the memorial tells the narratives of the victims and their sufferings. Louise Bourgeois' burning chair is a constant reminder to the atrocities that were once committed. In the big glass cube, the chair and the flames are also reflected in seven gigantic mirrors surrounding the chair. While the burning flame and the historical sources connect to an historical past, these mirrors, by their shape provide associations with modern science as it is represented in laboratories, surgery rooms, and other institutions related to investigation and research. For the visitor, these mirrors sometimes reflect the flames and the chair, sometimes the surrounding landscape, and sometimes the visitor her/himself as a spectator. The reflections can carry references to illegitimate uses of power and atrocities being committed in our own time. On the other hand, Peter Zumthor's Memorial Hall for the individuals who lost their lives during these witchcraft trials in the extreme north of the Scandinavian Arctic reminds us of the fragility of historical facts. The amassed historical sources about this gruesome experience are organized as a hanging textile corridor, suspended from scaffolds above the earth, like victims in the most vulnerable position. Walking inside the construction, one can literally feel how it is the object of external forces when the wind makes the corridor move.

We have seen that the noaidi's drum has been interpreted and reinterpreted, decontextualized and recontextualized, as it has been developed as an object of several transculturations. Out of these encounters between changing actors and versions of the drum, new contexts have been formed, while some of the old narratives have been retained. The old narratives of the Sami noaidi, the missionary reports on the "ungodly" spiritual leaders of the "heathen" Sami, the museums' frozen exhibitions, modern Sami artists' fascination with, and creative interpretations of the imagery world of the old noaidis' drums, New Age reinterpretations of the old Sami noaidi into a version of world shamanism, and tourism's commodification of Sami spiritual culture: all of these influences are in some way or another implicated in the production of a virtual Sami noaidi at the Sápmi Park's Magic Theatre in Kárášjohka. But as we have seen, they all in a sense have connections to the same older historical presentations of Sami beliefs and spirituality.

But in this way the digitalized version of the old Sami shaman in Sápmi Park's Magic Theatre also gets caught in several dilemmas, and some of these dilemmas can be traced back to the older descriptions of Sami spirituality discussed in this chapter. On the one hand, the presentation evokes ideas of the Sami as primitive and ignoble children of nature with pre-Christian beliefs. Even the planning of the theme park raised protests among conservative Christian congregations in the area, who feared that the new center would disseminate old "heathen" ideas among the population of the area, and in that way become destructive to Christian work among the Sami. On the other hand, the ever-recurring European understanding of the Sami as a kind of Noble Savage must also be seen as equally far removed from the contemporary realities in the Sami area. The ideas of Sami spirituality as a unique indigenous concern for nature in fact leave a very limited space for Sami prospects in a modern world. Often tied to global New Age ideas of aboriginal nature-bound connections, these ideas and myths fasten a group of already colonized people to roles determined by the very myths of European majority populations. The myths of a widespread Western romantic imagination have a privileged position, and have to be met with strategic dialogue.

In this way, the picture of the child noaidi in the hotel room in Anár/ Inari should perhaps not only be interpreted as a romantic image meant for the tourist market. It also expresses some of the inherent ambiguity that always follows the image of the Sami noaidi, as it has been outlined above. Important historical sources (even when they are strongly biased) testify to the fact that the Sami have an important spiritual heritage relating to noaidevuotha. But the narratives and presentations relating to these spiritual traditions have always been influenced by colonializing forces from the outside world, and from the power relations that have been developed over time in the border zone. Legal, religious, archival, museum, literary, artistic, and touristic contexts can all be understood as parts of these processes. Commodification of noaidevuohta develops commercial contexts, in which the serialization of rune drums in souvenir shops, with relatively cheap versions for sale in a variety of sizes, also influences the use of the drum in artistic and literary contexts. The ambiguity relating to Sami spirituality must be acknowledged as part of any discourse related to this field of knowledge. Subsequently, one might say that the itineraries of the noaidevuotha-knowledge, represented by the rune drum traveling through different discourses and entering various contexts, are not only circular like the drum itself, but have in effect formed patterns more intricate and complicated than those painted with red alder bark on the rune drum skin. Different layers of meaning and different interpretations are constantly being mixed, recontextualized, and reinterpreted.

References

Bakhtin, Mikhail M. 1981: *The Dialogic Imagination*. Austin: University of Texas Press.

Bendix, Regina. 2000. "After Identity: Ethnicity between Commodification and Cultural Commentary," in Regina Bendix and Herman Roodenburg (eds.) *Managing Ethnicity. Perspectives from folklore studies, history and anthropology*. Amsterdam: Het Spinhuis, 77–95.

Bourgeois, Louise, and Peter Zumthor. 2011. *Steilneset Memorial: To the Victims of the Finnmark Witchcraft Trials*. Oslo: Forlaget Press.

Clifford, James, 1997. *Routes: Travel and Translation in the Late Twentieth Century*. Cambridge: Harvard University Press.

Comaroff, John L., and Jean Comaroff. 2009. *Ethnicity, Inc*. Chicago: University of Chicago Press.

Dana, Kathleen Osgood. 2003. "Áillohaš the Shaman-Poet and His Govadas-Image Drum." Academic dissertation. Oulu: Oulu University.

Dicks, Bella. 2003. *Culture on Display: The Production of Contemporary Visitability*. Berkshire: Open University Press.

Friis, J. A. 1871. *Lappisk Mytologi*. Christiania: Alb. Cammermeyer.

Fonneland, Trude. 2012. Spiritual Entrepreneurship in a Northern Landscape: Spirituality, Tourism and Politics. *Temenos: Nordic Journal of Comparative Religion* 48: 155–178.

Hagen, Rune. 2002. Harmløs dissenter eller djevelsk trollmann? Trolldomsprosessen mot samen Anders Poulsen i 1692. *Historisk tidsskrift* 81: 319–346.

———. 2003. "Kildene til og resepsjonen av trolldomskapitlet (kap. 21) i Knud Leems Beskrivelse over Finmarkens Lapper 1767," in Jan Ragnar Hagland og Steinar Supphellen (eds.) *Knud Leem og det samiske. Foredrag holdt ved et seminar i regi av Det Kongelige Norske Videnskabers Selskab 11.-12. oktober 2002* (Det Kongelige Norske Videnskabers Selskab Skrifter 2, 2003) Trondheim: Tapir akademisk forlag, 79–93.

Hirvonen, Vuokko. 2008. "Bild och text hand i hand. Om mångkunniga samiska författare," in Christina Westergren and Eva Silvén (eds.) *För Sápmi i tiden* (Fataburen. Nordiska museets och Skansens årsbok 2008) Stockholm: Nordiska museets förlag, 186–203.

Kraft, Siv Ellen. 2009. "Sami Indigenous Spirituality: Religion and Nationbuilding in Norwegian Sápmi." *Temenos: Nordic Journal of Comparative Religion* 45: 179–206.

Leem, Knud. 1767. *Beskrivelse over Finmarkens Lapper, deres Tungemaal, Levemaade og forrige Afgudsdyrkelse.* Kiøbenhavn: Det Kongel. Waisenhuses Bogtrykkerie.

Manker, Ernst. 1938. *Die Lappische Zaubertrommel. Eine ethnologische Monographie. 1. Die Trommel als Denkmal materieller Kultur.* (Acta Lapponica 1) Stockholm: Nordiska museet.

———. 1950. *Die Lappische Zaubertrommel. Eine ethnologische Monographie. 2. Die Trommel als Urkunde geistigen Lebens.* (Acta Lapponica 6) Stockholm: Nordiska museet.

———. 1965. *Nåjdkonst: Trolltrummans bildvärld.* Stockholm: LTs förlag.

———. 1971. *Samefolkets konst.* Halmstad: Askild & Kärnekull.

Mathisen, Stein R. 2004a. "Hegemonic Representations of Sámi Culture: From Narratives of Noble Savages to Discourses on Ecological Sámi," in Anna-Leena Siikala, Barbro Klein, and Stein R. Mathisen (eds.) *Creating Diversities: Folklore, Religion and the Politics of Heritage.* Helsinki: Finnish Literature Society, 17–30.

———. 2004b. "Representasjoner av kulturell forskjell. Fortelling, makt og autoritet i utstillinger av samisk kultur." *Tidsskrift for kulturforskning* 3/3: 5–25.

———. 2010. "Indigenous Spirituality in the Touristic Borderzone: Virtual Performances of Sámi Shamanism in Sápmi Park." *Temenos: Nordic Journal of Comparative Religion* 46: 53–72.

Olsen, Kjell. 2004. "The Touristic Construction of the 'Emblematic' Sámi," in Anna-Leena Siikala, Barbro Klein, and Stein R. Mathisen (eds.) *Creating Diversities: Folklore, Religion and the Politics of Heritage.* Helsinki: Finnish Literature Society, 292–305.

Pinkerton, John. 1810. *A General Collection of the Best and Most Interesting Voyages and Travels, in all Parts of the World,* vol. I. (Account of Danish Lapland, by Knud Leems) Philadelphia: Kimber and Conrad (First English edition London 1808), 376–490.

Pratt, Mary Louise. 1992. *Imperial Eyes: Travel Writing and Transculturation.* London: Routledge.

Rydving, Håkan. 1991. "The Saami Drums and the Religious Encounter in the 17th and 18th Centuries," in Tore Ahlbäck and Jan Bergman (eds.) *The Saami Shaman Drum.* Åbo: The Donner Institute, 28–51.

————. 1993. *The End of Drum-Time: Religious Change among the Lule Saami, 1670s–1740s*. Uppsala: Uppsala University.

Scheffy, Zoë-Hateehc Durrah. 2004. "Sámi Religion in Museums and Artistry," in Anna-Leena Siikala, Barbro Klein, and Stein R. Mathisen (eds.) *Creating Diversities: Folklore, Religion and the Politics of Heritage*, Helsinki: Finnish Literature Society, 225–259.

Silvén, Eva. 2012. "Contested Sami Heritage: Drums and Sieidis on the Move," in Domenique Poulot, José Maria Lanzarote Guiral, and Felicity Bodenstein (eds.) *National Museums and the Negotiation of Difficult Pasts* (EuNaMuse Report No. 8) Linköping: Linköping University Electronic Press, 173–186. (http://www.ep.liu.se/ecp_home/index.en.aspx?issue=082)

Thomas, Nicholas. 1994. *Colonialism's Culture: Anthropology, Travel and Government*. Cambridge: Polity Press.

Ucko, Peter. 2002. "Who Owns the Cultural Heritage?—'Heritage' and 'Indigenous Peoples' in the 21st Century," in *Vem äger kulturarvet?* (Duoddaris 20) Jokkmokk: Ájtte, Duottar- ja Sámemusea, 39–49.

Valkeapää, Nils-Aslak. 1988. *Beaivi, áhčážan*. (English translation 1997: *The Sun, My Father*) Guodageaidnu: DAT.

Willumsen, Liv Helene (ed.). 2010. *The Witchcraft Trials in Finnmark, Northern Norway*. Bergen: Skald/Varanger Museum.

————. 2013. *Witches of the North: Scotland and Finnmark* (Studies in Medieval and Reformation Traditions 170) Leiden: Brill 2013.

————. s.a. *Memorial to the Witches burned in Finnmark: Guidebook*. Vardø: Varanger Museum IKS.

Web pages

BRC Imagination Arts: homepage (http://brcweb.com); information on Sápmi Magic Theatre (http://brcweb.com/Projects/sapmi-magic-theater/) (visited December 12, 2013)

NRK Sápmi: October 30, 2008: "Brenner ikke kofter" (http://www.nrk.no/kanal /nrk_sapmi/1.6287555) (visited May 29, 2012)

November 4, 2008: "Vil verne om samisk kultur" (http://www.nrk.no/kanal /nrk_sapmi/1.6293956) (visited May 29, 2012)

Sápmi Park: (http://www.visitsapmi.no/) (visited December 10, 2013)

"SSN Protest against the Exploitation of Sami Culture": (http://boreale.konto .itv.se/rovaniemi.htm) (visited December 10, 2013)

Steilneset Memorial, National Tourist Routes in Norway: (http://www.nasjonal-eturistveger.no/en/varanger/) (visited November 18, 2013)

11

The Festival Isogaisa: Neoshamanism in New Arenas

Trude Fonneland

What Is Isogaisa?

Preface

"In Bardufoss, the war drum is replaced by the Sami drum (*runebomme*)," NRK Sami radio announced on September 8, 2010. A stone's throw away from the fenced and guarded military area near the welfare arena *Istindportalen*, green-clad young soldiers have company. People donning traditional Sami garb from Russia and Norway as well as 150 excited festival goers have found their way to the festival area. Three big *lavvu* (Sami traditional tents) are raised on the field outside, and smoke from the bonfire lies over the area. In the middle of the crowd, a man starts to *joik* (a traditional Sami way of singing). A Sami drum is passed along from hand to hand and ends up by an opening near the bonfire. This is where Mayor Viggo Fossum and festival leader Ronald Kvernmo take over; with a beat of the drum, they declare the first Sami shamanic festival in history to be open.

Isogaisa, which is presented as being an indigenous festival focusing on the spiritual, was held for the first time on September 3–5, 2010. For the first two years, the festival was arranged in Heggelia, both inside and outside of the military arena Istindportalen in the Målselv municipality of Nord-Troms. After 2012, the festival was moved to the guesthouse Fjellkysten in Lavangen, where it is now permanently located. The establishment of a winter festival arena in Fjellkysten is also in the cards: the Isogaisa *siida* (a traditional Sami community) will consist of an

Figure 11.1   Festival Poster 2012.

octagon—an eight-sided lavvu and eight peat *goahti*s (traditional Sami turf huts) for overnight stays.[1]

The modern shaman Kvernmo is behind Isogaisa. Having recently finished a bachelor's degree in marketing from BI (Norwegian Business School) in Oslo, he wants to put the theories he learned in school into practice.[2] Kvernmo invites the audience to take part in an annual festival weekend of inner travel—to magical adventures in a Sami landscape.

According to the festival program, the motivation behind the festival is to unite a pre-Christian Sami worldview with modern ways of thinking, and thus create "a spiritual meeting place where different cultures are brought together."[3]

Isogaisa is an innovative festival concept. On the basis of Sami pre-Christian religion and neoshamanic philosophy, the festival uses symbols, rituals, and ideas to enrich the experience of the audience. In this way, Isogaisa also exemplifies cultural production through reinterpreting and redefining the past. One of the products that takes shape in this way is Sami spiritual and cultural heritage, which can be seen not only as part of one's personal negotiation of identity (see Lowenthal 1998) but also as part of the marketing of the local, which is conveyed as being beyond—and thus of interest to—postmodern society (see Kirshenblatt-Gimblett 1998: 149–153).

In this chapter, I will look into the types of narratives, products, and services that take shape and that are put into practice when a shamanic festival opens its doors to an audience for the first time. I ask what is included and what is being defined in the marketing of Isogaisa as an attractive festival venue, and investigate the roles that the past and Sami pre-Christian religion play in the thematic production. Focusing on the local aspect, I further explore how the local and distinctive features of Isogaisa are highlighted based upon global structures and organizations to generate interest for a specific product and a specific destination.[4]

This chapter is based upon my own fieldwork at Isogaisa in 2010 and 2012, as well as meetings and interviews with the festival leader Kvernmo. The information about the festival presented on Isogaisa's home page and Facebook page is also a key part of my analysis.[5]

The chapter begins with a discussion about the limits of the festival genre, and moves on to discuss how the Sami neoshamanic movement has evolved from its early days to the celebrations of the present day at the Isogaisa festival. I will also present the structure of Isogaisa and the role of the festival in local revitalization processes—in creating new images and dreams about the high north.

Isogaisa—a Newcomer to the Festival Arena?

By virtue of being the first Norwegian festival oriented toward New Age spirituality, Isogaisa contributes to a broadening of the religious landscape in Norway. The festival can be characterized as a manifestation of spiritual entrepreneurship that combines New Age core values with pre-Christian symbols and stories. Isogaisa is also a key arena for the further development of Sami shamanism in a specifically North Norwegian environment.

When I characterize Isogaisa as being a newcomer on the festival scene, one might well ask, What about the many "alternative fairs" (*Alternativmesser*) that are arranged annually in both big and small Norwegian cities? Are not these also arrangements that focus on exactly the same types of religious sentiments that come into play at Isogaisa? Although the boundaries are not sharp, in my opinion the Norwegian "alternative fairs" fall outside of the festival genre. The arrangements and products featured at alternative fairs are the same all over the country, with only minor seasonal and local variations. These fairs are primarily marketplaces for a plethora of New Age products and services that are global in scope. The unique aspect of a festival of Isogaisa's type, on the other hand, is precisely the local connection and the emphasis on the particular and local flavor—the unique local culture and local religious traditions. Like the Norwegian alternative fairs, Isogaisa is an arena for promoting New Age ideas and trends, but the products on offer here have a glow of authenticity by virtue of their connection with a local place and local history. As ethnologist and festival researcher Kjell Hansen says, festivals are embraced as tools for promoting local and regional development (2002: 20). In this way, the festival genre has clear links with the tourist industry (Yeoman 2004). The organizers of these events use the festival to conjure up an attractive aura around their cities and districts. In combining catchy slogans with spectacular images of local nature and culture, and by connecting these with annual events, the objective is to create an attractive brand that will generate economic as well as cultural-social growth (see O'Dell 2010: 25).

The festivals also welcome an audience that increasingly acts as a body of tourists looking for spectacular events and instant adventure. The objective of Isogaisa organizers is to reach as many interested people as possible by tailoring a festival program that targets all age groups. When asked what type of audience Isogaisa is intended for, Kvernmo says,

> People of all ages, from all parts of society, from all countries! Some go there to meet like-minded people, some go there to attend seminars and workshops, and some go because they are curious. Isogaisa is suitable for families. There are arrangements for children, young people and adults. The volume of the music will be comfortable, and there are no age restrictions.[6]

Over the past two years we have seen that around 500 people visit the festival. The majority of these are women of a certain age group. People working in the health sector also constitute a large portion of attendees.

This is comparable with the demographics of those who attend Norwegian alternative fairs and New Age workshops and seminars (see Hammer 1997: 27–29). However, there is one area in which Isogaisa deviates from the traditional interest in New Age activities, which attract tourists in the form of Norwegian and international travelers to the region. To them, Isogaisa is probably not primarily regarded as a New Age gathering, but rather as an event that allows them to experience local religious and cultural traditions.

Isogaisa—a Center for a Growing Sami Shamanic Movement

Sami pre-Christian religious expressions, symbols, and narratives—the so-called *noaidevuohta*—serve as inspirational sources for the program and for the products on offer. At the same time, festival organizers say they want to communicate these expressions in a modern language and adapt them to contemporary life.[7] In this way, Isogaisa can be seen as a significant contributor to the growing and evolving Sami neoshamanic scene.

Festival organizer and shaman Kvernmo has been apprenticed to Ailo Gaup, who was the first to look seriously into Sami pre-Christian religion as an inspiration for modern shamans (see Fonneland, this volume). Kvernmo became part of this neoshamanic movement at a time when Sami neoshamanism was in its infancy. Like Gaup, he was eager to revive and recreate bits and parts of the Sami pre-Christian religious past, and, in 2008, he arranged his first workshop on Sami neoshamanism at a Sami school in the Målselv municipality in Nord-Troms.

The Isogaisa festival is presented as a celebration of the new local scene of Sami neoshamanism, and, according to the organizer, is intended to contribute to further development in this field. In order to create room for growth and development, Isogaisa allows for the gathering and uniting of Sami religious traditions from all of Sápmi, the Fennoscandian Sami region.

Each year, a specially selected group of Sami people is invited to take part in the event. In 2010, eight shamans from the Murmansk region participated: one interpreter, two shamans, two dancers, and three *duodji* performers. In 2011, the youth organization Nurash from Lovozero was invited, in addition to some of the Sami cultural workers and shamans who had participated in the festival the year before. The purpose of these invitations, which are financially supported by the Barents Secretariat, is to establish a bond between Sami shamans in Norway and Russia.[8] "Mini Isogaisa" festivals also take place throughout the year in both Norway and Russia, and the objective is the same, that is, to spread information about the festival and to link different Sami cultures. The program of the "Mini Isogaisas" spans the course of one day and focuses on socializing and on the performing of rituals, and usually concludes with a concert featuring Sami performers.

In this way, the festival and the festival landscape are transformed into serving as a cradle for Sami spiritual cultural heritage and a locally rooted Sami identity, which is used as a strategy and counterpoint to the global neoshamanic scene. In our conversation, Kvernmo stresses this point:

> the things that are coming from USA via Michael Harner, that's a lot of stuff; that's where the main beacon is. But we don't have to go further than just past Murmansk, to the Komi and Nenets peoples—and then there's the Sami; that's three different people in a small geographical area just over the border, and they...at least the Nenets people, many of them haven't had contact with the Russians, so shamanism is a living culture among many of the people within the tribe. There's a lot of solid culture to be found there, plain and simple. So, the things that have been lost to the Sami can be borrowed from them, because they are so close. And it feels so much more natural than that American thing. I mean, Michael Harner has done a great job....He has, in a way, mixed together a lot of cultures, and that's when you get that kind of world shamanism. But being a good Sami activist, I'm not sure I like it (laughter). I prefer to turn it the other way around: if we are to make a festival, we should rather base ourselves on the Norwegian, the local, the Sami region. And if we are to borrow from other cultures, we should go to Sami areas in Russia or the South Sami regions. If we have to go even further, it shouldn't be any further than to the next people who may be regarded as distant relatives. That would feel a lot more natural than taking something from the USA, or South America or Peru or Africa, or wherever. (Interview, my translation)

In emphasizing the connection with local, similar religious traditions, the festival sets itself apart from its American roots and supports a brand of shamanism that is becoming increasingly locally rooted. The Russian delegations are assigned the role of bridging new and old shamanic traditions, and are presented by Kvernmo as being important vessels of traditions and authorities on this subject. In this turn toward the local, festival organizers emphasize that the type of neoshamanism that is practiced at Isogaisa is not artificial or constructed; rather, it is founded on traditions rooted in a local and recent past.

The creation of a Sami neoshamanic milieu that is being formed at Isogaisa is a matter of writing oneself into a local tradition, and creating narratives about the local place and local religious traditions. The festival takes part in the global by highlighting the local. Global New Age currents are colored by local tradition and culture, and transformed into something that the practitioners can present as being local and unique. In this way, the festival becomes a resource when it meets the global New

Age culture, by making a distinction between what is considered to be locally authentic and what is considered universal.

Isogaisa—Indigenous Festival with a Spiritual Focus

Festivals are a break from the daily routine and, according to Hansen, they offer a narrative structure that cannot be comprehended solely by reading about it; it has to be experienced through action and participation (2002: 21). This was my experience as well when I got on the bus to Målselv one September morning in 2010 to observe and take part in the Isogaisa neoshamanic festival, and similarly when I participated in the festival weekend in Fjellkysten at Lavangen in 2012. Although I had studied the program and sought information from the Facebook page and home page in advance, it was only after I was present and actively taking part in the festival that the events there became comprehensible to me.

I will try to impart what Isogaisa is like and what the festival can offer by way of stories, by describing the atmosphere and values, and by the observations I made during these visits. The analysis of the festival will be based upon four different sections and events that in sum make up the core of Isogaisa, namely, seminars, the alternative fair, entertainment, and ceremonies. These events are presented separately on the festival posters, and although some of them overlap to an extent and are arranged simultaneously, I have chosen to present them separately in order to provide a comprehensive idea of the experiences that are generated in the thematic production of the festival.

Seminars

The Isogaisa festival weekend has so far had a fairly fixed program, beginning with a keynote seminar focused on a specific topic. In the two first years of the festival, the general theme of the seminars was "similarities and differences between conventional medicine and the traditional practices of indigenous peoples." The seminar was organized as a series of lectures with three invited speakers, and was rounded off by a panel discussion in which the audience was invited to ask questions related to the theme of the seminar. In order to shed light on this theme, in 2010 the organizers invited shaman Ailo Gaup, postdoctoral research fellow in clinical medicine Randall Sexton, and pedagogue and Sami researcher Jens Ivar Nergård. Gaup opened his talk by stressing how it was an historical moment, and pointed out how the opening of the festival marked a milestone in Sami history. He went on to express how the "time is ripe for a gathering such as this. In a place like this. The fact that people are summoned to this landscape; to this part of the country."[9] Sexton took the opportunity to talk about the experience he had gained from his fieldwork and practice in the region, and stressed that the World Health Organization (WHO) encourages cooperation between conventional medicine and local practitioners. Nergård, for his part, pointed out how, although cooperation is being encouraged, there is little dialogue between the two traditions in Norway. He moved on to say that Sami narratives of how the Sami relate to nature are met with little sympathy by conventional medicine, and that this may have consequences such as malpractice and prescribing the wrong medication. This is a recurring issue in his own research, among other things in his book, *The Living Experience: A Study of the Sami Traditional Knowledge* (2006)—(*Den levende erfaring: En studie i samisk kunnskapstradisjon*).[10]

In addition to the regular festivalgoers and the Russian delegation, the 2010 seminar audience consisted of people who work in the health sector in the Troms and northern Nordland municipalities. Their attendance at the festival had been paid for by their employers, and most of them only attended this part of the program. It is rare to have Norwegian municipalities fund shamanic seminars for their employees! What made the seminar appealing to this particular target group was probably the connection between neoshamanism and science. Kvernmo comments on the motivation behind the seminar in this way:

> In this seminar, we raise the spiritual up to a scientific level; we find research-ers who defend our practice and give it some kind of acceptance. This is very important. Those who attended the seminar were mainly people from the municipal health sector. They have a relaxed attitude towards what we are doing. Traditionally it's been, like, if a patient suddenly receives a visit by their grandmother who has been dead for ten years, then they have been regarded as having a problem. Then you're hallucinating and schizophrenic and need to be medicated. Of course, there's a lot of good psychiatric practice going on, but they are a wee bit afraid of spiritual things. It is sufficient to say, "Oh. So what did she want?" She's a helper, that's all. And then it's no longer a problem; it's a resource. That's part of the point; they were supposed to raise this to a dif-ferent level.

In many ways, the seminar demonstrates what religious historian Olav Hammer identifies as a central discursive strategy that he believes is com-monly utilized in New Age circles as a legitimizing factor for New Age products and services, namely, to appeal to rationality and science (2001: 201–330). In this seminar, Sexton and Nergård served as spokesmen for neoshamanic practices, and their presence has contributed to legitimizing the field. At the same time, the boundaries between neoshamanism and conventional medicine are blurred.

The three speakers also provided public relations to the local area and local religious traditions. The seminar was portrayed as an historical event, regarding both the topic being discussed and the place where the seminar was held. In various ways, the three speakers shook up established stereotypes and conceptions of the north Norwegian region as a superstitious and uncivilized place, far from modern life and progress. The new narratives that were thus being shaped also challenged power and status relationships by imparting a message of how the indigenous peoples' cultural and religious traditions form a center and serve as a resource in our postmodern world.

In addition to the main seminar, the festival also offered smaller seminars and workshops arranged by different exhibitors. In 2010, the neoshamans Ailo Gaup and Eirik Myrhaug offered workshops based upon their courses on neoshamanism, while Sexton taught holotropic breathwork—a practice in which breathing is considered a tool for altering one's consciousness and opening up underlying emotions and energies. For the past three years, the festival has also held a workshop in which people are invited to make their own Isogaisa drum, which, according to festival organizer Kvernmo, "will be a very special and exclusive drum with enormous energy."[11] The workshop is arranged by the modern shaman and drummaker Fredrik Prost from Kiruna. This workshop requires preregistration and begins as early as Thursday afternoon. The participants are handed materials from which they are supposed to make their own drum for use at the festival.

In the process of shaping and developing cultural heritage, there is a clear focus on objects. At Isogaisa, the traditional Sami drums (*runebomme)* are used as the basis for the new drums constructed by the participants, and they become a symbol of continuity with traditions of the past. In the words of the geographer David Lowenthal, "To be certain there was a past we must see at least some of its traces" (1985: 247). The Sami runebomme is one such trace. In providing participants a place to shape their festival drums, Isogaisa also offers the audience access to a firsthand taste of the past. The object, the Sami drum, is in this context a messenger that enables a dialogue between the past and the present. As folklorist Jonas Frykman says about the role of objects in cultural production: "Things like this—and many more—have become something more than symbols. They bear secrets and have to be induced to speak" (2002: 49).

At Isogaisa, the Sami drum no longer has the stigma of being a reminder of a pagan past; it is instead a powerful, authentic, and magical symbol of a vital Sami culture (see Mathisen 2011). Using the drum in a festival setting contributes its establishment as both an object that is to be displayed, as well as a living national and spiritual symbol.

The Alternative Fair

The second main part of the festival program is an alternative fair, which operates in parallel with the other festival activities right up until the festival concludes on Sunday afternoon. Compared with the alternative fairs (*Alternativmesser*) that are held annually in small and large Norwegian cities, this festival fair is a "mini alternative fair" with about 30 exhibitors. Whereas the alternative fairs gather a wide range of New Age exhibitors and performers, the main focus of the Isogaisa fair revolves around the Sami tradition, selling Sami drums, brass rings, duodji, Sami art, and other products related to the practice of Sami neoshamanism.

As festival organizers have chosen to have an alternative fair be one of the main parts of the festival, the dialogue Isogaisa has with the New Age milieu is highlighted. An alternative fair is a New Age market in miniature, which, despite its wide range of topics and products, conveys a standard repertoire that provides insight into the core values of the community—the New Age lingua franca (Kraft 2011). In a study of people who offer alternative treatments in Denmark, religious historian Lars Ahlin characterizes the New Age core in terms of four points, namely, self-spirituality, self-authority, self-responsibility, and holism (2007). At the festival fair, just as at other alternative fairs, various healers and therapists place weight on the *self* as a divine being within humanity, which is absolutely sovereign with regard to one's own judgment and choices. The neoshamans who have found their way to the festival fair venue and who receive festivalgoers for consultation and treatment, regard illness as a sign that something is wrong with the *whole* person. As therapists, they market their role as *guides*; it is the patients themselves who are responsible for their own healing.

Despite the fact that Isogaisa embraces the core principles of the New Age milieu, festival organizers also want to distance themselves from traditional alternative markets. Kvernmo emphasizes,

I don't know of any other events like Isogaisa. The local alternative fairs do try; but they lack the cultural bit. There are many good alternative events here in northern Norway, but you don't have any core culture; that's my impression. My impression is, not that I want to say anything bad about how the alternative fairs are organized, that it's a lot about business. "We sell what people want." We, on the other hand, don't do a lot of that. We try to convey a message that highlights Sami culture and neoshamanism; whereas, the alternative fairs are more like putting all sorts of stuff together under the same roof, and there's a lot of variety. Of course, we have to have some variety at Isogaisa, too; there will be bonfires, lavvu and Sami music....

Kvernmo has adopted the critique that many scholars and media express toward the alternative market, namely, that there is too much emphasis on business and there are too many religious traditions mixed together. In this way, the New Age movement appears to be a low-class culture (see Kraft 2011). In their focus on Sami culture and tradition, the festival fair makes a move to mark a distance from low culture.

New Age spirituality and Sami indigenous spirituality are portrayed as symbolizing two different sets of values: whereas the New Age movement is criticized for lacking roots and traditions, Sami indigenous spirituality holds a special status, and is connected with values such as wisdom, the ancients, cultural heritage, environmental protection, and natural insight. By marking their distance from typical New Age markets, and by linking the religious aspects of the festival to Sami culture rather than to the New Age, festival organizers boost the status of Isogaisa as both a festival and a business. In contrast with the New Age, the links to a Sami past and Sami indigenous spiritual traditions become a resource that attracts attention and guarantees a unique product, service, and experience.

Ceremonies

The many large and small ceremonies that are performed both inside and outside of the festival area constitute the third main event at Isogaisa. The festival begins with an opening ceremony, and is followed by a hunting ceremony, a children's ceremony, a chocolate ceremony, and various types of drumming journeys. Additionally, the announcement for the 2013 festival indicated that it would include a ceremony greeting the dawn, a tea ceremony, a pipe ceremony, and of course a closing ceremony.

The opening ceremony at Isogaisa 2012 was an event lasting three hours. At dusk on the first day of the festival, over 200 people gathered outside of the octagon, and before entering every participant had to go through a short act of purification in which sage smoke was passed over his or her body. Inside the octagon festival, attendees gathered in a big circle around an unlit bonfire. Then all the invited indigenous representatives from New Zealand, Canada, Russia, and Norway, together with festival leader Kvernmo, the municipality mayor, and musicians who were drumming and joiking, entered the center of the circle in a procession. While the music was playing, four people who were standing in opposite places were chosen to light the fire while invoking the spirits from the different corners of the world, from north, south, east, and west. The festival fire, Kvernmo announced, was a holy fire meant to burn until the end of the festival, and people were encouraged to come and sacrifice here during their stay. Then talks were given by the mayor, some of the indigenous representatives, and Kvernmo himself, who finished his speech by declaring that the Isogaisa festival 2012 was open. The rest of the opening ceremony was filled with theater performances and Sami folk music performed by invited groups and established Sami folk musicians. As the formal program came to an end, festival participants joined in, singing and dancing.

Activities are a core part of all types of festivals. The audience is not a group of festival spectators, but rather, they are festival *participants*. This implies an active and tangible relationship with the products on offer as well as the place in which they are offered. Additionally, the series of ceremonies marketed by Isogaisa facilitates other types of activities than we usually associate with the adventure economy of our time. Whereas theme parks, which were the subject of analysis in Joseph B. Pine and James H. Gilmore's book *The Experience Economy* (1999), allow for immediate satisfaction of the senses, Isogaisa, in contrast, allows for experiences of a slower kind—experiences that are supposed to affect the participants on an inner, psychological level. The various ceremonies are experiences laden with expectations of how they will, in one way or another, give the festival audience a feeling of increased energy—of inner growth and development (see O'Dell 2010: 31).

Although the activities offered at food festivals, literature festivals, and music festivals may also offer experiences for the senses that will influence and change those who participate, the numerous ceremonies of Isogaisa offer an additional dimension that more "worldly festivals" do not provide in the same way. The pipe ceremony, the hunting ceremony, the tea ceremony, and the many drumming journeys offer ritual passages in which the sensing of the landscape, the sound of the drum, tastes, and scents represent a liminality, transformation, and inner self-development. Isogaisa is thus not a festival in which the audience is supposed to just come and be entertained; the objective is to come, experience, and *be changed*.

The ceremony and interactive theater performance, "Those Who See," were among the activities that attracted many people in 2010. It focused on this change, and was staged as a rite of passage. The performance was created by Haugen Productions, and was also a part of the program of the indigenous festival Riddu Riđđu in Mandalen in 2007, under the name Mátki (the journey).[12]

At Isogaisa, the starting point of the performance was located in the woods behind Istindportalen. On Saturday and Sunday afternoons, groups of eight persons were dispatched every 30 minutes to go into nature and meet actors, healers, dancers, clowns, neoshamans, and musicians. The participants followed a forest trail that combined elements from Sami mythology and natural medicine from various parts of the world. They took part in drumming journeys aimed at finding their power animals, cleansing ceremonies, joik, and various creative challenges such as painting and dancing. The objective of the performance was, according to the organizers, that participants were to experience ancient indigenous traditions, and, through these, they would assess their own lives by asking questions such as: who am I, where do I stand today, what is my path? "Those Who See" places weight on how inspiration from indigenous peoples' religious tradition is a resource in the present day. This, according to the organizers, is something we in the Western world have lost and something we should rediscover.

Isogaisa presents itself as being precisely this type of learning arena, in which those with inquiring minds may acquire the values they feel we lack in Western culture. The festival offers a perceptible access to the Sami past, and thus forms a bond between the past and the present. The festival generates a feeling of how *it all happened here*, and that *here it is all happening now*. It is loaded with powerful symbols, which not only bring us back in time, presenting tales from the past, but also convey information about which types of values we regard as important in the present (see Eriksen 1999: 87ff). In this way, Isogaisa can be said to be a monument to Sami pre-Christian traditions that are being created within a certain framework every year. As a monument, Isogaisa contributes to a "coding" of the local place, which can be deciphered by the participants at the festival. The Isogaisa monument is not, however, solely based on the local landscape, but is meant to represent contemporary Sami neoshamanism in all Sami cultures.

The past, which is revived during the festival, is not the past we know from history books and the discourses of scholars. At Isogaisa, the link between memory and the imaginary world that is staged (Lowenthal 1985). Here, the past is not a closed chapter; it is a process that extends into the present and reaches into the future (Frykman 2002: 54).

Entertainment

Festivals are primarily social arenas in which people come together, maintain, and expand their social circles, and relax in a nice atmosphere while enjoying the entertainment. Entertainment is also the final item listed on the festival program. Isogaisa offers musical performances such as joik, dance, poetry readings, storytelling, and of course socializing around the bonfire. This type of entertainment can best be described as "ritual entertainment"—it has an additional dimension related to each participant's self-development.

One of the highlights of the entertainment section of the Isogaisa 2011 program was a festival dance for the general audience accompanied by joik chanting. The dance was published on YouTube prior to the festival, and on the Isogaisa home page people were encouraged to learn the steps before the festival. The dance and the joik visualized the journey to the Isogaisa festival by mimicking the movements and sounds of various Arctic animals. In the festival area, the dance and the joik contributed to a sense of community. The simple dance steps symbolized a project of coming together, in which participants of all age groups could take part according to their abilities. The Isogaisa dance and joik also served to highlight how formerly taboo cultural expressions are currently entering popular culture.

Norwegian festivals are generally known for having a relatively high level of alcohol consumption, where alcohol is an essential tool for setting the mood for the scheduled entertainment. The connection between alcohol and festival life is something from which the Isogaisa festival organizers wish to distance themselves, and they have chosen to market the festival as being a non-alcoholic event. There are probably several reasons for this.

From a historical perspective, alcohol is associated with colonization, with being a bad influence, and with exploitation by Norwegian authorities. Hard liquor was a frequently used trade commodity. This created a codependent relationship, which over time indebted people. History tells of Sami families who lost all their possessions because of this form of trade: of social misery, poverty, and conflict.

In addition to such perspectives on colonization, Kvernmo, in an interview with the newspaper *Troms Folkeblad*, also highlights a religious argument: "I am a shaman; and although I am not personally a teetotaller, I believe a spiritual practice such as neoshamanism cannot be combined with alcohol" (September 1, 2010). The homepage of the festival has this to say on the subject:

All the older Sami shamans I have talked to agree on this one thing: Inebriation has never been part of Sami shamanism! All of them also agree that we, too, should abstain from mixing shamanism with inebriation! So please, respect our ancient Sami culture and tradition. Do come to the festival! Come as you are! You're really more pleasant when sober![13]

In addition to confronting historical stereotypes, the festival leader's goal to create a festival in which participants abstain from alcohol, involves a wish to be taken seriously and to be on par with other, more established religious traditions. According to Kvernmo, neoshamanism is a serious spiritual practice in which all the senses must remain sharp, and is not taken lightly. Thus at the festival, one is to obtain intoxication from spiritual experience, which creates entertainment and serves as the basis for a neoshamanic movement that is growing and evolving.

Isogaisa in the Media

Several Norwegian and Sami regional newspapers have covered the Isogaisa festival.[14] *Troms Folkeblad* presented it as being Norway's first shamanic festival (September 6, 2010), and *Salangen Nyheter* announced that the festival was a "Drumming Success" (August 27, 2012), while *Nordlys*, in its January 14, 2013, article "Healing the World," pointed out that Isogaisa is lauded all over the world for its healing power. In 2010, the same newspaper had a feature article on the main seminar of the festival, and presented the seminar as an historical moment: "it is probably the first time in history that conventional psychiatric medicine is being held up against shamanism in this way" (September 8, 2010). All of the media stories were completely positive in their festival reviews. This media angle on the Isogaisa festival is probably due to the fact that the festival is regarded as a Sami indigenous event rather than New Age. Festival leader Kvernmo had previously been very clear about his Sami background in the same media. In this way, the festival is also linked to a Sami indigenous context. As Siv Ellen Kraft points out, this type of media coverage can be seen as an expression of a postcolonial consciousness, which has made one cautious regarding how indigenous peoples are portrayed in the media (2011). The way the festival is profiled in the media can thus be seen as contributing to legitimizing the festival as both a channel for entertainment and a player in regional development processes.

"Isogaisa: the Beating Heart of a Counterculture"

Festivals are events that serve to profile and expand the local, says Kjell Hansen in his article "Festivals, Spatiality and the New Europe" (2002). The special aspect of festivals is that they are indeed taking *place* (2002: 20). Isogaisa, too, takes place in a specially selected landscape. During the festival weekend, the local north Norwegian landscape is transformed into a spiritual hub for Sami culture, both nationally and internationally. When I asked Kvernmo what he considers the most important aspect of Isogaisa, he replied, "The forming of bonds. We are in the centre, the south Sami area is represented there, and Russia is also there." From having been peripheral, Isogaisa transforms the place where the festival is held into a creative cross-national hub for religious innovation and a focal point in Sápmi.

The prerequisite for having Isogaisa's landscape take the shape of a center is to market the place as being unique—as being different from all other places. In most cases, this type of marketing is done by creating a clear local connection, and the easiest way to do this is through its name (ibid.: 29). The name Isogaisa means "big peak," or "the biggest peak among many big mountains." The word is also familiar from several poems and songs. The festival organizers aim to use the festival to make "Isogaisa" a brand name, covering not only the festival itself but also the growing, evolving Sami neoshamanic movement in general. Kvernmo says,

> Branding. The name Isogaisa.... now we are establishing the term Isogaisa, we are anchoring it in the "top of the mind" of people. So the next time people think of shamanism, the name Isogaisa should come up, and it should be a broad term. It's not only a festival; it's a shamanic center. We may even launch a CD soon, which is going to be called the "Power of Isogaisa."

By marketing and spreading the name Isogaisa and its local connection, the objective is to expand the local by making the municipality a hub for practitioners of Sami neoshamanism.

The construction of and the dream of having religious experiences at often remote centers has been a prevalent pattern in religious history. The tales and visions of journeys to holy places such as Jerusalem, Rome, and Mecca have been many. In the postmodern religious landscape, the distance to these centers has grown shorter, and the number of centers has increased in step with developments within the religious sphere (see Kraft 2011). Isogaisa is a clear example of how the northern Norwegian region is marketed as being such a spiritual center. North Norway, which in the past was marketed and known for its magnificent nature, gains an added dimension at Isogaisa, namely, the promise of personal reward in the form of inner self-development.

The connection between local development and the marketing of spiritual values makes the festival an agent of change in extended cultural innovation and development processes. At Isogaisa, the identity of the region is recast in a way that replaces the traditional image of North Norway as being "peripheral," and as being a politically, economically, and culturally repressed region. For this reason, Isogaisa is not situated in a political vacuum, despite the fact that the festival is primarily intended to be an arena of activity and entertainment (see Hall 2007: 306, Hansen 2002: 28). This is highlighted by the statement made by festivalgoer and exhibitor Wilhelm Strindberg in the heading above: "Isogaisa: creator of a separate identity and a sense of pride but also a spearhead of counterculture. Isogaisa: the beating heart of the counterculture."[15] Isogaisa, with its seminars, alternative fair, ceremonies, and entertainment, is like other festivals in that it is a place for socializing, enjoyment, and leisure. Nevertheless, it is also a place where the local and global are merged, where power relationships come into play, where political interests are materialized, where cultural identities are tested, and where new dreams take shape.

Notes

1. In the long term, the organizers of the festival want to have Isogaisa Siida evolve into a spiritual center focusing on indigenous culture.
2. The topic of Kvernmo's bachelor thesis was the development process of a shamanic centre in Målselv in Nord-Troms.
3. http://www.isogaisa.org/, accessed 17/06/2011.
4. This chapter is based partially on a previous article, published in Norwegian in *Aura* (Fonneland 2013).
5. On their web page, one can find information on this year's and last year's programs, exhibitors, central themes, practical information, and registration forms for volunteer workers. On their home page, one can also find a YouTube link where those who are interested may see, listen, and take part in a special Isogaisa dance, which is accompanied with a special festival *joik*.
6. http://www.isogaisa.org/, accessed June 28, 2011.
7. The festival organizers are part of foreininga Isogaisa, which is headed by festival leader Ronald Kvernmo. Ingebrigt Pedersen serves as cashier; Monica Dragset is responsible for the expo part of the program; Bente Arntsen is responsible for the volunteer workers; Eli Sabbasen is the supervisor of the duty lists; and Inger Anne Kristoffersen deals with the seminars. Several of these individuals have prior experience in organizing festivals in North Norway. Isogaisa also hosts several co-organizers; among them are Spansdalen Sameforening and Foreningen Kystsamene
8. See http://www.isogaisa.org/default.asp?show=news&artid=2688, accessed June 28, 2011.
9. From my field notes.
10. The book has been criticized for lacking a descriptive angle and for being a scientific contribution that naturalizes and contributes to the construction of mythological ideas. Kraft claims that the book is "yet another contribution to the discourse about 'the natural Sami', and thereby to the primitivistic tradition" (2007: 60).
11. http.www.isogaisa.no, accessed June 17, 2011.

12. Haugen Productions was founded in 2003 by the sisters Liv Hanne Haugen and Anne Katrine Haugen. They are both dancers, and stand behind several productions and performances (see http://www.haugenproduksjoner. no/).
13. http://www.isogaisa.org/default.asp?pageid=14679 accessed June 17, 2011, my translation.
14. A search of the term "Isogaisa" in Atekst on January 14, 2013 yielded 70 results.
15. http://www.isogaisa.org/default.asp?pageid=14674 accessed June 28, 2011, my translation.

References

Ahlin, Lars. 2007. *Krop, Sind—Eller Ånd? Alternative behandlere og spiritualitet i Danmark*, Højbjerg: Forlaget Univers.
Beyer, Peter. 1998. "Globalization and the Religion of Nature," in J. Pearson and G. Samuel (eds.) *Nature Religion Today: Paganism in the Modern World*, Edinburgh: Edinburgh University Press, 11–21.
Christensen, Cato. 2005. *Urfolk på det nyreligiøse markedet. En analyse av Alternativt Nettverk,* Masteroppgåve i religionsvitskap, Universitetet i Tromsø.
———. 2007. "Urfolksspiritualitet på det nyreligiøse markedet. En analyse av tidsskriftet Visjon/Alternativt Nettverk." *Din. Tidsskrift for religion og kultur* 1: 63–78.
Christensen, Cato and Siv Ellen Kraft. 2010. "Religion i Kautokeino-opprøret. En analyse av samisk urfolksspiritualitet", *Nytt norsk tidsskrift* 1: 19–27.
Eriksen, Anne. 1999. *Historie, Minne og Myte*, Oslo: Pax Forlag AS.
Fonneland, Trude. 2010. *Samisk nysjamanisme. I dialog med (for)tid og stad.* Doktoravhandling: Universitetet i Bergen.
———. 2007. "Med fokus på det nære og lokale. Tromsø—ein samisk urfolksby?". *Din. Tidsskrift for religion og kultur* 1: 79–88.
———. 2013. "Isogaisa: Samisk sjamanisme i festivaldrakt." *Aura. Tidsskrift for nyreligiøse studier* 5: 102–131.
Frykman, Jonas. 2002. "Place for Something Else: Analysing a Cultural Imaginary," *Ethnologia Europea* 32(2): 47–68.
Gaup, Ailo. 2006. *Sjamansonen.* Oslo: Tre bjørner forlag.
———. 2007. *Inn i naturen. Utsyn fra Sjamansonen.* Oslo: Tre bjørner forlag.
Hall, Michael. 2007. "Politics, Power and Indigenous Tourism," in Richard Butler and Tom Hinch (eds.), *Tourism and Indigenous Peoples.* Oxford: Elsevier, 305–318.
Hammer, Olav. 1997. *På spaning efter helheten. New Age en ny folketro?* Stockholm: Wahlström & Widstrand.
———. 2001. *Claiming Knowledge: Strategies of Epistemology from Theosopy to the New Age.* Leiden, Boston & Köln: Brill.
Hansen, Kjell. 2002. "Festivals, Spatiality and the New Europe." *Ethnologia Europea* 32(2): 19–36.

Harner, Michael. 1980. *The Way of the Shaman: A Guide to Power and Healing*, San Francisco: Harper & Row.

Kalland, Arne. 2003. "Environmentalism and Images of the Other," in H. Selin (ed.), *Nature across Cultures: Views of Nature and the Environment in Non-Western Cultures*, Amsterdam: Kluwer Academic Publishers, 1–17.

Kirshenblatt-Gimblett, Barbara. 1998. *Destination Culture: Tourism, Museums, and Heritage.* Oakland: University of California Press.

Kraft, Siv Ellen. 2007. "Natur, spiritualitet og tradisjon. Om akademisk romantisering og feilslåtte primitivismeoppgjør. Review-artikkel om Jens Ivar Nergårds *Den levende erfaring* (2006)." *Din. Tidsskrift for religion og kultur* 1: 53–62.

———. 2009. "Sami Indigenous Spirituality: Religion and Nation Building in Norwegian Sápmi." *Temenos*, 45(2): 179–206.

———. 2011. *Hva er nyreligiøsitet.* Oslo: Universitetsforlaget.

Kristiansen, Roald. 2005. *Samisk religion og læstadianisme.* Bergen: Fagbokforlaget 2005.

Lowenthal, David. 1985. *The Past Is a Foreign Country.* Cambridge: Cambridge University Press.

———. 1998. *The Heritage Crusade and the Spoils of History.* Cambridge: Cambridge University Press.

Mathisen, Stein R. 2011. "Indigenous Spirituality in the Touristic Borderzone." *Temenos*, 53–72.

Nergård, Jens-Ivar. 2006. *Den levende erfaring. En studie i samisk kunnskapstradisjon,* Oslo: Cappelen Akademisk Forlag.

O'Dell, Tom. 2010. "Experiencescapes: Blurring Borders and Testing Connections," in Tom O'Dell and Peter Billing (eds.), *Experiencescapes: Tourism, Culture, and Economy*, Køge: Copenhagen Business School Press, 11–34.

Pine, Joseph B., and James H. Gilmore. 1999. *The Experience Economy.* Boston: Harvard Business Scholl Press.

Reksten Kapstad, Connie. 2007. "Når poesien tar plass. Om Olav H. Hauge, litteratur og festival," in Torunn Selberg and Nils Gilje (eds.). *Kulturelle landskap. Sted, forteljing og materiell kultur.* Bergen: Fagbokforlaget, 156–178.

Stuckrad, Kocku von. 2005. "Harner Michael—and the Foundation for Shamanic Studies," in Bron Taylor (ed.), *The Encyclopedia of Religion and Nature*, vol. 1, London: Thoemmes Continuum.

Taylor, Charles. 2007. *A Secular Age.* Cambridge: Harvard University Press.

Yeoman, Ian. 2004. *Festivals and Events Management: An international Arts and Culture Perspective.* Amsterdam: Butterworth-Heinemann.

Media

Troms Folkeblad September 6, 2010
Troms Folkeblad September 1, 2010
Nordlys September 8, 2010
Klassekampen March 11–12, 2006

Internet Sources

http://www.isogaisa.org/
http://www.facebook.com/#!/event.php?eid=184680388209837
http://www.norwayfestivals.com/
http://ec.europa.eu/research/social-sciences/pdf/policy_reviews/euro-festival-report_en.pdf.

12

Shamanism and Indigenous Soundscapes: The Case of Mari Boine

Siv Ellen Kraft

Mari Boine (b. 1956) grew up in a tiny Sami village in the Norwegian high north, in a world ruled by the strict Christian god of her parents and the politics of assimilation on the part of the Norwegian state. She has later described a sin-oriented religion, an ever-present threat of dooms-day, and a never-ending list of taboos and forbiddens—including music. All forms of music except hymns were forbidden. *Joik*—an ancient form of Sami music—was connected to the devil himself, due partly to its connection with the pre-Christian Sami religion. She has also described her shame in regard to all things Sami, and—as she grew older—her increasing rage, anger, and rebellion.

Today, in her mid-fifties, Boine is a leading world music artist, one of Norway's most influential musicians, and probably the best-known ambassador of Sami culture in Norway and internationally. Sápmi has changed dramatically since the time of her childhood in Finnmark, and Boine is commonly credited for her contribution—to healing processes, to the rebuilding of partly lost traditions and identities, and to the repo-sitioning of stigmatized symbols and practices. Artists like Boine, Ole Henrik Magga, the first president of the Sami parliament, has claimed, "have done more in many arenas for the breakthrough of political power than our hundreds of resolutions which I myself have been a part of writing" (quoted in Hilder 2010: 55).

This chapter deals with the religious dimension of Boine's contribution, which she refers to as shamanism, and recognizable as part of a broader neoshamanistic milieu, albeit with unusual twists. The use of music as the primary method and source of shamanism is one such twist.

Connections to Sami cultural revival and to indigenous peoples are other twists. As a respected high-culture musician, Boine also disturbs established notions of neoshamanism as the religious equivalent of "low culture." A major theme of this chapter is that her music has helped soften resistance against shamanism in Sami circles and contributed to the establishment of a cultural heritage version of Sami shamanism.

I will be concerned mainly with the public face of Boine's shamanism, as she has presented it in media interviews, documentaries, on her official home page, in a recent biography, and in her song lyrics, albums, and performances, many of which are available on YouTube.[1] References will occasionally be made to interviews she has given in academic contexts and that have been published in texts with a more limited public scope. However, my main concern is Boine's public self—the self she has decided to share and present. All translations from Norwegian have been done by me, but vernacular formulations are in footnotes, in order for the translations to be as transparent as possible.

Mari Boine (b. 1956)—A Biographical Sketch

Boine has told her life story many times, in numerous interviews, documentaries, and television shows. This story has, as is commonly the case with stories that are retold, gained a standardized form and structure, with the same episodes referred to, often in almost the exact same formulations. There is no reason to question the sincerity of these stories, but many reasons to believe that Boine tells them publicly for a reason—that they are intended to shed light upon the broader contexts to which they belong.

The politics of assimilation and forced Norwegenization belong to this level of shared premises. Boine grew up with little knowledge of Sami history and culture beyond the limits of her family, and like many other children of the 1950s and '60s she experienced her Sami identity as a social stigma (Eidheim 1998, 1971). Identity as Sami had in certain areas more or less disappeared as a result of assimilatory strategies on the part of Norwegian authorities,[2] and many parents shielded their children from a culture they had learned to consider as shameful and backward.

Læstadianism is a conservative Lutheran revival movement that spread during the mid-nineteenth century and that has been a stronghold among the Sami ever since.[3] Boine has described her parents as unusually strict followers, and their world as dominated by the Bible and doomsday: "I never really reached my father. Bible and doomsday. It was something that was always there, as a dark shadow"[4] (Amundsen 2003, NRK radio).[5] It stayed with her, she later recalled, as a heritage that she has spent much of her life trying to overcome and free herself from (Oksnes, *Dagbladet* May 8, 2006).

By her early twenties, Boine had married, given birth to a child, and started her studies at the teacher education college in Alta. During this same period, the Norwegian government plans to build a hydro-electro dam led to conflicts and heated debate among the local population, and eventually to massive demonstrations both on the banks of the Alta river and in front of the Norwegian parliament in Oslo. Having started out as an issue involving local people in Alta and Norwegian environmental organizations, the saving of the river became a Sami cause, and, in addition, the first Sami cause to be framed in terms of indigenous rights. The Alta case is commonly regarded as a turning point with regard to public recognition and Norwegian politics toward the Sami. It was followed by important political changes, including the establishment of a Sami parliament in 1989, and it led—perhaps most importantly—to consciousness-raising among a new generation.

Boine was not among the protesters at the banks of the river. Tonstad's (authorized) biography describes her as at this point a bashful young woman, full of shame, doubt, and unresolved tensions (Tonstad 2012). Boine has in interviews spoken of her shame with respect to anything Sami, and of wanting to get away from it all, even the language (Amundsen, NRK radio 2003). Boine and her first husband grew up with Sami as their first language, but spoke Norwegian with each other and with their firstborn son (Amundsen 2003).

The political unrest nevertheless shaped her (ibid.), and as a teacher-student she was introduced to Sami history and taught by Sami teachers, as well as introduced to positive perspectives on joik, a Sami way of singing she had learned to see as primitive and heathen.[6] "You have now sold yourself to the devil," Boine's father told her when she took up joiking" (NN 2005). He died in 1995, without ever accepting her choice of lifestyle and career (ibid.). The death of her parents left her with grief but also "with some sort of freedom" and new feelings of emotional closeness—"I feel that after they died, I felt closer to them than before" (Amundsen 2003):

> We become a part of nature when we die, according to shamanism, so we have a very good communication now. I walk in nature and talk to my dead parents. I can feel that they are there. (ibid.)[7]

Boine's first album, *Jaskatvuoða maŋŋá* (After the silence), reveals a stronger and angrier woman, who clearly takes a political stance. Released in 1985, *Jaskatvuoða maŋŋá* confronts the school system, the Norwegian state's treatment of the Sami, and what Boine has regularly referred to as *den samiske skammen*—internalized feelings of shame and stigma. This first record has been connected primarily to the so-called northern Norwegian folksong wave, a movement that sought to reposition a culture that in the national context had been marginalized (Thomassen 2010: 30). In her breakthrough release, *Gula Gula, The Voice of the Foremothers* (1989), Boine turned to joik, and combined this with jazz and elements from various indigenous musical traditions, a turn that placed her in the recently established category "world music" and opened the door to a global market (ibid.: 38).[8] Since then, indigeneity and world music have been trademarks of her career, with respect to lyrics, soundscape, and the choice of musicians. For *Gula Gula*, for instance, the band consisted of musicians from Peru, Sweden, Norway, and Sápmi, and they used instruments from a variety of indigenous cultures, including breath drone drum, quen breat, and claypot (ibid.).[9]

By 2014, Boine had produced 12 albums, given hundreds of concerts, performed at numerous Sami and indigenous festivals in Norway and internationally,[10] and received several prestigious awards, including the honorary award of the Sami Council (1992) and the Nordic Council Music Prize in 2003. She was in 2009 appointed knight, first class, in the Royal Norwegian Order of St. Olav; in 2012 became *statsstipendiat*—an artist with permanent national funding; and was in 2005 one of ten candidates for the position "most important Norwegian of the century."

Bridging the Past and the Present

The development of Sami neoshamanism coincided with Boine's early career. Boine in her (authorized) biography describes how during the 1990s she found comfort in poems by Ailo Gaup, who later would become known as the founder of Sami neoshamanism, and how they opened a door for her to powers of which she had been aware during her youth, but never had understood or dared to take seriously (Tonstad 2012: 238). Boine later participated in one of Gaup's recently established shamanist courses in Tromsø (ibid.: 239). This provided her with building blocks, and with knowledge of her power animals: the eagle, turtle, and wolf—her helpers during drum journeys, and sources to which to turn when she felt scared: "she could [then] send the wolf to eat the threats. She felt that this helped and gave her strength" (ibid.: 239).[11] Boine later referred to her grandmother, who died when she was 14, as her lifelong guide and helper, and the single most important person in her life (NN 2014).

Neoshamanism appears just as crucial to Boine's sense of continuity—in her own life and Sami history. New religions share with nations a concern with origins and continuity. The challenge of nation-building, folklorist Anne Eriksen has argued, is not merely to document that a given nation is old but to an equal degree that throughout its extensive history it has preserved a cultural distinctiveness, that "'we' are still the same" (1999).

Sami neoshamanism was born as an offspring of Michael Harner's core shamanism during the late 1980s, some 300 years after the Christianization of the Sami (see Fonneland and Kraft 2013), but it was from the start connected to the pre-Christian Sami religion, through accounts offered by scholarly sources. The bridging of past and present has been based partly on notions of a primal source—available to shamans in the past and the present. Additionally, what scholars refer to as "the preservation thesis" (Minde 2008a) has offered a "factual" basis for notions of continuity. This thesis does not question that important changes have taken place. It is well documented that the building of churches became part of a conscious colonizing effort starting in the sixteenth century, and that by the seventeenth century a systematic and active Christian mission was established, including the systematic collection and destruction of *runebomme,* drums used by the *noaidi*—Sami religious specialists—during ritual journeys. Historian of religion Håkan Rydving, in the title of what has become a classical study of the Lule Sami, refers to this latter period as *The End of Drum Time* (1995).

Literally beneath these changes, central elements of Sami drum time lived on, the preservation thesis claims. Crucial to this theory is the claim that Læstadianism provided "a sanctuary for the minority populations, at a time—from 1870 down to World War II—when the authorities were tightening the screw of Norwegianisation in the name of Social Darwinism and nationalism" (Minde 2008a: 9). What Historian Henry Minde refers to as a radical and romantic version of this thesis further expands these perspectives, by way of links to the pre-Christian past (ibid.). The old religion never really disappeared, this version claims. Rather, it went underground. The noaidi found shelter under the garb of the Læstadian *leser* (a healer and religious expert); the trance journey of the noaidi lived on as *rørelse* (ecstatic outbursts known to occur during Læstadian ceremonies);[12] and joik—the musical expressions of the noaidi, lived on as folk-religious practices, outside of the Church.[13]

In Boine's interpretation, music constitutes the main medium of continuity. Boine describes Læstadianism as a heavy burden from which she has spent much of her life trying to free herself, and also as a carrier of elements from the Sami religion of the past, introduced to her during her upbringing, and present as "an almost invisible thread—from the pre-Christian religion of the Sami to Læstadianism, the singing of psalms

and Christianity" (Tonstad 2012: 264). She remembers rørelse as the
highlight of prayer house meetings:

> Among the things I liked the best was what we called *likhahuset*, in Norwegian
> *rørelse*—but which I believe is a residue from shamanistic rituals. At the end of
> the meeting they would sing and sing till they reached a kind of trance. It was
> probably the closest they came to dancing. Asked each other for forgiveness. I
> have talked to other people who grew up with this—who found it frightening,
> but to me it was the highlight. (Amundsen NRK radio 2003)[14]

Looking back (in 2012), Boine described rørelse as crucial to her development; "*Rørelse* is at the bottom of all that I have. *Rørelsen,* the singing
of psalms and the forbidden *joik*" (qtd. in Thomassen 2012: 70).[15] Her
propensity for repetition in her music, similarly, is connected to a longing
for the trance-like state of rørelse:[16]

> There have been reviews too, [claiming] that this is terribly monotonous.
> And so one has gradually realized that there is—if one dares to let one self be
> touched by it, that there is another door, one that is more related to—not the
> intellectual, the thought. . . . I had a longing for the trance, which came from
> my childhood, and the *rørelsene* I grew up with. (interview with Thomassen
> 2010: 45)[17]

These same forces are at play during her concerts, Boine claims, moving
herself and her audiences. During concerts she seeks to create "an atmosphere in which the audience opens the doors to their innermost being
and become susceptible to spirits and journeys" (Tonstad 2012: 109).[18]

Joik was not part of Boine's upbringing, but is subjected to a similar interpretation as that of rørelse, here through the singing of psalms.
Boine notes of the first joik that she "dared to take into her mouth," that
she had grown up thinking that joik was forbidden, and "probably gradually took over the attitudes of my parents" (qtd. in Thomassen 2010:
38). By the early 1990s, she had come to see a link between Læstadian
psalms and Sami joik traditions, similar to that between rørelse and a
trance journey:

> Day after day, for several hours, she sat in the Tromsø Museum, listening
> to traditional *joik*. She had to approach this well, this source of dreams, the
> mother of fantasy and the inner secrets of the Sami people. It was condemned
> by the Church and missionaries, trampled upon and cursed, but it was a life
> nerve that could not be broken. And there was an almost invisible thread—
> from the pre-Christian religion of the Sami and shamanism to Læstadianism,
> the singing of psalms and Christianity—this she grasped for (Tonstad 2012:
> 264, my translation). [19]

Joik is many things, according to Boine's descriptions: a source of wisdom, a connection to the past, a trance technique used for (shamanistic)
traveling, and even a trance-like state. It is customary to talk of joiking
"something" (as opposed to singing "about"). Boine adds to this a notion
of *becoming one* with the tone:

> She could enter the *joik* and stay there, become one with the tone. The joik
> opened a door in to a room with power and energy, she felt that she flew on the
> wings of *joik* on stage. A people who is in contact with this power cannot be
> easily manipulated and controlled. (Tonstad 2012: 315)[20]

The idea of a deep level of continuity is common to Boine, neoshamanism in general, and a select groups of scholars. The heritage from the
past is located in particular musical and ritual forms: joik, psalms and
rørelse, and at the same time in the subconscious depths of the Sami, or
at least those among the Sami who have grown up with Sami culture
and Læstadian traditions. One may, from this perspective, acknowledge
radical differences between the *then* and *now*, the ancient shamans and
contemporary versions, and at the same time maintain a notion of connection and continuity. Sami shamanism *almost* disappeared, but never
fully or totally. In the words of Boine's biographer,

> Magic is alive in the consciousness of many Sami. The unexplainable has a
> status. It is there, usually, as a positive force, able to help people in various situ-
> ations. The shaman is by no means dead.... This has also to Mari been a hid-
> den treasure. She has dared to open it and to gradually make use of it. Today's
> shamans follow a long Sami tradition that was almost destroyed by Christian
> missionaries. (Tonstad 2012: 41)[21]

Current usage of the terms shaman/noaidi and trance/rørelse offer further support for notions of continuity. It has, since at least the early
1990s, been common to use these concepts more or less interchangeably,
and to allow for *shamanism* to frame and account for the pre-Christian
past. Shaman and noaidi are commonly used as synonyms, and in highly
inclusive ways, as designations of not only the religious specialists of pre-
Christian Sami religion and so-called shamanistic religions but also of
Sami religious specialists generally, including Læstadian *lesere* and New
Age-inspired healers. The late Johan Kaaven (1836–1918), for instance, is
commonly referred to as a shaman and "the last of the noaides." Kaaven
has been the subject of a number of books, [22] but there is—to my knowledge—no evidence of his ever using drums, performing trance journeys,
or being connected to other typical ingredients of "shamanism." His position as a noaidi/shaman appears to be based on the combination of being

Sami and having supernatural powers, including—one of the most well-known stories claims—the ability to stop the coastal ferry *Hurtigruta*. The grandfather of the well-known actor and Sami neoshaman Mikkel Gaup, similarly, was known as a famous læstadian leser, but is today referred to as a shaman by Gaup himself and in public media (Fonneland and Kraft 2013). Ester Utsi, to provide a contemporary example, has since 1997 offered lodging, healing, and self-development courses at Polmakmoen Guesthouse, in Tana, Finnmark County. The products that are provided are in other contexts known to journalists as typically New Age, a form of religion situated near the bottom of Norwegian media evaluations of religion (Døving and Kraft 2013). Located in rural areas of Sàpmi, however, they are commonly connected to the ancient shaman-istic traditions of the Sami, and in positive ways, as part of Sami cultural revival (Fonneland and Kraft 2013).

A broad concept of shamanism and the shaman is hardly unique to the Sami.[23] Rather, "the shaman" has internationally become an umbrella term for religious specialists among people today referred to as "indig-enous," more or less regardless of the content of their expertise and prac-tices. In the case of the Sami, processes of translation and synonymization probably date back to the 1970s and later, in the wake of the develop-ment of neoshamanism internationally. Folklorist Marit Anne Hauan interviewed the above-mentioned Gaup during the 1970s.[24] At that time, she claims, he was known as a leser and healer, and referred to himself by this title.[25] Folklorist Bente Alver interviewed Gaup's daughter during the mid-1980s. By then, both Gaup and his daughter (Ellen Marit) called themselves shamans, and even "the last true shamans in Finnmark" (see Alver: 143, this volume). At some point during this decade, Gaup, whose healing powers were famous internationally, had also been visited by Harner and a Finnish colleague (ibid.). The above-mentioned Ailo Gaup is a relative of Mikkel Gaup. He also visited him during this period, and retrospectively refers to him as a great shaman.

Indigenous Connections

Læstadians are not likely to sympathize with the undercover version of (Læstadian) shamanism. Sami Christians in the south of Norway have experimented with the use of drums, joik, and outdoor ceremonies on traditionally sacred sites. Liberal Sami theologians from this area have also argued that the old Sami religion constitutes the Old Testament of the Sami (Kraft 2009b). Læstadians further north, however, have remained opposed to anything connected to the religion of their ancestors, includ-ing the noaidi, joik, drums, and sacred sites.[26]

Outside of Læstadian circles, joik is known as an ancient Sami way of singing, and as a marker of Sami identity. Joik is today classified as Sami indigenous knowledge, along with duodji (Sami art) and Sami folk medicine (Hilder 2010: 86), and has even served as "evidence" of indigeneity. A frequently cited story claims that the famous multiartist Nils-Aslak Valkeapää, during the first meeting of the World Council of indigenous Peoples in Port Alberni, Canada, in 1975, "used yoik to prove that he and the Sami delegation really were an indigenous people":

> Several of the indigenous representatives from other places in the world were, in fact, skeptical about the Sami because of their white skin color; but when Valkeapää performed a yoik for the assembly the skepticism was blown away and the Sami were accepted on a par with the others. (Gaski 2008: 358)

The processes through which joik became recognizable as "indigenous" (in the contemporary sense of the term) lies outside of the limits of this chapter. However, it is reasonable to assume that the international indigenous movement, along with the world music industry, has contributed to such processes. Scholar of Sami literature Harald Gaski has claimed of the indigenous movement that musical performances have from the start been a more or less standard ingredient of meetings and conferences. They have been followed by indigenous festivals and digital arenas of musical contact and exchange, including the world music industry. The result, Gaski claims, is music as "the cultural area that globalization has had the greatest impact on within indigenous cultures," including mutual inspiration across different indigenous people (2008: 247).[27] Hilder, along similar lines, notes that "indigenous musicians (have) identified a commonality of cultural expression," transformed local traditions and built "a global indigenous soundscape" (2010: 114–115). He adds of the Sami section of this soundscape, that representations of shamanism have become increasingly popular, including the noaidi, the drum, and spiritual notions of *joik* (ibid. :135), and that world music has become a regular and frequent feature on Sami music channels (2010: 85). The Sami, due partly to this development, "have come to see themselves as possessing a music heritage within a wider global arena of music traditions. Indeed, particular to the 'ethnic' list is a focus on famous indigenous musicians such as Buffy Sainte-Marie and other bands that have played at the Riddu Riddu festival. Indigenous music on Sami radio therefore not only mirrors the emergence of Sami solidarity with other indigenous people, but have also played a vital role in building a sense of musical and political connection to their indigenous sisters and brothers" (2010: 85–86).

The Sami musicians interviewed by Hilder agree that through music they have "felt a connection"; have realized that "there are many

similarities," that—in the words of Sami musician Antte Ailu Gaup—
"We spoke the same language" (ibid.: 113). The Norwegian musician
and musicologist Tellef Kvifte has referred to the resulting sound of such
encounters as "generally ethnic" (2001).[28]
Boine has expressed similar a viewpoint in interviews. She seems, moreover, to consider similarities as not merely the result of recent encounters
between indigenous peoples but as originating from a common source.
Asked by Hilder how she understands the relationship between joik and
musical traditions among other indigenous people, Boine explained that
it "has to do with 'the primeval' (urmenneskelige) and its connection to
nature":

> This quality, she reiterated, can be heard in joik, especially [Inga] Juuso's voice.
> Like with joik and other "related"…vocal traditions, Boine continued, it is
> the way one uses the voice. Whereas "Western" vocal traditions are descrip-
> tive and are removed from and outside of what they are singing about, the
> "primal-voice"…is the very thing it sings, she reasoned. It is only through joik
> and related traditions that the "primeval" can be achieved, and it is thus the
> "primal-voice" that Boine has been in search of through her musical develop-
> ment. (Hilder 2010: 120)[29]

Boine's use of "Western vocal traditions" as a contrast indicates that the
"related vocal traditions" are those of indigenous peoples. Her song texts
further elaborate upon musical connections between indigenous people,
and the contrast between indigenous- and western people, or what she
on some occasions has termed "Western A4." Consider, for instance,
Gula Gula—perhaps her most famous song, on the album by the same
name. Gula Gula means "hear, hear," but Boine translated it as "Hear
the voices of the foremothers" because, she notes in a radio documentary, "it says more" (Amundsen 2003, NRK radio). Gula Gula speaks
of brothers and sisters from around the indigenous world: "You have
brothers. You have sisters. In the rain forests of South America, on the
barren coast of Greenland"[30] (Boine, Gula Gula).[31] The song starts with
an invocation of antiquity and traditional knowledge, and continues with
other widely used markers of indigeneity, such as environmentalism, the
notion of nature people, and a holistic worldview.[32] Indigenous people
are presented as the children of Mother Earth, a notion commonly associated with the earth as a living being, and with creation and creativity as
embodied processes. Finally, there is a call for revival and responsibility
("again they want to remind you, that the earth is our mother. If we take
her life we die with her," Gula Gula).[33]

The "Western world" constitutes the other in this song text. The Sami
are not explicitly held accountable for the pollution of Mother Earth,
merely for allowing it to happen ("why have you let the Earth become

polluted," *Gula Gula*). They are asked to rise to their responsibility as her sons and daughters, but responsibility for the crisis appears to be attributed to Western people, to those who have suppressed and colonized Mother Earth and her children, those—to quote the title of two other songs on *Gula Gula*—who are *White thieves* and have claimed the position of the *Master Race*[34]

The contrast between Western- and indigenous people is repeated in many of Boine's songs. In "Gods of Nature," for instance (on *Room of Worship*), the stiff and machine-like ways of Western people are contrasted to the holistic and dynamic ways of indigenous people:

> their hardened talk, their hardened state, their hardened smile, their hardened laws drain me; suffocate me; raging rivers, howling winds; lightening flashes; gods of nature; embody them; with Earth Mother Spirit. ("Gods of Nature," on the album *Room of Worship*)

Accompanying the distinction between Western and indigenous perspectives in her song texts are repeated references to nature, often in the shape of elemental forms like the sun, water, mountains, and animals, particularly birds, and in ways that highlight flow, fluidity, and connections. Similar notions are expressed through album covers and performances, many of which are also available on YouTube. Boine often wears a large shawl during performances, and has become known for her "wheeling dance," with arm movements "evocative of a gliding bird" (Cronshaw 2013). Two of her album covers offer variations on this theme. On *Eagle Brother*, a swirling movement is indicated through the image of three women shading into each other, one of them blindfolded and standing still, the other two spreading their arms in a wheeling fashion. On the cover of *Sterna Paradise* she is pictured with a feather-like shawl, doing a swirl-like dance, outdoors—and with the one end of her shawl spreading over the back cover, where, in an exaggerated image, it flies over what appears to be a mountain.

A comparison with traditional Sami national emblems indicates both continuity with former discourses and a more recent turn to pan-indigenous vocabularies. The Sami national anthem, published for the first time in 1906, draws upon a pre-Christian motif of the Sami as "sons of the Sun." In Boine's music, the sons are partly replaced by daughters and foremothers, while the "family" is extended from that of the Sami to that of indigenous peoples. True to the genre of national anthems, the Sami version ends with a reference to their land as their land: "Remember the ancestor's word. Saamiland for Saami." In *Gula Gula*, the land of the Sami is replaced by the geographically more extensive notion of Mother Earth—of homeland as universal and indivisible, while "owning" is replaced by notions of shared responsibility and the lack of clear boundaries between nature and people—of brothers and sisters who take care of their mother, and of a mother who secures their very existence. Indigeneity is still connected to local lands and traditions, but here as part of their shared connections to Mother Earth. References to nature, to Mother Earth, and to environmentalism belong to what is perhaps the single most important theme in Boine's song texts, performances and interviews.

Sacred Claims

Boine is clearly aware of and concerned with the political impact of her music, and of her artistic and political integrity. In 1994 she turned down a request to perform at the opening ceremony of the Lillehammer Olympics, on the basis that she would not play the role of "exotic garnish and alibi." Nor would she, according to later interviews, be reduced to "a cosy entertainer" (Oksnes, Dagbladet 2006). Asked by Thomassen about political intentions behind her music, however, Boine appeared as "more tentative than agitative" (Thomassen 2010: 71). She confirmed political intentions in *Recipe for a Master Race* (*Oppskrift for Herrefolket*), but for the song *Gula Gula*, for instance—illustrated on YouTube with atomic bomb explosions and similar scenes of destruction—"she would not immediately confirm a political agenda" (ibid.). Rather, she told Thomassen, "I believe that many of the texts are written for myself sort of to find the way" (ibid.). She chose indigenous musicians, similarly, because she liked them, not as an act of solidarity: "It is something I have understood afterwards. This is why one sees, intuition is much, much wiser than oneself, than the head" (ibid.).[35]

Similar references to her "inner voice" or intuition have been repeated in other interviews. Consider for instance the following extract from an interview with a music journalist:

> I very much use intuition. I don't think first, I just follow a feeling, and it has a wisdom that is much more wise than the intellectual wisdom. So it's not that I sit and think "I should do this," but I follow this feeling, then afterwards I can see also with my intellect, I can see a course—"yes, now I understand with my intellect what this is." (Cronshaw 2013)

The ability to understand and follow one's intuition is, she says in an interview with Thomassen, connected to the distinction between indigenous and Western people, and to reminders from the past:

> You know, we are raised to become very Norwegian and very westernized, and this text is more like...when these melodies started coming, it was like a voice,

a reminder from those who have been before us. I didn't see it very clearly then, but later on seeing the text, it is like a...like a reminder from them not to—not to forget your legacy. And also, this about when you are raised by school and everything to become very westernized, then other indigenous people become very distant. And one of the lines here is that, you know, that we have brothers and sisters in Latin America and on Greenland. (Boine, in Thomassen 2010: 80–81, my translation)[36]

Boine, in a 2009 documentary on NRK-radio, speaks in similar ways of her songs as "coming" ("the shamanistic music started coming through me"), and of her "inner voice," "intuition," and "those who have been before us" as their origin.

What historian of religion Greg Johnson has referred to as "sacred claims" offer clues to this combination of depths, tradition-based authority, and a downplaying of political motives (2007). Johnson's context is North American Indians, and their use of religious language in legal contexts concerning repatriation. He describes "sacred claims" as a particular kind of speech, characterized by a combination of depth and metaphorical playfulness (ibid.: 24). Indigenous speakers

are compelled to present themselves on legal stages as "authentic" subjects/ objects who, despite their manifest engagement in political processes, must maintain an appearance of disinterestedness, as signs of "interest" may be viewed by audiences as undercutting claims to authenticity. (ibid.: 22).

Boine operates on a different stage, but the basic logic of "sacred = authentic" = not profaned by engaging in politics" (ibid.) may to some extent be transferable. Boine does not deny political engagements, only that they lack relevance for the coming into being of her music. The latter is based on the authority of Sami- and indigenous traditions and on voices from outside her rational self—ancient foremothers and the (subconscious) depths of her own being. The logic resembles her experience-based recognition of shamanism in Læstadian music and rituals, as traditions outside and inside of herself. The sacred = authentic = not profaned by engaging in politics, in these contexts. And they are sacred in a Durkheimian sense of the term, as that which is beyond dispute and negotiation, anchored in spheres of absolute truths.

Audience Responses

There are two types of shamanistic music, Ailo Gaup claims on his home pages, one used for the ritual journey, and one used for relaxation and pleasure (www.sjaman-sonen.no). That Boine is "an artist rooted in shamanism is clear to most people," he adds. The same goes for Nils Aslak

Valkeapää, described by Gaup as the great star before her. In fact, he concludes, "I know of not one Sami artist today who is not aware of this connection and draws inspiration from these sources" (ibid.).[37]

Leaving aside for the moment the issue of whether this is a reasonable conclusion, trained neoshamans can easily find their notions of shamanism in Boine's music, and can rely on her own testimonies that it is so. We have here the main ritual instruments of Sami shamanism, the runebomme and joik, along with experiences of trance and a primeval voice, all of it performed by a Sami musician and rooted in Sami religious traditions. We have, moreover, notions of indigenous brothers and sisters, of environmental responsibility, and of nature's all-encompassing importance—all of which are central to core shamanism.

These same elements can account for the negative view of Boine among Læstadians. Boine, in addition to her harsh criticism of their religion, has based her career on what has traditionally been some of its top-level forbiddens: joik, drums, and trance journeys. She has done so in highly profiled settings, including national mega-events like the wedding of Crown Prince Håkon Magnus and Mette Marit Tjessem Høyby in 2001. Worst of all, perhaps, she has regularly played in Christian sanctuaries, and even combined Christian and shamanic elements. At the wedding of the crown prince, she did both, through the performance of what was referred to in the media as a joik-version of a Christian hymn, in Oslo Cathedral (Oslo *domkirke*)—in the presence of (in principle) the entire country.

The range of possible responses to Boine's music includes a complete lack of interest in—or recognition of—shamanistic elements, along with more diffuse notions of the "magic" or "spiritual." Boine, I have argued, regularly refers to religious beliefs in interviews. She sings primarily in Sami, a language unknown to the broader segment of her fans and audiences, but her albums and many YouTube clips come with Norwegian and English translations, and during concerts she regularly translates between Norwegian and Sami, telling her audience the name and content of the songs. Her Norwegian audiences can thus hardly fail to recognize a religious dimension in her music. However, knowledge of shamanism is fairly limited among ordinary Norwegians, implying that they may not recognize or interpret it as "shamanism." If they do, however, this may mean little to them personally. One need not be religious to enjoy religious music. Boine's shamanist language is in addition close to that of late modern psychology. Notions of "intuition" or the inner voice *can* be interpreted along the lines of secular vocabularies, and thus as secular wisdom, just as "indigenous brothers and sisters" can be understood as merely declarations of solidarity.

Reviews from the past couple of years indicate another perspective. References to the "shaman" or to "shamanism" are far less common in reviews of Boine's albums and concerts than words like "magic," "primal force" (*urkraft*), and "ecstasy." Unlike "shaman" and "shamanism," these belong to the more ambiguous world of what has been referred to as the "secular sacred" (Knott, Poole, and Taira 2013). News media references to "magic" have more to do with the extraordinary than with invisible forces and the ability to control them, but nevertheless carry a sense of the religious, sacred, or more-than-human. Used in reviews of Boine's concerts and albums, moreover, this latter sense is often supported by other similarly vague references to religion.

A few examples: Boine's concert in Kautokeino with the Norwegian Broadcasting Orchestra (Kringkastingsorkesteret) on March 28, 2012, and in association with a conference for the indigenous peoples television broadcasters, allegedly left "the audience in ecstasy" and the reviewer from NRK (Norwegian Broadcasting) "wildly excited" (Berg 2012). The reviewer used words like "her own aura," to describe Boine's unique charisma. He spoke of "primeval forces" and "magical moments," and of Boine and the orchestra "entering a higher union." Concerning the ballad "Elle," he stated that it is like one "senses the entire Sami history compressed into one single song, and manifested in a single representative of Sami culture."[38]

The reviewer of a concert in Tromsø on February 8, 2014, together with the Norrbotten Big Band, used the word *trollsk* in the headline, a word that is connected to "troll," but in a positive and religious sense—as in enchanted, mystical, or seductive (Larssen, *Nordlys*: February 9, 2014). Being at a concert with Boine, the ingress stated, "is like going along on a trip to the unknown spheres":[39]

> Boine in a magical way draws us into her world, and there hails the most powerful of all, nature. With her celestial[40] voice, she brings us along in the powerful world out there. And she has a unique way of conveying her message, a way that makes us listen to and live ourselves into her world—which she wishes to tell us about, even though we do not understand a single word. (ibid.)[41]

The reviewer of the north Swedish newspaper *NSD* was less impressed with the same concert program in Luleå, the week before. "Boine preached against the Kallak-mine," the headline stated, including in the text that followed, references to a "Sami revival meeting against mines" and "Boine as High Priest and preacher" (Larsen February 1, 2014, NRK).[42] Unlike his Norwegian colleagues, the Swedish reviewer chose terms from the negative register of religiosity, invoking Boine's control over her audiences and their religion-like willingness to submit to it. "High priest" is in the secular press a term of ridicule or concern—the laughable or threatening. Although used for an opposite purpose, it nevertheless supports the broader tendency among Boine's reviewers to draw upon religious vocabularies.

Adding to the above range of possible interpretations are discourses on shamanism as cultural heritage. I have in a previous study described an increasing interest in shamanism from this perspective, connected to Sami nation-building, and expressed through official and semiofficial institutions such as museums,[43] educational programs, festivals, tourism,[44] and place-branding strategies, as well as through film,[45] art, and music (Kraft 2009a). To define something as "cultural heritage" implies that it is separated from the flow of "ordinary history" and positioned as particularly valuable. In the Sami context, as with Christian cultural heritage in regard to Norwegianness, there is also a "we" involved, or even produced—as the heirs of the heritage concerned (Eriksen 2009, see also Selberg, this volume).

Joik belongs to the official category of Sami cultural heritage. Boine has contributed to the inclusion of the runebomme and the shaman in Sami heritage, and thus to the heritagization of Sami shamanism (see also Selberg, this volume). She has done so by regularly and publicly making visible, audible, and real this part of the past, and by linking it to other indigenous people, with (presumably) similar heritage from similar pasts. Boine's appearance (makeup, hair, and dress) will to many people be recognizable as what (regarding her sound) has been termed the "generally ethnic" or "indigenous" (Kvifte 2001). The runebomme can be connected both to indigeneity and to Sami shamanism. It today constitutes what is probably the most commonly recognizable marker of Sami shamanism, due partly to the fact that it (unlike joik) is connected exclusively to the noaidi.[46] Boine has made it a part of her public image. There are numerous pictures of her holding or playing a runebomme, and she regularly uses it during performances, even in settings in which its contribution as sound is more or less absent.

A series of concerts with the historian of religion Brita Polland is particularly interesting with respect to the productive ambiguity of Boine's music, as well as to the multisensory appeal of performances. Hilder, based on attending one of these concerts in Kautokeino in 2009, describes "a kind of musical and storytelling journey through the Sami pre-Christian religion" (2010: 136). The program alternated between singing (by Boine) and recitation of extracts from texts by missionaries, travelers, and researchers (by Polland), with each song exploring or subverting "the themes encountered in the preceding story" (ibid.: 137). Themes included the noaidi and Sami mythology, the burning of drums by missionaries and state authorities, the rise of Læstadianism, and the so-called Kautokeino rebellion in 1852 (ibid.: 136–137). Polland provided chronology and narrative coherence to the (necessarily) more fragmented and isolated story themes in Boine's song texts, and she added facticity to the narrated events through references to historical sources and to her own status as a historian of religion. Polland's role, Boine notes in a newspaper interview, was to provide a "spiritual backdrop" (*spirituelt bakteppe*) for her music, and—she added jokingly of the series—to contribute to public education and missionary goals (NN 2005, *Telemarksavisa*).

Boine's contribution involved *performance* of the stories narrated, including the trance journey of the shaman. Toward the end of the two-and-a-half-hour performance, Hilder notes, Boine's "soaring electric guitar…improvised high-pitched vocalisations of ecstasy induced a kind of trance in the audience" (ibid.: 137).

Musical performances are multisensory experiences, based on a combination of aural, visual, and ideological effects and impressions. Members of the audience may or may not have had trance-like experiences, but Boine must (with Polland's contribution) have been recognizable to them in the role of the shaman, regardless of whether this was interpreted as theatrical performance, religious ritual, or both. Neoshamans will commonly recognize role-playing as a dimension of their rituals. Make believe is central to neoshamanistic rituals, as probably to most rituals. Make-believe in a ritual or theater-like context (like concerts) may be merely that, a playing of roles, but can also imply the enactment, or even the creation of belief. The theatrical dimension probably lowers the threshold for religious make-believe. People who may not consider signing up for a course in shamanism may, nevertheless—in a concert setting—accept the roles granted to them.

Music-style Shamanism—Concluding Comments

Boine's life story reflects some of the broader issues and changes in recent Sami history—the politics of assimilation, the feelings of shame and inferiority that it created, rebellion against unfair conditions, the organized search for nationhood, and the discovery of a broader family of indigenous peoples—people with whom they share a similar fate as victims of colonialism. Similar processes of resistance and revival have during the past decades taken place among many indigenous peoples. An international trend in the sense that they occur in local communities around the world, such processes are also linked through various contact zones that have been established during this period, including legal arenas, conferences, festivals, websites, and (new) popular genres like indigenous film, art, and music. Social anthropologist Ronald Niezen has referred to notions of an indigenous *we* (2003, 2009, 2010) as one outcome of such processes. Several scholars, including Niezen, have also referred to a religious dimension of such identity-making,[47] variously termed "indigenous spirituality" or "indigenous religion," and consisting of elements such as shamanism and animism, sacred places, environmental awareness, and holistic worldviews. Niezen defines "indigenous religion" as "a conceptual and performative secondary elaboration of the indigenous peoples concept" (2012:13). During the last several decades, he claims, "the notion of 'indigenous religion' has been so thoroughly conventionalized that most Euro-American lay people presented with it would likely have some notion of what is meant by it, probably by drawing upon related ideas associated with such things as shamanism and forest spirituality" (119).

The question of whether this is in fact a globalizing trend—a global religion in the making—awaits further research. Boine's shamanism constitutes one example of what it may look like from a local perspective, and it constitutes an example of unusually extensive opportunities for indigenous identity- and religion-making. Her shamanism, I have argued in this chapter, has been shaped by various local and global influences. Boine has participated in numerous indigenous festivals, events, and concerts around the world, and worked with band members and music from other indigenous traditions. Her background in core shamanism has equipped her with a flexible set of religious resources, including notions of a primal voice, of power animals and helpers, of sacred landscapes and holistic perspectives, and of distinctions between Western and indigenous ways of being and thinking. Similar notions appear to be widespread in the indigenous soundscapes that have framed her career, along with concepts of connected musical traditions, and supported both by the world music industry and the indigenous movement internationally. Her music, in turn, has contributed to the religio-cultural dimension of Sami nation-building processes—as a way of performing, articulating, and reclaiming Sami identity within the broader frames of global indigeneity.[48] And it has contributed to issues and concerns highlighted by the international indigenous movement and the movement for Sami revival: the healing of colonial wounds, the revival of partly lost traditions and the repositioning of stigmatized symbols. Boine herself appears to consider music as important to all these levels of restoration, healing, and development.

Shamanism in Sàpmi is far from the position of Christianity—as the favored choice of faith and religious practice—but interest in neoshamanism appears to be increasing. It is currently a visible movement, and has recently been officially certified as a religion, implying, among other things, that it can offer and perform rites of passage (see Fonneland, this volume). Shamanism as cultural heritage, similarly, can hardly compete with the position of Christianity as cultural heritage in Norwegian discourse—backed up by state-church traditions and defined in the constitution as the foundation of "our values." But it has, over a relatively short period of time, become an established part of nation-building endeavors.

Thomassen has noted regarding the political potential of music that the very qualities that make it effective—its communicative polysemy and emotional impact—undermine its suitability for the "dissemination of one-dimensional political messages" (2010: 21). In the case of Boine's music, this same combination would seem to constitute an asset, an allowance for different interpretations and thus for sense-making potential among a religiously diverse and pluralistic population.[49] Shamanism can be many things, according to the perspectives performed and articulated by Boine, along different tracks, with different degrees of involvement and intensity, and in combination with various religious, political, and artistic issues.

Notes

1. There have been, to my knowledge, no studies of Boine by historians of religion, or studies focusing primarily on the religious dimension of her music. There exists, however, an extensive body of media interviews and documentaries covering her career, personal life, and views on religion. Additionally, religion is an important theme in Per Lars Tonstad`s (authorized) biography, *Mari Boine: Fly med meg (Mari Boine: fly with me)*. Tonstad is a freelance journalist originally from the south of Norway, who has worked as a journalist in Northern Norway for the past 30 years, and has known Boine during most of this time.

   Interview-based sources by scholars include Ivar Thomassen's master's thesis, "Hør stammødrenes stemmer: En kontekstuell analyse av Mari Boines album Gula Gula" (Hear the voices of the ancestral mothers: A contextual analysis of Mari Boine's album *Gula Gula*), from the Department of Music Science at Nesna college (2010). Thomassen has a background as a musician in Finnmark. My second, interview-based academic source is Thomas Richard Hilder's doctoral thesis, from the music department at Royal Holloway, at the University of London, entitled "Sami Soundscapes: Music and the Politics of Indigeneity in Arctic Europe" (2010). Hilder interviewed Boine and several other Sami musicians during fieldwork in Northern Norway from May 2007 to December 2008.

2. To give only one example, Ivar Bjørklund in a study of the coastal area Kvænangen, based on censuses, found that 1,200 were registered as Sami or Kven (descendants of Finnish people) in 1930. In 1950, the number had been reduced to 5 (Bjørklund 1985).

3. For studies of Læstadianism, see Olsen 2008, Hepokoski 2000.
4. Original citation in Norwegian: "Jeg nådde egentlig aldri min far. Bibelen og dommedag. Det var noe som alltid lå der, som en mørk skygge."
5. Birger Amundsen received an award for this documentary (*Jævelsens verk*), as best radio documentary in Europe 2014.
6. For introductions to joik, see Hilder 2010, Gaski 2008, and Graff 1996. On the so-called *joik*-renessaince, see Jones-Bamman 2006.
7. Citation in Norwegian: "Ifølge sjamanismen blir vi en del av naturen når vi dør, så nå har vi en veldig bra kommunikasjon. Jeg går ut i naturen og snakker med mine avdøde foreldre. Jeg merker at de er der."
8. See Thomassen 2010: 24–25 for a further description of the concept of world music, and the world music industry.
9. According to Thomassen 2010, the *quena* is a bamboo flute from the Andes. "Quena breath" he interprets as a percussive effect in which the breath sounds are more central than the tone. The "claypot" is a rhythm instrument resembling a clay jar (ibid.).
10. Boine has performed regularly at the main Sami and indigenous festivals in Norway such as Riddu Riddu and Markomeannu (both in Troms county), and the Easter festivals in Kautokeino and Karasjok (Hilder 2010: 117).
11. The original citation in Norwegian: "Når hun følte frykt, kunne hun sende ulven ut for å spise opp det som truet. Hun følte det hjalp henne, og ga henne styrke."
12. *Rørelse* denotes a condition characterized by violent emotional outbreaks and expressions, such as crying, screaming, jumping, and shaking (Olsen 2008: 11), and is connected to the revival dimension of Læstadianism. Historian of religion Torjer Olsen describes its inner logic as based on the creation of sin remorse (*syndeanger*) connected to the strict teachings of Læstadianism. Promises of salvation through correct repentance will, then, lead to a will to confessions and rørelse—as a result of the joy at receiving grace (ibid.).
13. The romantic version of the preservation thesis is today marginal in academic circles, but has been supported by a few publicly influential scholars, among these—and probably the most important—Professor of Pedagogics Jens Ivar Nergård (see, for instance, Nergård 2006), author of several articles and books on Sami culture and religiosity, and a frequent contributor to regional news- and popular media. Boine may have been introduced to the preservation thesis through Nergård, through versions circulating among neo-shamans and at indigenous festivals, or through the historian of religion Brita Polland—who appears to favor similar views. Polland is a close friend of Boine. The two women have also appeared together on stage, through a series of 30 concerts in which music (by Boine) was accompanied by recitation from historical texts concerning the Sami (by Polland). Polland has a master's degree in the history of religion, has been employed temporarily at different scholarly departments in Norway, and has published extensively on Sami religion, including editorial responsibility for text collections and introductory chapters. See Polland 1993, 2002a and b, 2004, and 2005a and b.

Critics of the preservation thesis have focused partly on the time gap between the "end of drum time" and the rise of Læstadianism. The Læstadian revival took place among people who had been Christians for a long time. Second, Læstadianism was gradually Norwegianized, both through the politics of Norwegianization and through ethnic Norwegian converts, and third—it is far from clear—in the romantic version of the preservation thesis—how continuity and religion are to be understood. For a more detailed critique of this, see Kraft 2007.

14. Original citation in Norwegian: "Noe av det jeg likte best var det vi kalte likhahuset, på norsk rørelse—men som jeg tror er en rest av sjamanistiske ritualer. På slutten av samlingen sang og sang de til de kom i en slags transe. Det var vel det nærmeste de kom dans. Bad hverandre om tilgivelse. Jeg har snakket med andre som vokste opp med det—som syntes det var skremmende, men jeg syntes det var høydepunktet."

15. Original citation in Norwegian: "D'e rørelsen som ligger i bunnen av alt det jeg har. Rørelsen, salmesangen og den forbudte joiken."

16. The album Sterna paradisea (2009) includes a song titled Likhahusat, the Sami term for what in Norwegian is known as rørelse (Thomassen 2010: 37, the English title of the song is "Enchanted").

17. Original citation in Norwegian: "Det har jo vært en del anmeldelser også, at dette er forferdelig monotont. Og så har man etter hvert skjønt at det fins—hvis man tør å la seg berøre av det, så fins det en annen dør, som går mer på—ikke det intellektuelle, det tenkte....—jeg hadde en lengsel etter transen, som kom fra min barndom, og de rørelsene jeg vokste opp med."

18. Original citation in Norwegian: "Det er denne følelsen fra barndommens 'likhahusat' hun søker på konsertene. En slags utenom-fysisk opplevelse, en atmosfære der publikum åpner dørene til sitt innerste og er mottakelige for ånd og reise."

19. Original citation in Norwegian: "Dag etter dag, i mange timer, satt hun på Tromsø Museum og lyttet til tradisjonell joik. Hun måtte nærme seg denne brønnen, denne kilden til drømmer, fantasiens mor og samefolkets innerste hemmelighet. Den var fordømt av kirken og misjonærene, trampet på og utskjelt, men den var en livsnerve som ikke kunne slites over. Og det fantes en nesten usynlig tråd—fra samenes førkristne religion og sjamanisme til læstadianisme, salmesang og kristendom—den grep hun fatt i."

20. Original citation in Norwegian: "Hun ble mer og mer klar over at joik er tilstedeværelse, et nærvær, hun kunne gå inn i joiken og bli der, gå i ett med tonen. Joiken åpnet en dør inn til et rom med kraft og energy, hun følte hun fløy på joikens vinger på scenen. Et folk som er i kontakt med denne kraften, kan ikke være så lett å manipulere og styre."

21. Original citation in Norwegian: "Magi lever i mange samers bevissthet. Det uforklarlige har en status. Det er til stede som regel som en positiv kraft som hjelper mennesker i ulike situasjoner. Sjamanen er på ingen måte død....Dagens sjamaner følger opp en lang samisk tradisjon som nesten ble utryddet av kristne misjonærer."

22. See Bergh 1990 and Flåten 2009. There is also an entry on Kaaven on Wikipedia (wikipedia.or/wiki/johan_kaaven).

23. For a critical approach to such inclusiveness among scholars, see Sidky 2010.

24. Information from a research seminar at the Department of Religious Studies, University of Tromsø, spring 2008.

25. The synonymization of Læstadian rørelse and trance is supported by older traditions of translation. Johan Turi's *Muitalus sámiid birra* (An account of the Sami), originally published in Sami and Danish in 1910 and the first secular work published by a Sami author in a Sami language, uses the term *rørelse* (in Sami *Likhahusat*) to describe the state of the noaidi during "*noaidi* acts" (*noaidekunster*). During the nineteenth century, noaidi acts were described as hysterical or ecstatic attacks, followed by complete exhaustion. "Arctic hysteria" or winter depression were diagnoses granted to such behavior, along with the nervous and easily excitable moods of nature people (Hagen 2002: 21). More recent scholarship has questioned whether trance, ecstacy, and travels to other worlds were *ever* a widespread part of Sami religious practices, or—rather—were fabricated by the priests and missionaries who first put their religion into script, and did so in order to eradicate it (ibid.).

26. There are no recent studies of the status of joik among Læstadians, but joik is still formally forbidden in many north Sami churches (*Nrk Sapmi* December 31, 2013). During the past decades, moreover, high-profile examples of joik used in Christian settings have been met with harsh criticism from these same circles. In November 2013, to give a recent example, the performance of what newspapers referred to as a "*joik*-like" song by the famous violinist Ole Edvard Antonsen in the church in Kautokeino during a concert led to a heated debate in national and local newspapers (Kveseth, *Altaposten* October 15, 2013). I contributed to this debate, in the form of a piece in the liberal Christian daily *Vårt Land* under the headline "striden om joik" (the controversy over *joik*). The head of Kautokeino menighet in public interviews and in an email to me denied that their views on joik had anything to do with the pre-Christian Sami religion, stating that it is not considered as shameful or a sin, but merely does not belong in church and Christian circumstances. Other members of the board claimed (publicly) that they had nothing against joik, only against performing it in churches. It remained unclear why other musical forms (like rock) are considered as acceptable in concerts on church grounds, while joik is not. Secular critics, on the other hand, claimed that Edvard Antonsen's song had nothing to do with joik, and that Sami musicians should stay away from a church that has never properly made a settlement with the Sami.

27. Gaski considers this as a natural side effect of the festivals and conferences organized since the late 1970s, "where groups have met and exchanged experiences and created a new political and cultural platform" (2008: 347). He adds that "most political conferences have also functioned as cultural meeting places, with performances by musicians, dancers and poets. In that way, one can say that culture and politics to a large extent have gone hand in hand for indigenous groups in recent decades" (ibid.)

28. In Boine's song *Du lahka* (on *Gula Gula*), for instance, there are clear associations to joik as well as to the powwow music of North American Indians.

Boine has also been compared to the Red Bull singer Buffy Sainte-Marie, both in regard to so-called pentatone tonality, to sullabene such as "hey ja" and "ho-ia-ha-ia," and due to what Thomassen terms the "funk meets indigenous people" tone of vocal expressions (2010).

29. The reference to a primeval voice has been repeated in newspaper interviews. In an interview in *Aftenposten*, for instance, in connection with the premier of *Joikefeber*—a film about a young Sami woman who learns to joik, Boine notes that she is pleased that more people are becoming interested in joik, and "seek[ing] their own primal voice" (Rapp 2014).

30. Citation in Norwegian: "Du har brødre. Du har søstre. I Sør-Amerikas regnskoger. På Grønlands karrige kyst. Har du glemt hvor du kommer fra."

31. Both Hilder and Thomassen emphasize the environmentalist theme of *Gula Gula*.

32. On the prevalence of these themes, see Niezen 2012, Karlsson 2003, Pedersen 1995, Rønnow 2011.

33. Hilder discusses some of these same connections, including the ways in which the lyrics not only draw on Sami mythology, "but tap into a pan-indigenous rhetoric" (2010: 164).

34. The songs are called "White Thiefs" and *Recipe for a Master Race*. "Master race" is the English term used by her in the English version of the text (printed on the cover of *Gula Gula*. In the Norwegian version she uses the term *herrefolket*.

35. The original citation in Norwegian: "Det er noe som jeg har skjønt etterpå. Det e derfor man ser, intuisjonen er mye, mye klokere enn en sjøl, enn hodet."

36. The original citation in Norwegian: "Vi er jo oppdratt til å bli veldig norske og veldig vestlige, og den teksten er mer sånn der at... når disse melodiene begynte å komme, var det som en sånn stemme, en påminnelse fra de som har vært før oss. Jeg så det ikke så veldig klart da, men etterpå når jeg ser på teksten, så er det jo en slags sånn... akkurat som det er en påminnelse fra de om at ikke... ikke glem den arven dokker har. Og også det her med at når du blir veldig oppdratt av skolen og alt til å bli vestlig, så blir andre urfolk veldig fremmede. Og en av de linjene er jo at, ikke sant, at vi har brødre og søstre i Latin-Amerika og på Grønland."

37. Citation in Norwegian: "At Mari Boine er en artist med røtter i sjamanisme er tydelig for de fleste. Nils-Aslak Valkeapää, som var den store stjernen før henne, dyrket kanskje i ennå større grad denne arven som sitt særpreg. Jeg vet ikke om en samisk artist i dag som ikke er klar over denne forbindelsen til sjamanismen og som henter inspirasjon i fra disse kildene."

38. Original citation in Norwegian: "fornemmer hele den samiske historien komprimert inn i en enkelt sang, og manifestert i én enkelt representant for den samiske kulturen."

39. Original citation in Norwegian: "Å være på en konsert med Mari Boine er som å bli med på en reise til de ukjente sfærer."

40. The term *overjordisk* means literally "above ground," and usually in a religious sense, as in supernatural, ethereal, or celestial.

41. Original citation in Norwegian: "På en magisk måte trekker Mari Boine oss med inn i sin verden der hun hyller det mektigste av alt, naturen. Men sin overjordiske stemme får hun oss med i den mektige verden der ute. Og hun har en helt spesiell måte å formidle sitt budskap på, en måte som får oss til å lytte til å leve oss inn i hennes verden som hun vil fortelle oss om, selv om vi ikke skjønner et eneste ord."

42. Boine during the concert in Tromsø (which I attended) brought up this review, noting that her father would have been thrilled to know that at least one of his children had ended up as a preacher. She added that she had sent the reviewer a message, thanking him for spreading her protests against the mine industry.

43. The noaidi is frequently included in representations of Sami musical performances in music exhibitions (Hilder 2010: 139).

44. Trude Fonneland is currently involved in a post doctoral study focusing on the relationship between Sami neo-shamanism, tourism, and place marketing. See Fonneland, 2012, 2011. For studies of references to religion in Sami institutions more broadly, see Kraft 2013, 2010, 2009 a and b.

45. For studies focusing on the relationship between Sami revitalization, film, and indigenous spirituality, see Cato Christensen 2013, 2012 a and b, 2010, and Christensen and Kraft 2011.

46. The runebomme is a membrane-covered oval or circular drum, made of wood (the base) and reindeer hide, and decorated with various symbols.

47. See, for instance, Niezen 2012, Brosius 1997, Karlsson 2003, Beyer 1998, 2007, Pedersen 1995, Rønnow 2011.

48. On the intersection between music and nation-building, see Post 2006.

49. The authenticity of Sami neo-shamans may, broadly speaking, be more acceptable in southern parts of Norway than in the Sami strongholds in the north. References to plastic shamans and to New Age connections have been fairly common among the latter, but remain rare in the former.

References

Beyer, Peter. 2007. "Globalization and Glocalization," in James A. Beckford and Nicholas J. Demerath (eds.). *The Sage Handbook of the Sociology of Religion*. Los Angeles: Sage, 98–117.

———. 1998. "Globalisation and the Religion of Nature," in J. Pearson, R. H. Roberts, and G. Samuel (eds.). *Nature Religion Today: Paganism in the Modern World*. Edinburgh: Edinburgh University Press, 11–22.

Bergh, Richard. 1990. *Mannen som stoppet Hurtigruta: Historier og sagn om Noaiden Johan Kaaven*. Oslo: Grøndahl.

Bjørklund, Ivar. 1985. "Local History in a Multi-ethnic Context. The Case of Kvænangen, Northern Norway. Some Remarks on the Relationship between History and Social Anthropology." *Acta Borealia* (1/2): 46–56.

Brosius, J. P. 1997. "Endangered Forest, Endangered People: Environmentalist Representations of Indigenous Knowledge." *Human Ecology*, 25(1): 47–69.

Christensen, Cato. 2013. *Religion som samisk identitetsmarkør. Fire studier av film*. PhD dissertation, Department of History and Religious studies, University of Tromsø.

———. 2012a. "Reclaiming the Past: On the Historymaking Significance of the Sámi film *The Kautokeino Rebellion*." *Acta Borealia* 29(1): 56–76.

———. 2012b. "Overtroen er stor blant viddenes folk: Om religion og koloniale relasjoner i samisk filmhistorie." *Tidsskrift for kulturforskning* 11(2): 5–25.

Christensen, Cato, and Siv Ellen Kraft. 2011. "Religion i Kautokeino-opprøret: en analyse av samisk urfolksspiritualitet." *Nytt norsk tidsskrift* 1: 18–27.

Døving, Cora Alexa, and Siv Ellen Kraft. 2013. *Religion i pressen*. Oslo: Universitetsforlaget.

Eidheim, H. 1998. "Ethno-Political Development among the Sami after World War II: The Invention of Selfhood," in Harald Gaski (ed.) *Sami Culture in a New Era: The Norwegian Sami Experience*. Karasjok: Davvi Girji, 29–61.

Eidheim, Harald. 1971. *Aspects of the Lappish Minority Situation*. Oslo: Universitetsforlaget.

———. 1999. *Historie, minne og myte*. Oslo: Pax Forlag.

———. 2009. "Kulturarv og kulturarvinger." *Nytt norsk tidsskrift* 3: 4.

Flåten, Edith. 2009. Johan Kaaven: *Fortellinger*. Alta: Nordnorsk Forlag.

Fonneland, Trude. 2011. "Sami Tour: urfolksspiritualitet i ei samisk turistnæring." *Chaos. Dansk-norsk tidsskrift for religionhistoriske studier* (55): 153–172.

———. 2012. "Spiritual Entrepreneurship in a Northern Landscape: Spirituality, Tourism and Politics." *Temenos* 48(2): 155–178.

———. 2013. "Sami Tourism and the Signposting of Spirituality: The Case of Sami Tour: A Spiritual Entrepreneur in the Contemporary Experience Economy." *Acta Borealia* 30: 190–208.

Fonneland, Trude, and Siv Ellen Kraft. 2013. "New Age, Sami Shamanism and Indigenous Spirituality," in Ingvild Sælid Gilhus and Steven J. Sutcliffe (eds.) *New Age Spirituality: Rethinking Religion*. Durham: Acumen, 132–145.

Gaup, Ailo. 2005. *Sjamansonen*. Oslo: Tre Bjørners Forlag.

———. 2007. *Inn i naturen: utsyn fra sjamansonen*. Oslo: Tre Bjørners Forlag.

Gaski, Harald. 2008. "Yoik—Sami Music in a Global World," in Henry Minde (ed.) *Indigenous Peoples: Self-determination, Knowledge, Indigeneity*. Delft: Eburon, pp. 347–360.

Graff, Ola. 1996. *Joik og Runebomme. Hvilken betydning hadde joikinga i de før-kristne seremoniene?* Tromsø: Universitetsmuseet i Tromsø.

Hagen, Rune Blix. 2002. "Harmløs dissenter eller djevelsk trollmann? Trolldomsprosessen mot samen Anders Poulsen i 1692." *Historisk tidsskrift* 81(2–3): 319–346.

Hepokoski, Warren. 2000: *The Laestadian Movement: Disputes and Divisions 1861–2000*. Culpeper, VA:

Hilder, Thomas Richard. 2010. *Sami Soundscapes: Music and the Politics of Indigeneity in Arctic Europe.* PhD thesis, Music Department at Royal Holloway, University of London.

Johnson, Greg. 2007. *Sacred Claims: Repatriation and Living Tradition.* Charlottesville and London: University of Virginia Press.

Jones-Bamman, Richard Wiren. 2006. "From 'I'm a Lapp' to I am Sami": Popular Music and Changing Images of Indigenous Ethnicity in Scandinavia," in J. C. Post (ed.) *Ethnomusicology: A Contemporary Reader.* New York: Routledge, 351–367.

Karlsson, Bengt G. 2003. "Anthropology and the 'Indigenous Slot': Claims to and Debates about Indigenous Peoples' Status in India." *Critique of Anthropology* 23(4): 403–423.

Knott, Kim, Elisabeth Poole, and Teemu Taira. 2013. *Media Portrayals of Religion and the Secular Sacred. Representations and Change.* Farnham: Ashgate.

Kraft, Siv Ellen. 2007, "Natur, spiritualitet og tradisjon. Om akademisk romantisering og feilslåtte primitivismeoppgjør, Review-artikkel om Jens Ivar Nergårds *Den levende erfaring. En studie i samisk kunnskapsproduksjon.*" *Din. Tidsskrift for religion og kultur.* 1: 53–62.

———. 2009a. "Sami Indigenous Spirituality. Religion and Nation Building in Norwegian Sápmi," *Temenos. Nordic Journal of Comparative Religion* 4: 179–206.

———. 2009b. "Kristendom, sjamanisme og urfolksspiritualitet i norsk Sápmi." *Chaos* 51: 29–52.

———. 2010. "The Making of a Sacred Mountain. Meanings of 'Nature' and 'Sacredness' in Sápmi and Northern Norway." *Religion. An International Journal* 40: 53–61.

———. 2014 (in press). "Sami Neo-shamanism—Colonial Grounds, Ethnic Revival and Pagan Pathways," in Kathryn Rountree (ed.) *Modern Pagan and Native Faith Movements in Europe.*

Kvifte, Tellef. 2001. "Hunting for the Gold at the end of the Rainbow: Identity and Global Romanticism. On the Roots of Ethnic Music." *Popular Musicology Online,* accessed September 2013

Minde, H. 2008. "Constructing 'Laestadianism': a Case for Sami Survival?". *Acta Borealia: A Nordic Journal of Circumpolar Societies* 15(1): 5–25.

Nergård, Jens Ivar. 2006. *Den Levende Erfaring: En Studie i Samisk Kunnskapsproduksjon.* Oslo: Cappelen.

Niezen, R. 2003. *The Origins of Indigenism: Human Rights and the Politics of Identity.* Berkeley: University of California Press.

Niezen, Ronald. 2009. *The Rediscovered Self. Indigenous Identity and Cultural Justice.* Montreal and Kingston: McGill-Queen's University Press.

———. 2010. "A New Global Phenomenon," in Margaret M. Bruchac, Siobhan M. Hart, H. Martin Wobst (eds.) *Indigenous Archaeologies: A Reader on Decolonialization.* Walnut Creek, CA: Left Coast Press, 33–37.

———. 2012. "Indigenous Religion and Human Rights," in John Witte and M. Christian Green (eds.) *Religion and Human Rights: An Introduction.* Oxford: Oxford University Press, 119–134.

Olsen, Torjer A. 2008. *Kall, skaperordning og makt: en analyse av kjønn i lyn-genlæstadianismen.* PhD dissertation, Department of History and Religious Studies, University of Tromsø.

Pedersen, Peder. 1995. "Nature, Religion and Cultural Identity—The Religious Environmentalist Paradigme," in O. Bruun and Arne Kalland (eds.) *Asian Perceptions of Nature: A Critical Approach.* København: Nordic Institute of Asian Studies, 258–273.

Polland, Brita 1993. *Samiske sjamaner. Religion og helbredelse.* Oslo: Gyldendal 2005.

———. 2002a. *Noaidier: historier om samiske sjamaner.* Utvalg, kommentarer og innledende essay, i *Verdens hellige skrifter,* De norske bokklubbene.

———. 2005a (ed.). *Samiske beretninger.* Innledning og språklig bearbeidelse ved Brita Polland. Oslo: Aschehoug.

———. 2005b. "Samisk religion i Norge," in Arne Bugge Amundsen (ed.) *Norsk religionshistorie.* Oslo: Universitetsforlaget, 414–456.

Polland, Brita, and Eirik Myrhaug. 2002b. "En nålevende samisk sjaman: møte med Eirik Myrhaug," in Brita Polland (ed.) *Noaidier: historier om samiske sjamaner. Utvalg, kommentarer og innledende essay,* in *Verdens hellige skrifter,* Oslo: De norske bokklubbene, 259–266.

Post, Jennifer. 2006 (ed.). *Ethnomusicology: A Contemporary Reader.* New York: Routledge.

Rydving, Håkan. 1995. *The End of Drum Time: Religious Change among the Lule Saami, 1670's–1740's.* Uppsala: Almqvist & Wiksell.

Rønnow, Tarjei. 2011. *Saving Nature: Religion as Environmentalism, Environmentalism as Religion.* Münster: LIT Verlag.

Sidky, Homayun. 2010. "On the Antiquity of Shamanism and Its Role in Human Religiosity," *Method and Theory in the Study of Religion* 22: 68–92.

Thomassen, Ivar. 2010. *Hør stammødrenes stemmer. En kontekstuell anal-yse av Mari Boines album Gula Gula.* Masteroppgave i Musikkvitenskap, Høgskolen i Nesna.

Tonstad, Per Lars. 2012. *Mari Boine. Fly med meg.* Oslo: Kagge Forlag.

Turi, Johan. 2011; 1910. *Min bok om samene,* Karasjok: Forfatternes Forlag.

———. 1931. *(Turi's) Book of Lappland.* Translated by E. G. Nash. New York: Harper & Collins.

Newspapers/home pages

Amundsen, Birger. 2003. "Jævelsens verk," NRK radiodokumentaren.

Berg, Arne. 2012. "Maris magiske aften," NRK Sápmi 29. March.

Cronshaw, Andrew. 2013. "Mari Boine—Not Waving, but Dancing." Andrew Cronshaw talks with the Sámi innovator. File:///Users/Siv/Documents/mari% boine/M.Boine. Interview.webarchive, accessed by me September 2013.

Graff, Ola. 2007. "Music," in *Sapmi—Becoming a Nation*—www.sapmi.uit.no

Kraft, Siv Ellen. 2014. "Striden om joik," *Vårt land* 5. January, available also at www.forskning.no

Kveseth, Magne. 2013. "Utestenges etter joiking i kirka," *Altaposten* 15.10.2013.

Larssen, Bjørn H. 2014. "Det er noe trolsk over henne når hun står på scenen," *Nordlys* February 9.

Larsen, Dan Robert. 2014. "Kalles yppersteprest og predikant," February 1, 2014, NRK.no, accessed February 14, 2014.

Larsson, Carl-Göran and Marie Elise Nystad. 2013. "Joikeforbud i disse kirkene," *NRK Sápmi,* December 31, 2013.

NN 2005. "En fri, samisk sangfugl," TA (Telemarksavisa), July 19, 2005, http://www.ta.no/pulsen/article1670038.ece, accessed February 2014.

NN 2014. "Mari Boines opplevelser," gjengitt fra Norsk Ukeblad 2009, i http://magic.no/magic-magasin/reportasjer/kjendisenes-overnaturlige-liv, accessed by me January 20, 2014.

Oksnes, Jakob. 2006. "Boines demoner," portrettintervju, *Dagbladet Magasinet,* May 8, 2006, file:///Users/siv/Documents/mari%20boine/Boines%20demoner%20-%20Portrettet%20-%20Dagbladet.no.webarchive, accessed September 2013.

Rapp, Ole Magnus. 2014. "På jakt etter urstemmen," *Aftenposten* January 16, 2014.

Mari Boine homepage: www.mariboine.no.

Ailo gaup's homepage: www.sjaman.com.

Isogaisa homepage: www.Isogaisa.org.

Riddu Riddu Festival homepage: www.riddu.no.

Contributors

Bente Gullveig Alver (born in Denmark 1941) is Professor of Folklore in the Department of Archaeology, History, Cultural Studies and Religion, University of Bergen. Her research interests revolve around folk religion, magic and sorcery, the use of rituals, cultural perspectives on health and illness, and the cultural history of folk medicine. Alver's latest publications include *Mellem mennesker og magter: Magi i hekseforfølgelsernes tid* (2008) and the biography of Anna Elisabeth Westerlund: *En fortelling* (2009). A particular field of interest is method development and ethical challenges in social studies, in which she has published books together with Tove Ingebjørg Fjell and Ørjar Øyen, as well as numerous articles.

Cato Christensen is currently Assistant Professor in the Department of International Studies and Interpreting at Oslo and Akershus University College of Applied Sciences. His research interests revolve around contemporary religion in Western societies, particularly New Age spirituality, indigenous spirituality, religion and popular culture, and religion in professional discourse and practice. His dissertation focused on the relationships among film, religion, and identity politics among the Sami in Norway. His latest publications include "Reclaiming the Past: On the History-making Significance of the Sámi film *The Kautokeino Rebellion*" (*Acta Borealia* 2012), and "'Superstition Is High among the People of the Tundra': On Religion and Colonial Relations in the Sami History of Film" (*Tidsskrift for kulturforskning* 2012).

Trude Fonneland is currently postdoctoral fellow in the Department of History and Religious studies at the University of Tromsø. Her research interests revolve around contemporary religion in society, particularly Sami shamanism, tourism, and popular culture. Her dissertation focused on the developments of modern Sami shamanism in Norway. She is also the author of several scholarly articles on the subject. Her latest publications include "Spiritual Entrepreneurship: Tourism, Spirituality and Politics" (*Temenos* 2012), "'The Seven Coffee Stops': Spiritual

Entrepreneurship in a Sami landscape" (*Tidsskrift for kulturforsking* 2012), and "Isogaisa—Shamanism in Festival Clothing" (*Aura* 2013).

Olav Hammer, Professor of the Study of Religions at the University of Southern Denmark, has published extensively in English and Swedish on New Age, and on religious innovation from the nineteenth century to the present. He is at present editor (with Henrik Bogdan) of an encyclopedic work on Western esotericism in the Scandinavian countries.

Merete Demant Jakobsen has been researching shamanism for more than 30 years, first for her master's degree in Nordic literature and ethnography and later for her doctorate at Oxford University. Her book *Shamanism: Traditional and Contemporary Approaches to the Mastery of Spirits and Healing* describes the role of the shaman in Greenland in the past centuries and how shamanism is presented to and experienced by modern course participants. She has also published a study of the experience of evil: *Negative Spiritual Experiences, Encounters with Evil*. This study looks at 4,000 letters describing spiritual experiences, which were collected in England in the 1960s and '70s by Professor Alister Hardy. Presently she is researching narrative implications of patients' first consultation with an oncologist.

Anne Kalvig is Associate Professor of Religious Studies at the University of Stavanger, Norway. She has published *Spiritual Health: Views of Life among Alternative Practitioners* (2013 in Norwegian) and various articles and chapters on themes within the field of alternative spirituality, such as alternative therapy, folk medicine, crop circles, spiritual tourism, spiritism, religion and media, popular culture, and death.

Siv Ellen Kraft is Professor of Religious Studies at the University of Tromsø, Norway's Arctic University. Major research interests include theosophy, New Age spiritualities, neo-paganism, and the increasing indigenization of the Sami, particularly with regard to religion. She has published four monographs (one of them with Cora Alexa Døving), several articles and book chapters, and has coedited four anthologies.

James R. Lewis is currently Professor of Religious Studies at the University of Tromsø. He is a highly published scholar of new religions and of the New Age. He is the coeditor of three book series: the Brill Handbooks on Contemporary Religion series, Ashgate's New Religions series, and Palgrave-Macmillan's Palgrave Studies in New and Alternative Religions. He is also general editor of the *Alternative Spirituality and Religion Review* and, until recently, the *Journal of Religion and Violence*.

Stein R. Mathisen is a folklorist and Associate Professor of Culture Studies at the Finnmark University College, Alta, Norway. Major research interests include folk medicine and folk belief, the role of narratives for the constitution of identity and ethnicity, questions of heritage politics and ethno-politics, and the history of cultural research in the northern areas. Recently published articles in English include "Narrated Sámi Sieidis: Heritage and Ownership in Ambiguous Border Zones" (2009), "Festivalising Heritage in the Borderlands: Constituting Ethnic Histories and Heritages under the Rule of the Finn Forest Republic" (2009); and "Indigenous Spirituality in the Touristic Borderzone: Virtual Performances of Sámi Shamanism in Sápmi Park" (2010).

Henno Erikson Parks is originally from New York City, and lived in Estonia for 16 years before moving to Turku, Finland, where he is a doctoral student of Comparative Religion at Åbo Akademi. A combination of an ancestral background in Estonia and an interest in the field of shamanism has led him to begin working on a dissertation entitled "Contemporary Shamanic Practices in Estonia: An Examination of the Reconstruction of Ancient Traditions within a Modern Context." In addition to focusing on current practices and beliefs in the country, he will also examine the broader influences from Russia, the Baltic States, and Scandinavia. He has published an article in *Báiki*, the North American Sami journal, as well as articles in the fields of developmental education, and politics.

Torunn Selberg, folklorist, is Professor in Cultural Studies, Department of Archaeology, History, Cultural Studies and Religion, University of Bergen. Her research interests revolve around folk religion, magic, ritualization, tourism, and cultural landscapes. Selberg is a prominent scholar of new religions in contemporary society and has written numerous chronicles, articles, and books focusing on contemporary religious phenomena, pilgrimage, festivals, and place construction.

Index

Printed and bound in the United States of America